Island Wings

Also by the Author

No Man in the House
Sleep On, Beloved
A Place Called Heaven:
The Meaning of Being Black in Canada
Slammin' Tar

Island Wings

a memoir

CECIL FOSTER

HarperCollins*Publishers*Ltd

http://www.harpercollins.com/canada

HarperCollins books may be purchased for educational, business, or
sales promotional use. For information please write: Special Markets
Department, HarperCollins Canada, 55 Avenue Road, Suite 2900,
Toronto, Ontario M5R 3L2.

First edition

Canadian Cataloguing in Publication Data

Foster, Cecil, 1954–
Island wings : a memoir

ISBN 0-00-255736-3 (bound)
ISBN 0-00-638572-9 (pbk.)

1. Foster, Cecil, 1954–   – Biography. 2. Barbados – Politics and government. 3. Authors, Canadian (English) – Biography.* I. Title.

PS8561.O7727Z53 1998   C818'.5409   C98-930604-6
PR9199.3.F572Z47

98 99 00 01 02 03 04 HC 10 9 8 7 6 5 4 3 2 1

Printed and bound in the United States

Contents

To Ann and Mervin — and to all who answered the call. Thanks.

For Stephen and Errol: always a special place in my heart. Only we know. Brothers always. Love.

To our children — so you may understand.

1

Keepers of a Promise

My mother cried that day on the Bridgetown Wharf as she walked off, leaving her three sons: Stephen, Errol and me, still a baby. My brothers tell me they didn't cry, but how could they not? If they didn't, maybe it was because they had already fallen victim to the pressure of never openly showing emotion.

Stephen was seven years of age and Errol almost five. Perhaps they didn't cry because they had been prepared for this separation. In anticipation of this eventful day, they were already living apart from my mother, staying with my father's family on another part of the island. And maybe they didn't cry because they had promised my mother to comfort and look after me, their little brother, almost two years old, until we could be reunited. Everybody had encouraged them to be men for our mother's sake.

Everyone who recalls the event tells me I bawled. I cried when my mother handed me to Grandmother after she heard the boarding announcement that one part of her had hoped would never come. The wharf that had become symbolic of the pain and yet also of the hope for her and so many islanders was where Barbadians met the world and where the world came to them, where the hopes for the future and the harsh reality of the past collided. This wharf was where human and other cargo had always moved: where the men with pushcarts laden with tropical fruits like bananas, mangoes and oranges from neighbouring islands, bags of flour and sugar and the like, loaded their goods onto lighters tied up at the side of the inlet. These small boats took the cargo to the ocean-going ships anchored just offshore and they brought back what the island didn't produce but needed.

It was on this wharf where, for centuries, people dressed in their finery had met for their social gatherings, especially to see the luckier ones among them leave to build the Panama Canal, to cut cane in Cuba or Florida, or to come back with trunks and valises brimming with foreign goods, with pockets lined with foreign currency and brains sharpened from the experience of just living in a foreign country. Several times before my mother had gone to this wharf to see friends and family escape the hardships of life on the island. On this day, the assembly was to see my mother, and others like her, step into the lighter and be rowed out to the ship waiting to take them away.

When the boarding announcement came, my mother walked off, crying softly, her teary eyes steadfastly fixed on the lighter that was to take her to the ship waiting offshore, and then across the ocean to England. I cried as she handed me over; I cried as they carried me away from the wharf; I cried on the bus that took us to our new home in Lodge Road; I cried myself to sleep and I woke up crying.

What was unusual about this scene on the wharf was that traditionally it was not the women and mothers who left their children behind, but the men who went abroad. The man's role was defined by his ability to provide financial support for the family. If it was necessary for men to leave the island in order to make a living, society had come to terms with this, in some ways. Men were expected to do what was needed to provide the money to live, while mothers were the nurturers. They took care of the home and the children. They kept watch when the men were away and they raised the children to understand the differences, to appreciate why often there was no man around.

Also crying at what should have been a celebration for a beloved sister escaping the trials of life in Barbados was Aunty Ann, then only twelve years old. Until this day of separations, she had effectively raised me, looking after her favourite sister's youngest boy while her beloved Dee worked long hours as a domestic servant in the home of rich white people on the south coast of Barbados. My mother always brought home the smell of onions from frying fish and other meats. It was an aroma my father said he always found endearing.

My mother handed her sons over to our father's family. This action in itself was a slap in the face to Aunty Ann and all the members of my mother's family because my mother's family and my father's family absolutely did not get along. My mother's family could not have approved of my mother's giving up her three children to people they didn't like and with whom they hardly spoke.

My mother was heading to England, supposedly to study nursing and, like so many young Caribbean women of her day, to work in British hospitals that faced acute shortages of labour after the Second World War. This was to be the opportunity for her to acquire professional skills that would improve her financial status and make her independent. Success in a foreign country also meant escaping the clutches of want so prevalent on the island in the 1950s. It was also supposed to be her social redemption. In truth, my mother was really chasing the man of her dreams, my father, Cleophus (Freddie) Goddard. Reputedly the best musician of his day in Barbados, he was supposedly so talented that after a *wicked* jam session on the Italian boat that had taken him to England a year earlier, he had been offered a job on the spot with the ship's band. Such offers were not new to him for he had been the lead musician in the Percy Green band, one of the biggest and most popular swing bands of the day. On his island, this had brought him prestige and notice, and great popularity with the young females.

My mother once told me of a special dance at the King George the Fifth Park, on the east coast of the island. She and a younger sister, Ruth, had sneaked out of the house and from under the watchful eyes of their parents. My mother, never much of a scrapper, had suddenly found herself in the middle of a fight over my father, when some girlfriend had seen my father dancing with her. While in the middle of the dance floor, she walked up to my mother and slapped her so hard my mother saw stars. She could only cry and hurry away. My mother did not retaliate, but in her own way she fought back to keep her man.

However, being the very fashionable and stylish *saga boy* that he was, in his arrogant and cocky way, my father had dismissed the offer to join the ship's band. As my mother

prepared to leave Barbados, she knew he was already working on the London Transport, like so many immigrants,
coupling trains on the tracks but hating every day on the
job. But soon he would be ensconced in the British Army,
a leading member of the military band playing the saxophone, clarinet, trumpet and even drums. And he would
enrol at the renowned Trinity College of Music in London,
with aspirations of someday studying music full-time at the
highest level—at Durham University, the top music school
in the country. My father's dream was to become the most
accomplished musician to ever live in Barbados. He wanted
to study music, not only conquering the popular genres
from the United States—jazz, swing, bebop—and the home-
grown calypso, but also the European classics. Supposedly,
nothing was going to deflect him from this course, a dream
that seemed so much closer with the security of a job in the
British military. This was a godsent opportunity to practise
his craft at the expense of Her Majesty's government, too!
And as a soldier boy in this colonial army, he knew that
status and pride of place awaited him when he decided to
return to his homeland, to the Caribbean island that was so
quintessentially British.

My father had left Barbados a few months after I was
born, staying around long enough to register and inflict on
me the middle name Adolphus, a name my mother only
heard about when the documents came home. It is a name
I have always hated. His other act of note was to gather all
the registration documents of his three sons and leave them
in the safekeeping of a close friend, Anderson (Peanuts)
Morrison, then considered a rising star in the community.
Peanuts was one of the first black boys in Lodge Road to

attend a grammar school, and had already secured an all-important civil service job, one of the limited opportunities on the island for a stable future, by rising through the ranks of the government service.

My brothers and I often talked about our parents, with their filling me in on what they remembered. They loved to tell me about the heroic feats of our father, whether it was on the cricket field as a wicketkeeper, or when, almost a year to the day of my birth, Hurricane Janet struck the island.

I was with my mother and she had sought refuge in a sturdy limestone house in her neighbourhood of Rockley. My brothers were already living with my father's family in Lodge Road. They recalled my father battling the violent hurricane winds and rains, and desperately trying to avoid the dangerous pieces of galvanized iron roof that were flying around him and that had supposedly impaled people, as he helped save a family from a house damaged badly by a fallen tree.

Later, he had rescued his own family from the Lodge Road Pilgrim Holiness Church, where he had found my brothers and an aunt cowering under the church benches. When a loud crack of thunder had sounded, Aunt Princess, my father's younger sister, had looked up to see the church ceiling splitting open. She had had just enough time to drag my brothers to safety under the benches before the ceiling crumbled. There, according to my brothers and Aunt Princess (who always relished her hero status), the three of them tried to wait out the hurricane. But, defying the high winds, the pelting rain and the lightning and thunder, my father arrived soon after and took them to another shelter. Then, like a true hero, he was off to look for other stricken people, and to aid in the government's efforts of ensuring that shipments of water and cans of corned beef got through to those in need. This was the story that my brothers always told me when I asked about this man, the father who, unlike me, my brothers always claimed to keep fresh in their memories.

When my father left Barbados, it was his intention to start his life anew. My mother would one day tell me how she had accidentally discovered that my father was leaving the island. She had rifled through his pockets while he was sleeping and found his passport and ticket. By then, my father had also made it clear that he wanted to end the relationship with my mother. He planned to go off to England, where a recent court ruling had thrown open the immigration floodgates to men and women of the British Empire. The ruling was that anyone in possession of a British passport, which any colonial subject was free to get, could enter and live in England. At the urging of local politicians, a stream of Caribbean youths had set out for places like London, Birmingham and Liverpool. They worked in health care and the service sectors: the women mainly as domestics, nurses and nursing assistants; the men as orderlies, drivers, conductors and mechanics on the London Transport, or they enlisted in the British military. Some of them used these jobs as stepping stones to university educations, primarily in the highly regarded professions of medicine and law. Several Barbadians who had sought legal careers later returned home as the next generation of political leaders. My brothers and I were living testament to this exodus, part of a generation left behind.

My mother, without invitation, went to the Bridgetown Wharf to see my father off to England. On hand were members of my father's family, his musician friends and the newest love of his life, Corrine. My mother told me that she had been ignored as she stood off to one side with me at her bosom, watching and dreaming of how she could turn her life around. Even at the time of his departure she had already decided that her fate and future rested with this musician, and that she would literally follow him to the ends of the earth. A year later, she left us behind, not sure if my father would be on hand to receive her when she arrived across the ocean, a perfect stranger in a strange land.

There may have been another reason, an even stronger force pushing my parents apart: the colours of their skin. My mother was high brown, showing some of the European blood that was a legacy from the days when white plantation owners sometimes ravished black workers. My father was jet black. As my maternal grandmother, Grand-Grand, often described him in anger, he was so black that even his gums were black. The palms of his hands were just too soft for a real man, Grand-Grand argued. And just as important, she said, he was too black to be trusted.

Neither family felt this was a fitting match. My father's mother felt that such a talented son deserved better for a wife; after all, he had his pick of the women on the island. He deserved more than just a domestic servant. In addition, she didn't know why that half-white devil with the cat's eyes would not leave her son alone. My mother's family felt that any man who made his living from playing music, who slept late into the day because of all-night gigs and who appeared to have hardly any money in his pockets was just plain lazy and idle. They felt, and often said so, that he was simply unaccustomed to hard work and was a poor choice for a bright young woman who could make something of her life by going to England and becoming a nurse.

But my mother's family also realized that my mother had little choice or bargaining clout. Social conditions didn't favour her or women in her situation. She had already produced three boys out of wedlock with this unemployed musician, shaming a family that had taken up important roles in St. Matthias Anglican Church as members of the Mothers' Union and the Church Army.

My mother had felt so outcast that at my birth she had had me christened outside the parish, at St. Paul's Anglican Church in Bridgetown, instead of at St. Matthias. And she told me that after my birth, realizing that her relationship with my father was rocky, she felt alone and afraid. She recalls that her father, a man known in the community alternately as Ball Starch, Greenie and, to his grandchildren, as Dadah—a carpenter and devout leader of the Church Army— had lifted me in his arms the first time he saw me and kept whispering to her: "Why, Dee? Why, Dee? Why another one? Why are you doing this to yourself?"

The Anglican church exercised tremendous influence over the daily lives of its members, and the island in general. The Church of England was then the established religion and Barbados received a string of expatriate, upper-class white priests to instill more acceptable mores on its people. The Anglican church dictated almost every aspect of life, and had the ability to reward, to punish, and even to confer on or revoke social standing. It blessed those starting out in life with a church christening and it ushered the specially blessed out of this world with a church funeral, with burial in a section of the cemetery set aside for confirmed Anglicans. In between birth and death, it might offer a scholarship to a needy student, help run the local vestry or municipal government, provide some schools of its own as well as oversee the administration of state-run schools. On leaving school, it was always wise for a young boy or girl to get a testimonial from the school's headmaster and from the parish priest. This character reference came in handy when the young person was looking for work.

My mother's father had attained social prestige in his area. This meant the church recognized his leadership role, singling him out as exceptional among the mainly poor and black worshippers who formed the Church Army and Mothers' Union. More so, this was testimony to his willingness to explain the church's teachings to other poor black people like himself. The Church Army helped to keep members compliant with the teachings of the church, thereby reinforcing the Anglican church's influence over their lives. The same was true for the Mothers' Union, which was aimed at the women in the church.

At special church events my grandfather was recognized. When the church members went into the byways and highways to testify about how their lives had changed and improved under the influence of the church, and to win souls as converts, it was Dadah who led the army of witnesses for Christ. When other armies from churches across the island visited St. Matthias, Dadah received them in his capacity as a church leader. Above all, my grandfather was expected to live an exemplary life, following the church doctrine and keeping his children in line, a missionary in his own house.

It was unthinkable that the daughters of such a high-profile lay preacher would ignore the church's ban on premarital sex and the procreation of children out of wedlock. But in a society where the majority of children are born without their parents having married, few people have had much success with the practical aspects of church teachings. Still, this was no excuse for the children of a Church Army captain or a leading member of the Mothers' Union, as was the case with my grandmother. This was neither the example expected by these two leaders nor the conformity demanded of their children. By the time I was born, my mother's older sister and a younger sister had both started families the proper way by first getting married. This could not have made my mother's life any easier.

Dadah realized he had little choice but to help my mother re-establish her life by escaping the island, and sold part of his land-holding—essentially what would turn out to be the inheritance for me and my two brothers—and shipped his beloved Dee off to England in the hope that she would somehow manage to marry the man she loved, and correct the mistakes in her life by giving her three sons their proper surname. Dadah and my mother were still holding onto a dream: that my mother and father would be freed from the pressures of their families and could get back together; that they would marry and send for their three boys, changing their names from Foster to Goddard; and that the reunited family would all live happily ever after in the mother country, England. They dreamt of a triumph of love and hope, strengthened by a bit of sacrifice and a few tears.

In clinging to the dream, my mother had to make some concessions. The main one was to my father's family. My father's mother would take care of her three grandsons until our father decided what he wanted to do with his life. Leaving us with our father's mother was also a financial decision reflective of the power struggle between men and women of that era in the Caribbean. Since it was expected that my father would be the one sending home the money to support us, it was better that he should entrust his hard-earned money to his mother, rather than send it to people who might only be plotting and scheming to trap him in marriage. With this came the notion that any spin-off from the money sent back for the benefit of my father's flesh and blood should be used only by those directly sharing his blood line. All the benefits of my father's money would be kept and shared within his mother's house. My brothers and I were left in the middle of this feud between the families. We always felt the tug to ally ourselves with one side of the family and to look askance on the other, our fate and future often tied to the size and frequency of the remittances sent from our father in London.

By the time she emigrated, my mother was able to cling to some hope of realizing her dream because of the letters my father had sent back to her. Yet, as she sailed away from us, taking the greatest gamble of her life, nothing was certain. The strain and stress from the uncertainty had made her thin, so thin that when she arrived in England my parents were able to pretend they were starting out together for the first time and did not yet have children. They did not correct this impression among their new-found friends, especially among colleagues and neighbours in the military communes and bases where they lived.

I grew to comfort myself by dreaming of joining my mother and father. But it was my mother I missed the most. Almost every day I stared at the pictures we had received from England and dreamt of living there happily with my parents. These were special pictures, especially the black-and-white one of my mother and father standing in bright sunshine on what looked like a church step. They are beaming: my father, a very dark man, immaculate in his military uniform, a big part down the middle of his head. Linking hands with him is an obviously happy woman in her white wedding dress, who everyone told me was my mother, a woman with a black mole on her forehead. In the picture, on this wonderful day that should have set the stage for the long-awaited family reunion, was someone described to me as Uncle John, my father's brother, and another man who was my mother's only blood relative in England.

Grandmother framed this picture of her son's surrender to the inevitable marital fate, and mounted it prominently on a side of our one-roof house. Beside it was another picture of a gentle-looking woman, almost white, dressed in her nursing uniform, sitting on the edge of a chair. She was absolutely the most beautiful woman in the world. This, too, was my mother. Almost every day I looked at that picture, of the woman smiling so tenderly, and wondered when I would be the object of this woman's smile and love. When would she be able to hug me? When would I be able to see her, just to talk with her, just to be able to call her Mom, or Mummy, or Ma, as other boys my age called their mothers? The answer was always the same: "Very soon you'll be going to England." I couldn't wait to join these people said to be my parents, people who, although strangers to me, became with each passing year more legendary: "Boy, that father of your'n was the best musician this island ever did had. He could blow sweet, sweet, sweet." And my mother: "Boy, you should hear your mother telling a joke; she'd break yuh up; make yuh laugh yuh belly full. And she's so beautify, with nice brown skin, just like your'n." I really missed them. And I kept crying for them.

2

A New Life

Grandmother sat on the bench by the table with the kerosene oil lamp. Minutes earlier, she had latched shut the door, checked the windows and ensured that the slats of the jalousie door were blocked tight. We were locked in for the night, all of us except Aunty Allison, or May as we called her, who was probably making her way home from work in the pitch darkness. Aunty Allison worked in Top Rock, one of the exclusive areas for the white and wealthy on the island, a neighbourhood hemmed in by thick limestone walls with razor-sharp cat or barbed wire, and broken glass embedded in the top. Behind these white-washed walls, the rich and influential lived in their impos-ing limestone walled houses with their well-manicured lawns, their trees with the fruits falling to the ground and their suspicion of the poor, working class people who surrounded them. Only the domestic servants, gardeners and watchmen moved openly behind these walls. Certainly, very few of us ventured into this exclusive area at night, not even when passing through would shorten a long walk home. We went out of our way to walk around Top Rock. When we had to pass through the area, we went at a very fast clip, for fear of being attacked by one of the big-teeth dogs snarling and barking at us from behind the iron fences and gates, or of being arrested and charged with loitering by the ever-present police patrolling on bicycles.

On this night, as Grandmother gathered around her Aunty Princess, Stephen, Errol and me, something was obviously bothering her. She sat on the bench, her legs spread with the bottom of her dress falling in folds between. Grandmother appeared tired and edgy, full of anticipation.

Then we heard it: the loud *tick-tick-tick* sound. It stopped in front the house. *Tick-tick-tick.* The sound stopped again. Next, we heard something dragging against the side of the house, near the door with the latches Grandmother had checked only moments earlier. Then, a rattling sound.

Grandmother could take it no longer. "Murder!"

We sat watching Grandmother, terrified. "Murder! Murder! Blue murder!" Grandmother kept shouting. "Somebody help us!"

The scraping sound became a loud thud as if something had been thrown against the side of the house. Grandmother screamed even louder, delirious. We heard footsteps running from the side of the house into the back-yard. Whoever was attacking us was approaching from the back, away from the unpaved road that ran in front of the house, where passers-by might witness the actions of whoever chose to prey on us under the cover of darkness.

"Murder! Murder! Blue murder!" Grandmother shouted. All of us joined in. We felt alone against the world. Someone started banging on the back door. Our cries of blue murder, long considered a universal no-nonsense appeal for help, intensified. Then, we heard the voice.

"Ma. Ma. Ma. What happening in there? Open the door quick, quick, quick. What happening?" The voice was familiar. It was Aunty Allison. Grandmother opened the back door and Aunty Allison ran into the house, not knowing what to expect. Grandmother stopped shouting and quickly recovered something of her composure.

"What happen? Why you and these idiots in here shouting for murder so?" Aunty Allison asked.

Grandmother explained how we had been spooked by the loud ticking sound and the noise outside the house.

"All o' you too foolish," Aunty Allison said, finally relaxing. "That was me. I rode a bicycle home and you must have heard the ticking sound from the wheel and then the noise from when I was leaning up the stupid bicycle against the house and it kept falling down." The explanation made sense: sometimes Aunty Allison got a ride home by car or bicycle. The young men, especially the gardeners for whom a bicycle was a status symbol, were extremely proud of their bikes, oiling and greasing the gears so that they emitted strong and powerful ticking sounds, so loud and clear that the young men could brag among themselves whose bicycle had a much desired one-tick, a two-tick, or as was most often the case, a tick-tick-tick sound.

Aunty Allison opened the back window and shouted across to the neighbours. "You heard these idiots in here carrying on?" She forced a laugh. "They too foolish. Scared for nothing." We saw the light from the lamp in the neighbour's house, but there was no movement. "Nothing ain't wrong," she told the darkness and the shut houses. "But everything's okay, they heard me coming home with a bicycle and got frightened, frightened, frightened."

From out of the darkness, a neighbour shouted something back to Aunty Allison. She closed the window and kept laughing at us to break the lingering tension. The pressures of living in Lodge Road had caused Grandmother to snap and to cry out for help. And, as she pointed out to us the next morning, while she might have ended up looking foolish because she thought we were under attack, at least she knew for sure who was willing to help us if we were ever in real trouble. None of the neighbours had come running when we called for help. "Let this be a lesson to you three boys," she said. "And to you, Princess, and you, May, too."

*   *   *

My earliest memories of life in Lodge Road are of Grandmother waking every morning to the task of getting us through one more day with as few compromises as possible. Would she be able to *trust*, on credit, a few more items of food from any of the four shops in the village? Was Mrs. Ashby going to hold off a bit longer for the rent that was always in arrears for the spot of land? And would Grandmother eventually find the money for an add-on to the one-roof shack that leaked on the six of us, a house already crowded with Grandmother's precious mahogany chairs—supposedly made by my father before he left the island—and which would not have had room for a second bed if she could have afforded one?

Grandmother had a chattel or board-and-shingle house, a common sight across the island. Chattel houses were constructed of wood sidings with a galvanized-sheet or wood-shingle roof. They were mounted on a groundsel of packed stones, usually with a large block of limestone at each corner to allow free circulation of air to cool the interior and to let the water run off unimpeded during a downpour. The houses were built so they could be dismantled and transported to another site at virtually a moment's notice, and for the task to be completed in one day. This was necessary because the houses occupied *spots* of land for which the home owner paid rent. This was a throwback to earlier times when slaves and, later, poorly paid workers, assembled houses on marginally productive agricultural land, but were expected to remove them if the landowner ordered, or if they fell behind with the rent. The houses were traditionally of one-roof, with the front symmetrically built—a main door in the middle with a jalousie window made of wooden slats on either side of the entrance. Usually a very poor family crowded into a one-roof house. As their circumstances improved, they might add another roof, called a shed-roof, and ultimately might end up adding three or four roofs to the home—each addition a further sign of improved financial standing.

Very often, Grandmother's biggest task was simply to thwart the threats of physical danger from a neighbour; of saying the right words of appeasement to stop some bully from feeling he had to prove himself by beating us, but a statement ambiguous enough to allow us to walk with our heads high, seemingly uncompromised.

And there are also the warm memories of food, and in tough times of the burning hunger from having nothing to eat. On a good morning, to the sweet smells of food, I would stir from my bedding on the floor, where I slept curled up between Errol and Stephen. We slept at the foot of the khus-khus grass bed that was reserved for Grandmother and her daughters. Once a year, when the bed had long gone flat and sagged from the breaking down of its contents into a powdery filler, a man turned up with a cart-load of grass and spread it in the backyard for drying. Then it was stuffed into the bed, Grandmother's substitute for the traditional coconut-husk stuffing that was used for beds in most of the houses. If nature called during the night, we all used the same *poe* or *topsy*, the night chamber that was kept under the bed. Well, the others did. Invariably, I soaked the bedding and Stephen and Errol, too. None of us wanted to go outside in the darkness.

A good day usually began with the sweet smells of morning tea. More sophisticated people called it breakfast, but for us it was morning tea—the common term for any hot beverage. My first task of the day was to pack away the heavy crocus bags and bits of old clothes that made up our bedding. The wet pieces I put out for sunning on the rocks used mainly for bleaching the laundry in a corner of the backyard. The dried rags and bags I bundled out of sight, usually under the bed behind a cloth blind that divided the house in two, supposedly shutting the private bedroom to prying eyes.

One night I woke up screaming. My head felt as if it was on fire. Grandmother turned up the lamp and inspected my head, but saw nothing that could have caused my pain. I just kept rubbing my head and crying. Nothing consoled me, not even when Grandmother, in desperation, started combing my hair. When she found nothing there, she carefully inspected our bedding. Hiding in the pillow was a big centipede, which had obviously stung me. The insect had probably entered the bedding from under the bed. After that, I took great care to inspect every piece of bedding before spreading it for the night.

Errol's chore was to take care of the sheep, so every morning he took them to Ashby's pasture in front of the house and staked them out. In lambing season, Grandmother always tried to stop the young from nursing as soon as they appeared weaned, before the mother's milk dried up. Every morning she milked the sheep, proclaiming that sheep's milk was the richest and most nutritious of any animal's. More importantly, it saved her from having to buy milk for our morning tea. Around midday, Princess took the sheep a pan of water, or a special feed supplement of *pollard* that became mash when mixed with water, and she moved the animals out of the sun. Errol brought them home just before sunset, after he had gone picking *meat*— the grass, vines and anything else for the animals to feed on overnight. It was everyone's task to be on the lookout for bits of wood or peelings of sugar cane for our cooking fires, and to help keep them dry overnight, just in case we woke to the misfortune of a sudden tropical downpour.

By the time we joined her in the backyard on mornings, Grandmother would have been up for hours. She was out of bed at the crack of dawn, getting an early start on the day, taking care of the *stocks*. Sometimes in our bed we heard her praying, often as she listened to one of the many who took literally the biblical admonition to go preaching in the highways and byways. These preachers, usually women, went from village to village warning that Christ was coming soon, and proclaiming destructions and damnation because of wickedness in people's hearts. In front of our house always seemed to be a popular spot to stop and spread the word, before they moved on to another point in the village. They preached at the top of their voices, their solemn message resonating in the early morning calm, with only the occasional cooing of a dove intruding in a moment of prayer.

These preachings were to be taken seriously, because we knew that when certain missionaries arrived it was usually a final warning to someone in the village an omen for that unnamed person to get his or her temporal affairs in order. When the preaching was accompanied by the cooing of doves, we knew death stalked the village and had picked its next victim. And if we had heard dogs crying at night, because we knew dogs could see ghosts and the like, it was only a matter of time waiting to find out whom in the village death had decided to carry away. By praying along with these preachers, Grandmother felt that she had interceded with God to let the angel of death pass over her house.

By the time we joined Grandmother on mornings, the dew glistening on the grass beyond the paling, beyond the sheep pen beside the outhouse, beyond the shaded area where she had emptied the poe to prevent the midday sun from accentuating the rank smells of the pee, she would have started her preparations for the day. She fed the *fowls* and turkeys and collected their eggs, which she sold to the rich white people on the south coast of the island.

Grandmother had a foolproof way of testing her fowls to determine how many more eggs she could expect by the end of the day. As they pecked the corn or discarded rice pickings, she would grab a hen and swiftly push her small finger into the bottom of the squawking fowl, in search of an egg. Should any hen consistently fail this test, Grandmother isolated it as having "laid out its lather." That chicken was tied with a string in the backyard and purged for a week, fed only water and grains, before it was killed and heavily marinated and cured with generous amounts of salt and lime juice, before becoming the centrepiece of our Sunday meal.

Sometimes, Grandmother's day started on a miserable note. She might have discovered one or two of her chickens or turkeys missing. Later, some of the neighbourhood boys would tease us about what a great stew the turkey or chicken had made for their family. Other times, Grandmother might select a prized turkey or chicken for sale. She would force-feed it, mixing pollard or cornmeal in the feed. Holding down the bird, she would force open its beak and shove balls of the feed down its gagging throat, pouring in water to wash it down. The chickens and turkeys were sold by weight. After such a feeding, the poor thing was often too heavy to walk. This way, however, Grandmother was always assured of the best possible price.

With feeding out of the way, Grandmother swept the yard, using a broom made from the long, hard spines of palm tree leaves. And she would have started the fire in the

backyard to ready our first meal of the day. If it was rain-
ing, Grandmother shielded the fire with a large piece of
galvanized tin. If a heavy downpour had left the yard water-
logged, she had no choice but to haul out the coal pot and
cook in the house. On those days our clothes smelled of
smoke and the foods she had cooked.

Most mornings we awoke to the intoxicating smell of
Écafe coffee, which came in small packages. She boiled the
coffee, and the sweet aroma was our morning wakeup call.
My favourite *tea* was made from rolled chocolate. This was
unrefined chocolate brought to Barbados from elsewhere
in the Caribbean. It was rolled in sticks and was usually
sold house to house by hawkers. Grandmother would
dissolve a stick or two in boiling water, together with a bay
leaf or some cinnamon, and produce a rich broth of chocolate tea with a thick creamy froth on the top. To make it
even tastier, she would add the milk of grated coconut and
a generous dollop of Carnation condensed milk. She always
swore by the Carnation brand, if only because it was
imported from England. A good breakfast for me was the
chocolate *tea* and a roasted sweet potato. This I got from
running out to greet Mrs. Campbell, the woman who sold
potatoes, yams, eddoes and other ground provisions from
the back of her donkey cart each morning. She liked me
and always gave me an extra medium-sized potato for free.
We placed them directly in the fire. The skins would burn
black, but the inside would be white, steaming and delicious. Sometimes, we even ate bits of the burnt skin, just
for the fun of it.

When she was in a happy mood, Grandmother boiled
flour drops in the chocolate. These small dumplings sank

to the bottom of the *tots*—tin cans with handles that we used as cups—and were the ultimate reward when we finally got to them. Or, instead of flour drops, she sometimes produced stacks of *bakes,* somewhat like fried pancakes, the batter made from flour, salt, sugar and baking powder. Or she made fried fish cakes containing either salted cod or the sprats that we bought in Oistins, a nearby town. Bakes were a main staple for many Bajans, but nobody willingly owned up to this as only the very poor ate them, and only the wretched of the earth had cold bakes for school lunches. We often had no choice, but we were discreet with our secrets. The same went for plain boiled rice, or white rice as we called it. No way we admitted to eating *scald* rice, as Grandmother had labelled it. The rice had to contain peas, beans or some vegetable such as okra, spinach or bits of meat and fish. When none of these was available, anything else became a likely substitute, even if it were diced potato and breadfruit.

Sometimes as a treat, Grandmother modified the recipe for bakes by kneading the batter into firm dough. Instead of frying it in lard oil, she cut the dough into firm balls, occasionally adding raisins or currants, and cooked them in her iron *buck* pot. The result was muffins, a kind of tea biscuit that was absolutely delicious and filling, and also socially more acceptable.

At other times we might very well wake up to the sizzling sounds of the frying pan, with Grandmother warming the leftovers from the previous night. Usually it was rice minus the sauce or gravy, which would turn sour overnight because we had no refrigeration. Other times, it might be crisp, fried slabs of the Barbadian national dish, *cou-cou*, a mixture of boiled cornmeal and okra. And if our father in England was generous, or the remittances from the British Army were coming on time and with dependable frequency, Grandmother might splurge a bit. Instead of selling all the eggs, she would hardboil a few for us.

*   *   *

Life was not easy for us in Lodge Road, a community nestled between several sugar cane plantations. Lodge Road was a relic from slavery, an outpost that had not changed much in the century that had passed since the ending of slavery and my arrival in the village. In many respects, Lodge Road was an isolated little pocket. Its spine was a narrow tarred road, which provided the main connection to Bridgetown, the capital with its parliament, law courts, rich people and the headquarters of the Pilgrim Holiness Church where we worshipped. The road also led to Oistins, a small town that was within walking distance. Oistins has a proud history of being the place where Barbadian settlers negotiated a peace treaty with Oliver Cromwell in 1651. These planters did not approve of the beheading of King Charles I and resisted all efforts by Cromwell to turn them into republicans without representation. To prove a point, they went ahead and issued a unilateral declaration of independence, essentially declaring that Barbados would remain independent until the British monarchy was restored, thereby creating quite a serious and auspicious precedent in British Commonwealth law. Cromwell immediately imposed a military blockade on the island—one of the first exacted on a Caribbean island and the forerunner of such things as the economic embargo that the United States of America imposed on Cuba some three hundred years later—and succeeded in forcing the Barbadians to surrender.

However, they did not go easily. The rebels negotiated an agreement that, among other things, ensured that Barbadians would always have a government freely elected by taxpayers—and this was before the famed Boston Tea Party in the American colonies—and that they would have the right to set up a parliament, the third oldest in the British Commonwealth, and to have law courts modelled on those in Britain. Recreated on this outpost called Little England were the institutions and norms of life that were mirror images of those in the mother country, England. These settlers, some of whom starting as miscreants exiled in this penal colony, were among some of the earliest outside England to claim the rights and privileges of the lauded Magna Carta.

As a result of this peace treaty, sometimes known as the Charter of Barbados, the island never became a crown colony. It stands out as the only English possession in the Caribbean never to be ruled directly from England. The British governor always had to seek approval of a legislative assembly. Barbados was one of the earliest Caribbean colonies to institute internal rule, a kind of apprenticeship for full political independence. For this, Barbados never had recourse to the British treasury. It always had to rely on its taxpayers for the maintenance and development of its local institutions and infrastructure.

These rights negotiated at Oistins in 1651 (ratified on August 18, 1652) eventually formed the basis for the Barbados constitution when the island gained independence in 1966, but long before then Barbadian colonists had spread the "freedoms and privileges" gained from the treaty throughout the Caribbean and the eastern United States. Later, my teachers would point out with pride that when Ian Smith in the then-named Rhodesia thumbed his nose at Britain and issued a unilateral declaration of independence in the 1960s, he was somewhat misusing a precedent that had had its beginning in British law from the treaty signed in Oistins. It is this pride, sense of achievement and political maturity expressed in the national motto, *Pride and Industry*, that every school child would learn in an independent Barbados.

Growing up in Lodge Road, we couldn't care less about the importance of such rights and privileges. Oistins was simply a beautiful beach where we went to play and frolic in the sea, or to bring home the white sands to spread around our homes at festive times. It was the main fishing village for us, where we could go in the afternoon and watch the men pull their *moses*, their fishing boats, up to the shore loaded with flying fish, shark, dolphin, barracuda, pot fish such as snapper and others caught in pots or traps set on the floor of the Atlantic Ocean: sea eggs, conga eels and occasionally a turtle. It was Oistins where we went to the noisy fish markets, where we learnt how to haggle over the prices as the sun set and the day's catch had to be disposed of speedily because there was no refrigeration. It was from Oistins where we knew the men on bicycles had come, with their boxes loaded with the fish they were selling. Oistins was also the site of the lone police station in the region, and the only cinema, public library, alms house and neo-natal clinic, or *babylea*, for women.

*　　*　　*

Although it wasn't much, Grandmother took great pride in her house. Whenever she could afford it, she splurged with some paint, or hauled the big mahogany chairs out into the backyard and got us to apply another coat of varnish. We covered the inside walls of the house with newspaper and magazine pages. I didn't know of any other house decorated like this, and when I asked her, Grandmother explained that in big countries, such as England and America, well-to-do people wallpapered the insides of their homes. Since she couldn't afford wallpaper, she said, she saw nothing wrong with substituting sheets of newspaper. "When yuh don't have a horse, yuh ride a cow," was one of her favourite aphorisms.

As I grew older, it became my task to scrub the floor, a job that I took over from Princess. Every Saturday, first thing in the morning, I scoured the pasture looking for white top bush, a hardy weed with reputed cleansing abilities. I sprinkled the floor with the detergent and water mixed with antiseptic Jeye's Fluid. On my knees and hands, I scrubbed away, using a big piece of cloth to soak up the dingy water and soap. When the floor dried, I sprinkled sand to absorb the grease from food that would fall on the floor or the dirt we brought into the house on our feet. At least that is what Grandmother told me.

My friends argued that the sand was really to keep *duppies* or spirits of the departed out of the house. Apparently, when a ghost arrives at a house and finds sand, the duppie is compelled to stop and count every grain. This was an impossible task to complete before the sun came up and the duppie had to flee. Also the cleansing smell of Jeye's Fluid was supposed to keep spirits away. Grandmother, claiming to be a woman of God and a proud member of the Pilgrim Holiness Church, simply dismissed such talk as foolishness from people believing in too much Obeah. "If yuh trust in the true and living God, the only Obeah that can trouble yuh is what you eat, not what somebody say or do."

The sand was transported from Oistins, in pails and buckets on our heads. This was when it was legal to simply walk onto any beach and cart away loads of this white gold, before beaches became a national treasure and tourism became the mainstay of the local economy. We piled the sand in one corner of the backyard, or instead of sand, we sometimes went to the limestone quarries in the area and brought home the marl, or crushed limestone. Grandmother liked the marl better, because it wasn't as gritty, wasn't as noticeable when it got into the food, and because she could bury any number of green limes in the marl and know that they would keep virtually forever.

Another corner of the yard was set aside for more personal use, and it was where we bathed. A large tub or basin was always close by, but it would never contain water until we were ready to use it. Grandmother absolutely forbade any of us from bathing in water that had been "sitting in the hot broiling sun all day long." Such water, for whatever reason, Grandmother argued, caused strokes. She made us bathe only with fresh water from the lone stand-pipe in our section of the village.

Grandmother had a problem getting us to bathe, as we preferred simply to *wash up*, or, as more common among boys of our age, to *wash our face'n'hands*, which sometimes included splashing water on our feet as well. However, Grandmother demanded that my brothers and I got a good bathing every Sunday. Princess would sit me in the wash-tub and scrub me from head to foot. Vaseline was applied to the hair to help comb out the kinks; applied elsewhere it served as lotion to stop dry skin and white soap film on the feet, arms and face. Stephen had the chore of bringing water from the pipe, often having to join the long evening lineup to await his turn. He had to make several trips to fill the water barrel in the backyard. The last bucket of water was for drinking. We kept it in the house, with a stick across the mouth of the pail and a white cloth thrown over it to keep out moths and ants during the night.

In the brightest corner of the yard, Grandmother had assembled a kind of rock garden. This was the area for bleaching clothes, including the washing that she occasionally took in from the white people on the south coast. Early in the morning, she would soak the clothes in a washtub. Later she *rubbed* them out with a *jucking* board. "See this jucking board here, boy?" Grandmother would say to me, bending over the board to get more leverage, the water from the wash soaking the front of her dress. "Your father, Freddie, make this for me. Before he left for England. He did also make a tub outta a barrel for me to wash in, but that tub mash up now." It was easy to find examples of my father's fine craftsmanship and other talents everywhere I looked. With time, his mastery appeared to extend to every possible area of life, and this made me pine to know who was this genius everyone said was my father.

To get the washing really clean, or to remove stains, Grandmother spread the soapy wet clothes on the stones and let the hot sun dry them. Intermittently, she splashed water on the clothes, waited for the sun to dry them, then splashed on more water, repeating this process several times during the day. Before catching the last of the sun, she dipped the clothes in water to which she had added starch from cassava roots—usually called balled starch because of the hawkers going from house to house selling the white balls—and hung them to dry on a line or a nearby bush. Grandmother swore that nothing beat the rocks for a good bleaching of the clothes.

Perhaps the pride of Grandmother's backyard was the large boulder with the smooth top that sat just beyond the back door. This served as a kind of throne for her, where she sat and stirred the rice or whatever she was cooking; where she often took time for herself to just think. Close by, she kept the wood and bits of paper and cardboard needed for the fire. Every so often she put a large piece of wood on the fire. We liked it when she had a piece of pine because the wood gave off a sweet smell. Grandmother kept the pine for burning at night, when we sat in the backyard. She used the pine sparingly for cooking, because it gave off lots of soot that blackened the cooking utensils and, she said, gave her more work scrubbing them clean.

We would sit around the fire with Grandmother enthroned on the big rock, her dress or skirt lapped between her legs, while she told us stories. She taught us about our family history and painted glowing pictures for Stephen, Errol and me about the great life awaiting us, when we joined our parents in England. And she told us about the nice English gentlemen and ladies she had met through the years; how we, too, were destined to be English gentlemen, but that we must always remember that we were black and that when we came back to Barbados to visit her, or more likely to attend her funeral or whatever, we shouldn't lose our natural Barbadian accent and appear too *poor-great* like some people she knew. We would sit in the backyard, under the bright open sky, with millions of stars twinkling at us, dreaming, laughing loudly and catching up on our individual experiences of the passing day. Many nights, she let me put my head in her lap and in the morning, I would stir from my bedding, not knowing at what point I had drifted off to sleep or who had put me to bed.

Despite these good times, it didn't take much to upset the routine, reminding us how vulnerable we were. We lived in dread of a heavy downpour, and the rainy season was the worst period for us. Our house was situated beside an unpaved cart road about two hundred yards off the main road. With the first heavy rain the cart road quickly became a series of water holes. Our house backed onto a small parcel of land which led into a cane field. In the rainy season the parcel of land became a pond, with water trapped against the high edge row of the cane field and draining onto our land.

The floodings drove Grandmother to desperation and made her grumble about why she was even paying rent to Ashby for this house spot. Over the years, she had begged

Ashby to dig a well, or *suckhole*, down to the natural water table to provide drainage during the rainy season. But nothing ever came of her plea. Worse, because the rented land was so prone to being waterlogged, Grandmother could not work it, which meant that she could not plant the beans, cassava, pumpkins, sweet potatoes, yams and other ground provisions, like her neighbours, and at least reduce her food bill.

When it rained, we shifted into the house, which really didn't provide much shelter as each downpour always seemed to discover new leaks. Often, they were not in the spots where Grandmother had strategically placed containers to catch the dripping water. She spent these nights worrying that rain would fall on the heated glass chimney of the kerosene lamp and cause it to split open or shatter. After these downpours, when the sun came out, we tried to pull tar from the road to plug the holes in the roof.

Another threat was usually more frightening. Several times, our family gatherings were interrupted by neighbours throwing stones at us. Or, from the darkness, they simply stoned the house, sending us scattering from the backyard.

*   *   *

By the time I arrived in Lodge Road, Errol and Stephen were already going to school. For me, it was just one long wait until I was old enough to join them at the age of five. I cried when they left home on mornings and I couldn't wait for them to get back home on evenings. Throughout the day, I fired a barrage of questions about school to

Princess and Grandmother. "Soon. Soon. Soon," Grandmother promised. "You soon going to school, like a big boy." Almost every night, I was after Stephen to teach me my A-B-Cs, or to help me to count to ten, so I'd be ready for school. I wore my brothers' navy blue school caps whenever I could and, to appease me, Grandmother promised fervently that it was just a matter of time before she bought me my own cap.

"Could you buy it now?" I asked.

"I guess so. I could buy it and put it down until you become a big boy. Wait until I next go into town to shop." Going into the capital, Bridgetown, to shop was one of the focal points of Grandmother's week. She steadfastly refused to buy anything but the essentials from the shops in the village, arguing that the local shopkeepers couldn't be trusted not to cheat her out of her money, and that the quality of what they sold was inferior and always more expensive. After the daily chores and morning tea, she headed off to the city, catching the bus that ran through Lodge Road. She bought all the foodstuff and anything necessary for the upkeep of the house, but more important, she bought the provisions that provided a living for her. Grandmother usually came back home with her basket laden down with all types of fruit—mangoes, bananas, golden apples, oranges and plums—which she later sold. Rather, she sold what we did not feast on. Grandmother made this trip into the city at least once during the week and on Saturdays. Her return home was always a treat for us.

Every trip, I looked for the cap when she came home, and every time, Grandmother said it had slipped her mind. Her forgetfulness, she said, was a sure sign that she was getting old and absent-minded, or perhaps it was because she always had so much business to conduct in the city. It became a question of how she and I could come up with a scheme to remind Grandmother to buy the cap. Finally, we settled on tying a string on her finger. Every week as she prepared to go to Bridgetown I reminded her of the string. Every week, though, she still forgot.

3

Sugar and Oatmeal

It was impossible to escape the legacy and importance of the sugar cane industry on the island. Just about every aspect of life in Lodge Road was in some way affected by the Ashby families, which must have been a holdover from the plantation era. There were the black Ashbys, who didn't have much money even if they lived better than we did. These were the Ashbys from whom Grandmother rented the house spot. Then there were the half-white Ashbys who owned large tracts of land. One of these Ashbys had a very senior job with government and was one of the first to own a car in our village.

The most influential Ashby lived on the outer edge of the village, where he had a big limestone house and fruit trees in the backyard. One morning Grandmother and I were out walking in the area when we got caught in a downpour. We took shelter in Ashby's garage, where I came across a piano. I had not seen a piano before; not even our church had one. I started pressing the keys and delighted myself with the resulting notes.

"Boy, you, like you is a real musician," Grandmother said. "Here you is playing the people piano as if you're your father self. And you sounding good, good, good, too. Boy, I like I have to watch you: you, like you is the next musician in the family. I can't wait to see what happen to you when you get with your father and he can teach you music. You'd like that, right?"

"Yes, Grandmother."

The rain ended and we went home. That night as we sat around the fire and Grandmother recalled my exploits, I triumphantly pulled from my pocket a keepsake I had been fingering and dreaming about all day: a black piano key. Grandmother frowned. We took it back the next morning.

But the Ashbys, especially the family that Grandmother rented the house spot from, were our link to the plantation and a reminder of what role villages like Lodge Road played in the local economy. Our village and community life was dictated by what happened on the plantations. The highlight occurred soon into the new year, when we noticed the sugar cane fields blooming and long arrows flowering at the top of the cane stalks. That was when I was likely to overhear Grandmother and the neighbours talking excitedly about the start of the crop season. The animated discussion was usually about which men in the village had decided to spend the season working for which plantations.

The first week of the crop season was ritualistic, beginning with services held the Sunday at the Anglican churches across the land, with the sermon from St. Michael's Cathedral in Bridgetown being broadcast on local radio. Monday morning, bright and early, the men trooped off to the plantation of choice and signed up for duty. They carried sharpened cane bills and machetes, and enamel or tin pails containing their lunch and water. The cane cutters were expected to work from sunup to sundown. They hacked and cut the long rows of canes, stacking them in neat rows for the women who followed them and loaded the canes onto the trucks and tractor carts. The women often had to *head* the canes, carrying large loads on their heads to the men who loaded the canes onto the cart or truck.

About the time the sun became scorching, other women turned up in the cane fields. They sold food and refreshments, especially the local drink *mauby*, which they kept cool in clay jars called monkeys that they transported on their heads. These women did everything with flair, while keeping up a steady stream of conversation and offering the odd joke to entertain the workers. One trick was to hold a glass or cup in one hand. While trying to finalize the next sale, the woman reached up and turned the spigot on the monkey. The mauby poured into the container, building a big foamy head, not spilling a drop, with the woman not missing a beat in her talking and haggling.

The crop season was a period for rejoicing and celebrating. On Saturday nights, the men assembled in the shops and spent freely. Usually, they talked a lot and bought large quantities of rum, much more than at any other time of the year. They purchased tinned sardines and biscuits, or smoked herring. Sometimes they bought tins of corned beef which they crushed and mixed with onions, black pepper and hot pepper sauce. They ate this with biscuits and drank rum. This was also a good time for the hawkers, especially those with the local delicacy, black pudding and souse. The vendors set up their coal pots outside the shop and did a licking business.

The crop season was when the local economy purred, when parents could afford to buy new shoes and clothes for the children, paint and furniture for the house. Importantly, this was when they were able to retire debts accumulated from *trusting* at the neighbourhood shops during the previous months of little or no work. Grandmother always swore that she and her children did not have the physical constitution for the slave labour associated with harvesting cane, but the sugar cane harvest was the main employment for the men and women in the area, especially those without a grammar school education. The better-off women worked as domestics, and for a rarity, might get a civil service position. Grandmother's aspiration was that her family should have the education and acumen to avoid working in the cane field, to avoid doing the same jobs as their slave ancestors.

Nights during the harvest, we sat in the backyard and savoured the sweet smells of the boiling sugar from the factory in the distance, as the aroma wafted across the island. This was a time to be alive in Lodge Road. And it was even more joyous when one of the workers at the sugar factory bought us a bottle of syrup, which we used mainly for making *swank* by adding water. Or we added lime juice for a kind of lemonade. Sometimes they brought us cracked liquor, the first boiling of the sugar cane juice, or molasses in any of its various forms. Throughout the day, and even into the night, we spent long hours *sucking*, really chewing, on the soft part of the cane and enjoying the sweet juice. Sometimes we sucked so much cane there was no room in our stomachs for the evening meal.

*　　*　　*

Danie and I were playing in his grandmother's backyard when he asked if I wanted to break a piece of cane. This meant doing something wrong; *to break cane* was the local parlance for raiding someone's field and stealing the cane—most often from breaking the cane across the knee. Watchmen at the plantations were always on the lookout for people breaking cane. When they caught them, the watchmen often used their hardwood night sticks on them. Or had them arrested.

"What you mean?" I asked, remembering Grandmother's stern admonition that I should not follow bad company or allow anyone to lead me into trouble.

"Come with me."

Danie led me into his grandmother's cane field, almost into the heart of the field, through the dry trash that tangled our feet and the long, sharp-edged cane leaves that cut our faces. Finally, we came to the desired spot. Standing before us were long, fat cane stalks. These were special pockets of cane—their colour was yellow, and everyone knew that the softest, sweetest and juiciest canes were yellow with long joints. Danie grabbed a cane and adeptly broke it, using his foot to first mash the stalk down, then breaking off the top. I followed him. Soon, we had cleared a spot among the cane thrash, *sucking* our bellies full of sweet, sticky juice. By the time we were finished, the area was well festooned with cane peelings and the pith we had chewed on.

Every day, I visited Danie. And every day, when we thought nobody was looking, we slipped into the field, found our favourite spot and broke cane.

"What the two o' you doing in the cane field?" a voice called to us as we snuck out one day. It was one of Danie's cousins. "I know, you've been breaking cane. I'm going to tell on you."

"Tell on me, nuh," Danie said dismissively, but I knew he was worried about being reported to his grandmother. To steal canes, especially his grandmother's, would warrant a beating for him and possibly a complaint to my grandmother, both of which were serious. For proof that we were sucking cane, they needed only to look at the dry white trails left by the juice that ran down the sides of our mouths and chin. They needed only to look closely at our palms for those fine thorn-like growths that stuck in our hands when we broke the cane; they had only to look at the sticky juice stains on our knees from where we had broken the long canes into more manageable pieces.

Danie's grandmother heard the complaint and surprised us.

"So what you would prefer he to do?" she asked. "You want him to go and break the plantation cane and get in trouble? No, I prefer that he break and suck my own cane than anybody else's. And even so, how much cane can the two o' them break out of a big cane field?"

Daily, until the men came with their machetes and flattened Danie's grandmother's field, I had an extra reason for leaving home and playing with him.

But the crop season wasn't all fun. Certainly, the cane fires were frightening experiences, and for me it was one of the most terrifying times of the year. I can still remember one fire very clearly.

The heavy, choking smoke from the fires darkened the afternoon sky and had long forced us from our homes. We were huddled in the shop at the side of the main road, waiting for either help or disaster to arrive. We felt the heat and heard the roaring and the loud popping noises the canes made as they fell before the flames. Some houses were in more immediate danger than ours. They were closer to the cane fields and sour grass pastures near the quarry and some of them had cane fields almost up to their back doors. Anticipating the worst, the occupants of the most threatened houses had removed furniture and other family valuables. The wall of fire had started some time earlier and was spreading with the aid of a strong breeze, heading right in our direction. We could only wait for the fire to consume our houses, or for the firefighters to come to our rescue.

Suddenly, in the distance, we heard the wailing sound of a fire engine siren. We saw it coming up Lodge Road, speeding towards us through the thick smoke. We could make out the men with black helmets and black plastic-looking uniforms and boots, with the big canvas hoses. The tension eased audibly, especially when the first fire engine swung off the main road, swerving past the shop where we had congregated and headed for the cane fields.

The tension had wrung us so tight that as the fire engine started up the unpaved road, I broke loose from the crowd and began running behind the fire engine, like some hypnotized moth towards the wall of fire. My actions were instinctive, unplanned. I was simply running.

"Where are you going?" Aunty Princess screamed after me. She was running full tilt to catch up to me. "Where you going?"

She grabbed me by the collar. We walked back to join the crowd, me with my heart still pounding in my chest, still breathing hard, still frightened. Slowly, the tension eased, abating as the smoke lightened, as the heat subsided, as the loud cracks and pops from the fire became less frightening, as the firemen—with the help of a shifting wind—removed the threat, until the next time.

For days, this near miss was all we talked about. The men went out and cut the burnt canes, giving them priority so the juice wouldn't ferment and spoil. About this time, I decided upon the job for me when I grew up: a fireman.

*   *   *

When the crop season finally wrapped up, its importance was marked with a great party celebrating the end of the harvest. The workers put on a big feast with much dancing and eating, with performances by fife and kettle drum troupes, called *tuk* bands, and by local calypso singers. Accompanying masquerade bands included men and women dancing on stilts or in a donkey costume. In another bow to the importance of tourism, this celebration has become the annual carnival called Crop Over, and attracts large numbers of visitors to the island.

Initially, tourism was encouraged to smooth out the hard times between the sugar crop seasons. These interims had been endured by the workers surviving with a few jobs, such as tilling or weeding the cane fields, or planting and reaping green peas, sweet potatoes and other ground provisions from fields resting between crops. The men might get a day's job planting corn on the plantation, but most of them would be on the look-out for construction work or gardening jobs. Others would go fishing or just wait out the hard times. The luckiest might get chosen by the government to go to North America to work as agricultural workers during the off season. Tourism was to break this dependence on sugar and to help undermine the hold plantations had on our lives. It was a contentious decision to diversify the economy. As a young boy, I couldn't help hearing the heated debate among the politicians that spilled over into the shops and even the churches and schools.

This debate became even more heated when Errol Barrow, then premier of the island and the man hoping to take the island into a new future as an independent nation, denounced the island's reliance on sugar cane. Barrow said he envisioned the day when a sugar cane blade would not cut his face, when the women of the island would no longer be reduced "to being beasts of burden" working in the cane fields in conditions no different from in the days of slavery. Even then some of his supporters felt he had gone too far: how could anyone denounce sugar cane, the main industry on the island for three centuries, and for what? Something as intangible as tourism?

We, too, discussed the statements. While Grandmother was indifferent to the sugar cane industry and chose not to work in the cane fields, she knew the economic hold the industry maintained on the island, and on the lives of everyone in the village.

* * *

Generally, the crop season and the availability of money led to other types of celebrations, such as weddings or services of songs. Traditionally, weddings were community events. Often, they marked the final decision by a man and woman to set their affairs in order, especially in the sight of God and the religious law of the land. Marriage seldom had much to do with family life or procreation, and it was not unusual for the bride and groom to have grown children. The marriage often took place after the man or the woman had "found Christ" and decided to give up on living in sin. Or it was a means to satisfy the law of the day on questions of inheritance.

It was not unusual for the wedding date to be set after a revival meeting at one of the churches, perhaps when marriage was the message for the week. The churches would be packed, with more people on the outside watching to see the "sinners" make their way to the altar and denounce their previous lifestyles.

Some of the most cynical regarded this as a spectacle, watching to see who would walk to the altar and taking bets as to how soon the new convert could be expected to backslide and return to the ingrained old ways. "But looka how Boysie, that old time brute all these years, going up there to the people altar and with long waters running outta he eyes saying how his life now change, that he ain't stealing no more, ain't cussing no more, ain't fighting no more and ain't drinking his liquors no more," was a typical comment. "Well, just let we wait and see. 'Cause Boysie like his liquors too bad. The rummakers would got to close down if he stop drinking and getting drunk, drunk, drunk. And his women, too, say he done with them, and he done got a child or two in every parish. Now, I guess, he gotta set heself straight with that woman he now live with."

Nonetheless, a marriage was an opportunity for celebration, and one wedding stands out in my mind.

We had been playing around, the older people in their homes, but all of us keeping an ear open. Then, we heard the horns sounding, signalling the bride and groom were coming home, and we started running. The procession of cars wound slowly through the village, with people running alongside, all of us coming from various directions to congregate at the home of the newlyweds. The families of the bride and groom arrived first and took their positions in front of the house. As long as I could remember, this was the first time that the front door and all the windows were thrown open. On the inside, we could see the colourful decorations, including specially made white curtains that flapped in the wind, some of them blowing through the door like a tongue teasingly slipping out of a mouth. Traditionally, what was called the front house of a Bajan home was used for special occasions only. This was where families kept their precious heirlooms and furniture, and the windows and doors were usually kept shut against prying eyes.

The bride and groom arrived. They smiled as they walked up the heavily marled path and stopped on the top step. The photographer set up his camera, family members and friends gathered around and flashbulbs started popping. Hundreds of photographs were taken, some to frame and hang in the house, several for the family album, others to give to friends and family in Barbados and abroad.

I noticed the little boys in their long-sleeved white shirts, ties and black pants and the girls in their frilly dresses, all trying to be on their best behaviour. More than that, they were feasting, moving around the backyard with plates of cake and puddings and glasses with drink. The boys and girls were acting as if they no longer knew us—those of us who had come running even though we weren't invited, and who were now standing outside the house happily joining in what had become a communal celebration.

Men and women arrived, passed through the waiting crowd and entered the house. They, too, were soon feasting. I watched the brother of the bride frantically chopping off the tops of coconuts, trying to keep up with the demand. In a corner of the backyard, great big bunches of water coconuts were in one heap. In another corner were the discarded shells from those that Basil had slashed in half so the guests could get at the soft, sweet jelly inside. Once the invited guests had had their fill, we onlookers would move in and take what was left.

Suddenly there was a loud scream and people started running to where Basil stood, holding a hand from which blood was dripping. He had chopped off the tip of his thumb and had to be rushed to hospital. As soon as the car disappeared, the celebration resumed, the formal part of the evening culminating with speeches and the *sticking* of the wedding cakes, when the newlyweds would cut the cake and, as a symbol of their union, exchange pieces by mouth to much applause. The wedding cake was now ready to be parceled out in the coming days, particularly to those who gave gifts. For a long time afterwards, Basil was a hero of sorts. Everybody commiserated with him for the great sacrifice of losing his thumb at his sister's wedding, and for not getting a chance to enjoy the feast of a lifetime because of having to spend the night at the hospital.

Whereas weddings were ostensibly for invited guests only, with spectators expected to stay at a distance, at least initially, and delight themselves by gawking and gossiping, the same was not true for services of songs. This was an opportunity for an enterprising business person to make a quick dollar. Someone would hoist a large tarpaulin tent in the backyard and invite the world to attend. Members of the local acappella choir, hired for the Sunday evening, came dressed in their best suits and gowns. They sang, the harmony ringing out in further invitation, and the host supplied food and drinks—at a price. Anyone could enter and sit around, as long as he or she paid the admission.

In Lodge Road the big dances of the week were on Saturday nights at Club Randal dance hall. Anyone could rent the hall and throw a dance, usually hiring the best available DJ and hi-fi set or a live band, such as the one in which my father had apparently been the lead musician.

*   *   *

Whenever possible, Grandmother chose to avoid these community events. She claimed that she had attended dances and services of song as a young girl, but that since she became a Christian, such things were behind her, and she made sure that *our* lives also revolved around the church. On Sunday mornings, she would head off to the service at the local Pilgrim Holiness Church, returning home to cook the meal of the week. The Sunday meal was always special. This was when she served a choice piece of meat, perhaps pork, lamb or beef ordered from the local butcher, or one of her turkeys or chickens. Even though cou-cou was deemed the national dish, there was no way she would serve such a low-class meal on Sundays. That was a Saturday meal, the same way that soups and *dry food*—boiled ground provisions usually served with butter sauce—were relegated for during the week. Fish was not generally served on the big day, either. The Sunday meal had to be special, so special that anyone passing in front the house would take notice of the sweet aroma.

This was the day when we got what was the closest to a healthy meal, with beets and a few lettuce leaves on the side, maybe some string beans, grated carrots or other vegetables. The staple of the meal was usually rice and peas, whether pigeon or dried. The entire meal was served on a heaping plate. The routine was to eat the rice and peas first, so that the best part, the meat, was kept for last. Sunday was also when Grandmother bought a block of ice from the truck that crisscrossed the island. I would buy the ice, add a generous coating of salt, wrap the block in a crocus bag, and store it in a container in a cool part of the house. On Sundays, we enjoyed special desserts, such as custards, soursop punch or any of Grandmother's various other delicacies. One of my favourites came from mixing evaporated milk, a red aerated drink—either a kola champagne type Fruitee or Ju-C—and coconut water, with the soft jelly from the coconut swimming between the pieces of ice. This, however, was a rare treat.

Then, it was time to relax for an hour or so before Stephen, Errol and I headed off for Sunday school. Grandmother attended the Sunday night service. During the week she would often take us along for the various services, or occasionally to an open-air meeting.

Every three months, Grandmother dressed me in my best clothes and took me with her into Bridgetown to attend the quarterly meeting of all the Pilgrim Holiness churches on the island. This was when the faithful met at the headquarters to celebrate and conduct church-related business. At first, I enjoyed the long drive into the city and the kind of picnic atmosphere, eating the sandwiches Grandmother had prepared for the occasion. But I hated the long services and the tiring drive back home. My presence at these meetings also served another purpose. It provided Grandmother with an opportunity to use me as a prop, to report to friends from various parts of the island on how well her son was doing in England, to remind people of Grandmother's pride at having a son who worked, not in the sugar cane fields, but in the British Army. A son who sent her pictures of his assignments in Europe, Africa and the Middle East. A son who was sending her back a little *tra-la* to put food on her table and to compensate her for raising his children.

"This is Freddie's last boy that I keeping for him until he can send for the three o' them," Grandmother told her friends. "And he's doing real, real good in England. He soon send for the three o' them now. And you know, the three boys' mother doing good, good, good sheself. The last they write me she's studying nursing at one o' them hospitals in England." The sisters and few brothers in the church would look on me, smile and compliment Grandmother for having such a successful son in England and for the great job she was doing raising the three of us. And they always warned me that when I got to England, in the lap of luxury, to remember the religious teaching to which I was being exposed at the church. Somehow, Stephen and Errol always seemed to escape having to attend these quarterly meetings.

There was, however, one aspect of church life that they never missed. It was the annual bus excursion, usually the final event of the long vacation before the new school year began. With much fanfare, the pastor would announce the date for the excursion to the congregation and set the prices for the adults and children to attend. The church would order the buses and with each approaching day the anticipation mounted. This was a dangerous period for Grandmother, when she had to keep close watch over her chickens and turkeys. Otherwise, some of them just might disappear a day or so before the excursion.

Grandmother often used the excursion to discipline us, threatening to "go and take back the excursion tickets to the church," if we didn't behave. For a while it worked, until we got older and realized the social importance of the excursion for her, as well as for us.

This was the time to display the latest fashions, for women and girls to spend nights straightening their hair with hot irons, styling it exquisitely; for the men and boys to get special haircuts. Next to Christmas, this was a *major* feast. Each family stacked a big basket or two with rice and peas, various stews, coconut breads and pudding, coconut water and other beverages, including alcohol for the men to imbibe when the pastor wasn't looking. The baskets were wrapped in big pieces of cloth or plastic to keep the food warm. Usually, the excursion was to the north of the island. It was an all-day affair and we had a special way of ending it. As we were nearing the village, everyone would start beating on the sides of the buses and singing at the top of his or her voice

> *Oh, Lord, me money gone*
> *In Maxwell pond.*

Also gone was the long vacation, of days playing cricket on Ashby's pasture or in competition with the boys from other villages, of frolicking at the beach, of setting *fly-stick* traps for wood doves or ground doves, of hunting the birds with gutta-percha slings. The next break from school would be for Christmas, but before then there was one major event that we had to celebrate.

In the months of September and October, we scoured the island for anything to make a bonfire. We were on the lookout for discarded tires from bicycles and cars, and felt extremely lucky if we found a big tire from a truck or a tractor. On the fifth of November we assembled in a pasture, poured kerosene on the tires and set a big bonfire, the burning of the balata tires lasting long into the night. The celebration of Guy Fawkes Day was the occasion for a fireworks display, and we particularly liked to set off our penny bombs, crackers and starlights. We also simulated the firing of cannons, the least expensive of the fireworks. All we needed was a can with a lid. We punctured a hole in the bottom and placed a piece of carbonate inside the can, spat on it and listened for the fizzing sound of the chemical reaction. When we touched a lit match to the hole in the bottom of the can, the resulting explosion sent the cover flying, just like a cannonball. Throughout the evening, we ate a special delicacy called *counkies* or stew dumplings. Among its ingredients were corn meal, grated sweet potato, coconuts, pumpkins, raisins and various spices. The mixture was wrapped in banana leaves and steam cooked. We couldn't get enough of them.

*   *   *

Grandmother finally remembered to buy my school cap. She brought it home and, after I tried it on to make sure it was the right fit, she placed it on a nail in the bedroom. The big day had finally come. With my cap on my head, I headed to Christ Church Boys' Elementary in Stephen's care. When he handed me off to the teachers, he took my cap for safe-keeping until the lunch break. My classroom was in a smaller building to the back of the main school. There, my classmates and I were delighted daily with some of the most wonderful stories told to us by a very amiable and oldish teacher, Mr. Moore, and a younger woman, Miss Small.

My going to school forced other changes on us. It soon became obvious that at five years old I could not make the quick dash home, eat lunch and run back to school, all in one hour. Stephen and Errol complained that I was causing them punishments as their teachers and the headmaster didn't hesitate to flog late arrivals. Grandmother came up with a plan, but it involved her making a big compromise. We would go next door to the school to Great-Grand's house, and Princess would bring our lunch there. This was not an easy thing for Grandmother, for even though Great-Grand was her mother and had supposedly raised my father, this mother and daughter never got along. But we met at Great-Grand's house, a stuffy smelling place that was always dark because the windows were kept closed. Great-Grand, who later died well past her century mark, was already getting on in age and this may have accounted for the conditions in the house. Then, I caused a crisis.

One day, Princess brought our lunch for us—piping hot oatmeal porridge. On such a hot day, in a closed-up house that was suffocating with heat because of the galvanized tin roof, I was sweating and could not stomach the porridge. I would not eat and started to cry.

"How Ermie expect these children to eat something like oatmeal porridge on a hot day like this?" Great-Grand asked angrily. Princess was in a bind.

"Look, I'll tell you what," Great-Grand offered. "Why don't you leave the oatmeal for later and let me make some lemonade for them."

I jumped at the offer, while Stephen and Errol kept their heads down over their steaming bowl.

"I . . . I . . . I don't know," Princess said.

"Except that I don't have any limes to make lemonade. I can only make sugar water."

I gladly accepted the cool sugared water and gulped it down, and headed back to school, except that Stephen and

Errol weren't any happier for getting back to school on time. I found out why when I got home.

"Fancy that," Grandmother scolded. "I send good, good, good oatmeal porridge for you and you let Great-Grand make you drink sugar water that ain't got anything nourishing in it for lunch. You too foolish." I had learned a valuable lesson: Grandmother had her pride and she expected us not to show her up.

*   *   *

Cars were rare in Lodge Road, and few people knew how to drive. One who could was Carl, who was a distant relative of Danie's. Carl worked in Bridgetown and he drove a small pick-up truck home every day at lunch. This was our treat. We gobbled down our lunches and waited until we heard him start the engine and sound the horn. We crowded into the back of the pick-up, so many of us crammed in that the springs cried louder than usual when the truck encountered its share of potholes. This was our thrill. While we sped down Lodge Road, we waved at those not so fortunate, those who had to walk on the hot tar road while we breezed by. And as the van neared the school gate, Carl played his part by ostentatiously *reading-down* the gears, expertly manipulating the clutch and speed by moving from fourth to third, second and first before stopping. We shouted our approval as we jumped off and boasted to our schoolmates for the rest of the day.

But just as suddenly our trump card disappeared. Someone must have complained about how unsafe it was for all of us crowded into the back of the pick-up, and how we added to the danger with our theatrics and misbehaving. Carl decided we could no longer ride in the pick-up.

Danie would have none of this. Carl got into the truck and sped off, not stopping to pick us up. Quick as a flash, Danie hopped onto the back and held on as the vehicle sped down Lodge Road. Soon it was gone from sight, with Danie still clinging onto the back bumper. Danie was now our newest hero. For days we talked about how he had hopped the pick-up. Each day, the story became more glorious. First, it was that Danie had hopped off soon after the truck disappeared from our sight. Then it was that he had hopped the van all the way to the school. Eventually, it was that he had hopped the van all the way to the city and that he might have even hopped it all the back home. I wished I were as bold as Danie, especially when he crouched over at the waist, held his hands up in front of his face, positioned his feet on an imaginary bumper and showed me how he had hopped the pick-up, how he had stuck to the back and Carl couldn't shake him no matter how fast he drove, and how he would do it again.

Grandmother heard the stories, too. But she must have heard a different version. How else to explain her decision to absolutely forbid any of us from even thinking of hopping a moving vehicle? Or why would she tell us about the foolish boys who hopped trucks and buses and who died when they fell and cracked opened their skulls so that their brains ran out, or when a vehicle ran over them. I suspect Danie must have got a similar warning, for despite his hero status and his proven ability to hop, I never heard of his trying this feat again.

It was about this time that I got drunk for the first time. It was Christmas, an open-house day across the island. For weeks, every home had prepared for the parties. Grandmother got into the act by making preparations for the best feast of the year. Lots of food and drinks, such as the traditional sorrel, were a must. To mark the occasion, Grandmother brought home the half-gallon bottle of rum that sat on the table for the entire day. A traditional drink was rum and *falernum*, a liquor made on the island from a supposedly secret recipe. People visited. In the spirit of Christmas charity just about anyone could show up on this day and freely help himself or herself to the drinks. This was great for children. Few of us ate at home on Christmas. Indeed, this was the one day Grandmother didn't mind our eating at the neighbours' houses. The early morning saw us at church, then we came home and moved from one home to another, feasting as we went. I liked eating at the neighbours as they usually had a big ham, something Grandmother never did. To me, the surest sign of Christmas was when the neighbours brought home the ham in the brown crocus bag and hung it from the roof of the kitchen. A few days before Christmas, they scraped the tar from the ham, soaked it to remove some of the salt, and boiled it. On that special day, ham, coconut bread and various cakes awaited everyone. And, when nobody was looking, we took a nip from the rum bottle, just like the adults. By mid-afternoon, the nipping had caught up with me. I staggered in the pasture in front of our house, trying to catch up to the boys going from house to house. But I couldn't. The pasture started to spin: the houses and faces looked distorted. "Look, Cecil like he drunk, yuh," was the last I heard someone saying before I toppled over into the khus-khus grass at the edge of the pasture and spent the rest of the day sleeping.

*   *   *

One day Mrs. Brown, the next door neighbour, saw me playing with her two sons and called me over to join the group of women sitting and talking in her shed-roof. For a six-year-old child this was special treatment, to be invited by big people to come and address them. I felt proud, even if Grandmother had warned us to be very careful about what we said in public so that we didn't carry news from home that bad-minded people could use against her. She didn't want us to accept food from them and would have stopped me from playing with their children if it would not have been so hard on me. Grandmother and the women who lived around us had frequent fallings-out when, for long periods, they didn't speak to one another.

"So, little boy," Mrs. Brown said. "Why is your Aunty Princess' belly looking so fat these days?" The women giggled knowingly.

"Well," I said, standing straight with importance, "it's from all the food she does eat." The women were now laughing uncontrollably. This drove me on. Indeed, until Mrs. Brown had asked, I hadn't noticed any change in Princess, but given this rare opportunity to speak with adults, I felt I had to show off.

"Grandmother keep telling her that she sleeps too much and that she does eat too much. I think it's the food."

"She eat too much, eh?" Mrs. Brown said, trying to control her own laughter. "All right. If you say so. She eat too much, eh? Well, let's wait a couple more months and see what happen to all that food in she belly."

I ran away to continue playing, feeling quite proud of myself, for I had made the grown-ups laugh.

*   *   *

I came through the paling door and saw him sitting there, talking with Grandmother. "Good evening, Dadah!" I cried.

"But look at you *doah, nuh*?" Grandfather feigned disapproval. "Coming home like that with your shirttail flying behind yuh?"

I quickly stuffed the back of the shirt into my pants. Dadah started laughing. "How you doing?" he said, standing back and looking at me quizzically, as if examining how much I had grown since the last time we had seen each other. "What you learn in school today?"

"Oh, nothing," I said.

"Nothing," he teased. "You mean to tell me you just sitting on the people's bench and warming it up, learning *nothing*?"

"No, you know what I mean. I mean I ain't learn anything . . . anything . . ." As I searched for the right word, Grandfather reached out and hugged me, slipping a coin into my palm. It was such a treat to talk to Dadah, either when he visited us or when we went to Rockley and spent time with him. Dadah always had a treat for us. In Rockley, within minutes of entering his house, we could always count on his reaching into his pocket, pulling out a coin and sending us running to the nearest shop to buy a large bottle of sweet drink. Grandmother seldom bought such drinks, preferring instead her own mauby, ginger beer and lemonade, but who as a child would not prefer a shop-bought treat over anything homemade? Often, I sat on his carpenter's bench and watched Dadah sharpen his tools, filing his saws and rubbing the tongue of his various planes on a flint stone on which he had poured some oil.

"Run along and play," he said. "I have some business to discuss with your grandmother." I disappeared to the approving mutterings of Grandmother and Dadah. A short time afterwards, a truck showed up at our house with several pieces of lumber. Grandmother announced that she was finally building the shed-roof add-on to the house. It would contain a bedroom for us and perhaps a bed, some place proper for the three of us to sleep until our parents sent for us. My mother's family saw the addition differently—as Dadah building a house for the enemy. Dadah seemed oblivious to the family feud. The next time he showed up, it was to examine how the addition was coming along, and to pull the metal measuring-tape from his pocket to confirm some sizes for himself.

*　*　*

One morning, Grandmother appeared preoccupied and seemed to be straining her ears to hear the neighbour's radio. May May Brown had turned up her Rediffusion louder than usual. We heard the music but could not make out the words.

"They just make the announcement," May May shouted across to Grandmother. "They say the funeral is this evening. They mention the boys' mother in England and how much grandchildren he had."

Grandmother finally broke the news to us. Dadah had died. The obituaries were read religiously on the radio each morning and this was the final confirmation. She told us to come right home at lunch and to tell our teachers that we would not be returning in the afternoon. She then went into the house and took down our best pants and shirts, and took our shoes from under the table and bed.

Grandmother kept checking the time, wondering what the holdup could be. The car had not arrived and she knew the ritual viewing of the body was well underway. She was anxious, wondering what people would say if we were not at the funeral. I had worries of my own. The neighbours had told me I should now expect night-time visits from Dadah's duppie. The only safeguard against them was to physically lift the youngest child in the house over the coffin. And it had to be done before the coffin was closed for good.

When we arrived at Grand-Grand's house, the coffin was being carried out. Nobody was happy. To accommodate us the family had obviously delayed the departure for the cemetery as long as possible. To my mother's family, this was the ultimate slight; in their view Grandmother had bad-mindedly kept us away from the funeral. And this was the funeral of the man *pulling his pocket* to put another roof on her house, an almost new house that she would have for her own uses when we went to England. Finally, the undertaker relented and re-opened the upper part of the coffin. Stephen, Errol and I filed up and took a last quick look at Dadah. The undertakers screwed the top back on and tried to push the procession along, as it was getting late for the burial. Nobody seemed to care about passing me over the coffin. Did this mean that I was now sentenced to endless nights of visits from the dead? We got back into the car and joined the procession to the cemetery. Relations between my mother's and father's families went into an even deeper freeze. The shed-roof would remain unfinished.

*   *   *

About a year after taking me to school, Stephen moved on from primary school. He got a place in Paragon High School in the city, which meant that he was one of the few boys in Lodge Road to go to high school. This was to be the beginning of great things for him, even though we all knew he was only marking time until we all went to England. But high school would help round him out for England. Indeed, our father had made us proud when he wrote a letter to the headmaster thanking him and his staff for taking such great care of us and promising that he would soon send for us. The headmaster had relayed the contents of the letter to the school assembly and invited the three of us into his office to receive the letters our father had written to each of us in care of the headmaster. We were floating on clouds as we ran home with the letters.

Stephen's going to Paragon showed the benefits of having a father in England in more tangible ways: school fees should not be a problem. This wasn't a case of where a son's or daughter's higher education depended on what a parent could scrape by on and save during the crop season. Neither should there be a problem getting the fancy school uniform: the khaki shirts and pants, the long khaki socks up to the knees, the brown shoes and the school tie. Except, as we soon found out, this was the case.

Errol and I continued in primary school, with no plans for high school, because we knew we would be in England long before secondary school entered the picture. Grandmother was talking in earnest about following through on our father's instructions to change our surname to Goddard. There was even much talk of the three of us going to England any day, if room could be found for us on one of the British military planes that so often visited Barbados. As children of military personnel, we apparently qualified for this air travel, or so our parents said in their letters. I didn't know it then, but with time it became very clear that the only possibility of my making anything of myself would depend on what I could achieve in high school, in Barbados.

4

Lodge Road

The plane that we imagined swooping down over Barbados and taking us to our new home across the Atlantic never arrived. There was always a reason, some excuse: maybe because our names had not been changed; our parents had not filled out the requisite forms; our parents wanted us to end the school year in Barbados and avoid the disruption of moving mid-term; or, as was most likely the case, our parents were too taken up with their travels in the British military, and with the growing demands of a quickly expanding *new* family in England. Or, they did not have the time and financial resources for us, the reminders of their previous lives and youthful imprudence that had produced three illegitimate children.

Instead of travel documents, our parents sent glossy coloured photographs of our brothers and sisters in England. In quick succession came pictures of two smiling boys, hair well greased and combed, and wearing sweaters. Then came family pictures that would eventually include three sisters. The pictures made me wonder if my mother would dress me the same way she dressed my siblings. How would I look in those V-necked sweaters, cardigans that resembled the ones our heroes on the West Indies cricket team wore when on tour in cold England? They were the same kind of clothes we saw important people wearing, the glimpses of life abroad coming to us via the mobile cinema that visited a pasture in our area approximately once every six weeks.

This was when a van from the Government Information Services turned up. A worker would hang a big white screen against the side of the van and set up a noisy projector with big reels of film. For several hours each visit we were entertained with a mixture of government propaganda on everything from combatting the ravishes of polio, to preparing for the hurricane season, or to such major world affairs as the funerals of President John F. Kennedy or Sir Winston Churchill, the latter shown with a heavy black border on the screen for the duration of the three-hour epic documentary.

No showing by the mobile cinema was complete or acceptable without a Bud and Lou funny as a finale. A night without the comic antics of Bud Abbott and Lou Costello was enough vexation to cause great despondency, as happened when the entire evening was devoted to the sombre, boring funeral of Sir Winston Churchill. We, the young colonials, didn't have much tolerance for all those scenes of soldiers marching, bells tolling and horses bearing the casket. This was not worth the price of *bottling dew*, the disparaging term for standing outside at night for any length of time. Everyone knew that too much dew and exposure to bright moonlight was a sure bet for catching a cold or a serious and crippling *passover* or stroke. For weeks following each screening we would regale one another by retelling the funny bits from Bud and Lou. We would remember, too, the government information on cleanliness, planting crops, conserving water or about some development in politics, but we waited impatiently for the announcement on the radio of when the mobile cinema would next be in our district, bringing us more Bud and Lou.

The clothes my younger brothers wore in the pictures my parents sent us looked nothing like what Stephen, Errol and I had. And we often felt envious when Grandmother admonished us to treat the one pair of dress pants and the few shirts we had with care. In my mind, where my parents lived, there were no pants with patches. Even little boys dressed well, wore shoes and sweaters to school, and ate at a big dinner table. At least, this was what I saw on the mobile cinema.

We responded to our parents with letters of how well we were doing in Barbados and how much we looked forward to living in England, reports usually dictated by Grandmother. Letter writing had became increasingly distant and sterile for us as the bond with our parents atrophied and diminished. What could we say in these letters? And, in my case, what words did you use—Mum or Ma, Mummy or Mama, Dad or Daddy—to address parents with whom you had never had a conversation? We avoided this chore until Grandmother caught up with us, always with the reprimand that this was the very last time she was helping us compose a letter. The next time, she threatened, we would have to write the letters on our own. Then she sat us down, one by one, and recited the traditional opening: *Dear Mum and Dad. How are you doing? I hope you are doing fine . . .*

Grandmother always found a creative way to get us to thank our parents for the infrequent pocket money they sent. Our father had suggested that one way to prepare us for life in England was to let us handle our own money, the way parents in England allowed their children to spend their allowances. The money he sent usually came in five-shilling postal orders with our names printed on them. At Christmas or for a birthday it might be ten shillings. Sometimes it was a one- or two-pound note, all with a smilling Queen of England promising to pay. We simply signed the postal order over to Grandmother. Then we *spent* the money with her, the same way workers in a village with a company store spent their money without any of it ever gracing the palms of their hands.

Grandmother argued it was better for her to *invest* the money wisely towards a shirt or pair of pants instead of letting us *lick* out the money on sweets. And since she was a hawker, she argued that it was better for us to buy fruits from her than from some stranger. As enticement, she reminded us that not only did she give us a better deal, allowing us to stretch the few *rare-mouth coppers* she was holding in trust, but that she kept us supplied with fruits even when our pockets were "dry, dry, dry."

For as long as we could, we kept alive the hope of one day having real allowances to spend at the shops in London, not realizing we were like thousands of other young children scattered across the Caribbean—the left-

behind children. Children, whose lives of parental abandonment and denial were the final sacrifice to a dying
colonial empire, the forerunners of what came to be known
as the "barrel culture." We were the children forced to
grow up orphan-like without the comforting presence of
our natural parents, who felt abandoned at the key points
in a child's life when we desperately needed the presence
or the soothing words of a parent, like when Errol joined
some of his friends hopping a water cart from one of the
plantations. Just as he hopped onto the back of the cart,
his feet slipped and he fell backwards, hitting his head.
Friends brought Errol home, still dazed. He revived after
someone threw some water on him, and had a big
headache for his foolishness. Over the years, Errol would
tell me that it was at this moment, when his frightened
friends brought him home and there were no adults to
receive him, that he missed our mother most. The same
way he missed her when he accidentally ran into Aunty
Allison just as she turned away from the fire with a cup of
boiling water. It spilled on him. Errol screamed so loud
that the next door neighbour, May May Brown, heard and
called over for Grandmother to apply butter on the big
black bubble that was already rising where the hot water
had scalded him. Perhaps even now, Errol carries the scars
on his chest and the feeling of abandonment in his heart.
He missed our mother then, too.

Children like us grew up eagerly awaiting the arrival of
the next barrel or hamper laden with food and clothes sent
by strangers, called parents, from some foreign country.
Barrels were the only real links between the children and
their absent parents.

Our parents did not send barrels, only the odd parcel. These boxes were wrapped in brown paper, with twine intricately knotted and Grandmother's address on the outside in big bold letters. Inside was the sweet smell of England, and neatly packed clothes (even if they *had* been described as old and used clothing for custom's purposes). In the parcel was the invariable tin of *Quality Streets* candies. In our eyes, these sweets were as British as a cup of tea must have been for a Londoner. This was the kind of stuff, not fruit, on which we were planning to spend our allowances in England. The tins also held and bestowed status, so that long after we had consumed the contents, the tins sat regally on a shelf as a kind of trophy, as prized baking pans or as the container for the safekeeping of important odds and ends.

Many of the professional people trained in England came back to the region and dared to dream of making something of the left-behind children. They talked about political independence to secure at home the prosperity sought abroad for generations. Symbolically, it was supposed to make the next generation of young men and women seriously consider the real option of staying home instead of leaving for some proverbial land of milk and honey. This dream was born crippled, for while independence brought national pride and opportunities for economic and social development, while it undermined the notion of a mother country, independence never really stanched the flow to foreign countries. We simply substituted a New York, Miami, Toronto, Montreal or Vancouver for a London or Liverpool. The only real difference was that we left home knowing we weren't going to the mother country.

For my brothers and me, effectively part of the first post-colonial generation, our cherished dream was to join our parents in this far-off land. This was our escape, but ever so slowly reality was forcing us to search for other options. Such would be the predicament of youths who unwittingly found themselves on the cusp of the independence movement. Dreams, handed down to us from our parents, were born in what was becoming a bygone era, even as we were growing up. Circumstances were pushing us into trying to fit our parents' aspirations into a totally different agenda. I was only four years old when the English-speaking Caribbean islands made a collective stab at independence, forming the ill-fated West Indies Federation, which igno-miniously collapsed in 1962 when Jamaica, and then Trinidad and Tobago, broke away from the new state to claim their own sovereignty and independence. Despite the death of the federation, the taste of political freedom had become too great for a return to colonial status. The following years witnessed a concerted rush on each Caribbean island, and in Guyana on the South American mainland, towards political independence.

As the excuses for why we weren't leaving became more creative, we noticed that people started to treat us differently. They began to assume that we were among the growing number of left-behinds. Worse was when the letters with the usual five-shilling note didn't arrive, or when the remittances from our father were interrupted and then, just stopped completely. Life turned uncertain and starkly difficult. Teachers publicly criticized us for coming to school without proper uniforms, or for not having shoes to wear to church on special days of worship. This was unacceptable behaviour, the teachers explained—or did they taunt?—especially for children with a father and mother in England. Showing up at school looking as poor as if we were from parents struggling to survive on the island was unexplainable to these teachers, and unacceptable. Not when we were supposed to have parents living in the lap of luxury. The implication of these statements and attitude was clear: what was the use of having parents in a mother country if the sacrifices of separating children and parents weren't compensated for in real and material ways? The notion of political independence, the changing intellectual awakening—even at the grass roots—was causing people to question old positions.

We noticed how the neighbours treated us, how they turned hard and took liberties. They taunted us, clearly signalling that without the protection of our parents we were defenceless. We were often forced to cower behind closed doors, whether from "big hard-back vagabonds," as Grandmother called the men preying on us, or from the bigger boys who knew we were easy pickings. Having parents abroad had become a liability rather than a cause for respect or advantage.

*   *   *

I must have been about four years old and was still following after Princess when she went to the defence of Stephen or Errol, who was in a scrap with a bully named Syl in the pasture in front our house. Princess chased after Syl and he scrambled about for stones to throw at her. For whatever reason, I was running behind Princess when one of the stones struck me full force in the head. In no time, my face and clothes were bathed in blood. I was bawling. Princess grabbed me and took me back to the house, while neighbours gathered around offering advice. The fight was over and everyone was concerned for me, even Syl apparently, who had disappeared. Princess washed off the blood and bandaged my head, keeping me inside the house to await Grandmother's return. On her arrival, Grandmother took one look and ordered Princess to take me to Doctor Ward, the only doctor within miles of Lodge Road. It was an especially long walk for Princess, who had to carry me part of the way. We waited in an office crowded with other people and I rested on Princess, occasionally napping, until the doctor could see me. Princess finally brought me home, bandaged and sore, to end one of the most harrowing days of my life.

The next day Grandmother came home extremely angry. She had run into Syl's father, a much-feared watchman at one of the plantations. She had sought *satisfaction* from him for his son's action, including "pelting a rock that chop loose" the head of a little boy like me. The father had refused, arguing that we deserved whatever we got, for this was the price to be paid for picking a fight with his son. If a little boy like me got in the way of the stone, well, that was too bad. There wasn't anything he could do about it, and neither could any of us.

Grandmother told us that the watchman's response was a reminder of how vulnerable we were and how we had to be very careful in whatever we did. Her main consolation was that I had not caught tetanus or been killed by the impact of the stone, something that had been a real possibility. "That vagabond, Syl, coulda kill you when he part loose your head with that rock-stone. But thank God, it didn't happen. And then for his father to get on that way." Grandmother never seemed to forget this incident. Whenever appropriate she would remind me of the danger of throwing stones. "Once a rock left your hand, you can't call it back," she warned one morning when we were out walking near a pond. I noticed frogs at the edge of the pond and I remembered the games of throwing stones at the frogs that boys of my age played. A direct hit would cause the frog to roll over onto its back, dead.

Grandmother didn't approve of this game, or maybe she still remembered the incident with Syl. "I want you to remember what the frog says to the little boy," she told me, ending one of her proverbs that she used to teach us the ways of life. "The frog said to the boy: what is fun for you is death for me. Don't throw stones. It's like a shot out of a gun." (Less than ten years later, this saying would have even more poignancy for me. My best friend would die after being struck with a stone in circumstances similar to the fight between Syl and Princess.) At the time I wasn't thinking of danger when Grandmother admonished us not to throw stones. I felt that a major concern for Grandmother was ensuring that word did not get to my parents in England—possibly through letters from my mother's family—about my near brush with death. Definitely, Grandmother didn't want to be in a position of having to explain anything that could reflect poorly on how she was raising us. We were vulnerable enough without adding danger brought about by our own accord.

*　　*　　*

I was sitting inside the house with Grandmother one day when we heard knocking. "Good evening, Mrs. Goddard," a voice called.

Grandmother went to the front window. Outside was Mrs. Gladys King and some of her family. "I've come to give you satisfaction, to find out how the little boy is doing."

Earlier in the day I had had yet another run-in with Mrs. King's dog. The animal often hid under the cellar, dashing out at anyone passing in front of the house. I hated having to pass Mrs. King's house, or having to deal with her yapping dog. I could never decide whether to try to outrun the dog or wait until the barking brought Mrs. King or someone from inside the house to control the animal. Somehow, this dog always seemed to be on the lookout for me.

At our last encounter, I had decided to outrun the dog. I had felt the dog's teeth sinking into my calf, just as someone came running from the house to call it back. Someone checked my calf and cleaned away the trickle of blood. When I got home, Grandmother slicked down the calf with heated Canadian Healing Oil, using a large feather to apply the medication. We were most surprised when Mrs. King showed up.

"Well, why don't you let him talk for himself to say how he really feeling," Grandmother said through the window. "For as you know, a dog bite can be a serious thing. Come here, Cecil, and tell Mistress King how your leg feeling."

I pushed my head through the window, my mind focused on remembering to show respect, the most important thing for any youngster—especially someone like me with a strict grandmother—when addressing an adult. I had learned many painful lessons from passing adults on the street and not showing respect by hailing them with a hearty good morning or good afternoon. It didn't matter if the adult didn't acknowledge my presence; it was mandatory that I show respect by speaking first and by addressing any woman of middle age or older as *mistress*, regardless of her married status. Grandmother always seemed to get reports whenever I was remiss in my manners. She was never pleased with this behaviour, scolding that she would not accept a little boy like me acting so *mannish* or impertinent, when dealing with people old enough to be my mother or father, people who knew me before I came out of the egg. "You and big people ain't no company, you hear me? You must be thinking these is people you pitch marbles with!" Speaking to Mrs. King was clearly my chance to impress Grandmother.

"Good evening, Mrs. King," I said loudly and clearly, thinking of how Grandmother would be extremely proud of my politeness.

"Good evening," she said. "And how are you feeling? You feeling okay?"

"Yes, Mrs. King!" I shouted, remembering the unspoken rule that we always told people who enquired that we were doing well, even when we weren't. Adults, Grandmother had always intimated, should not have to bother unduly with irritations of children who tended to exaggerate the scrapes and cuts that they would soon outgrow. I added, "My leg's fine. It's okay."

"It ain't hurting you, ain't it?"

"No, Mrs. King. My leg's fine, Mrs. King." I was sure Grandmother must have been smiling at my conduct, revelling in my display of the proper manners and decency she had instilled in me.

"I'm glad to hear that," she said. "I glad to hear the little boy is okay, Mrs. Goddard. Let me know if anything change." And she left.

Grandmother was not pleased with my answers. "How you could tell the woman that you' leg okay?" she asked. "You don't know a dog bite is worth something? And the woman came all the way over here to give me satisfaction and she probably had she mind made up to give you a little something for the dog bite. And you up and say you okay, that the foot ain't hurting."

*   *   *

Mr. Green, a conductor for the government bus service and supposedly a notorious man, arrived outside the paling, talking at the top of his voice and threatening what he planned to do to all of us in the house. This time, the caller was seeking satisfaction from Grandmother because Stephen had beaten his son. Except that Green wanted to dole out the punishment himself, on all of us.

This showdown was particularly scary as Green was feared around Lodge Road. Worse, Stephen had got us into trouble by disobeying Grandmother.

She had forbidden Stephen from joining the gang of school boys who spent their long vacations pulling weeds, or picking pond grass as we called it, from the cane fields.

Every day, the boys would take to the fields and, on hands and knees, pull the grass and weeds by their roots. For this labour they were paid cheaply, less than the plantations offered to mature men and women. Grandmother didn't believe such low-class work was appropriate for someone like Stephen, who was not only awaiting the call to go to England, but was also a decent high school boy. But Stephen had noticed how the boys his age had a bit of pocket money from picking grass. So he joined the gang.

Payday presented a huge problem: how would he explain the money to Grandmother? Stephen came up with the brilliant idea of hiding the money under a rock underneath the house's groundsel. Only his friend, Ivan Green, knew the location. When Stephen went back to get it, the money was gone. Stephen beat Ivan, who ran home and told his father.

In my memory, the older Green is outside the paling threatening us. The neighbours are looking on and, as the crowd grows, Green becomes even more enraged. He suddenly grabs a soft drink bottle and hurls it full force at the house. Grandmother manages to close the back door to the makeshift paling fence just in time. This door was really the top of a big black clothes grip, hanging from its leather straps. From behind the closed door, we heard the bottle shattering and the roar of the onlookers. We waited a long time to see if Green would follow through on his threat to drag us out of the house and beat us.

This incident gave Grandmother another opportunity to remind us of how vulnerable we were; of how life would have been different if we had had a father around to defend us; of how life would be better when we escaped to England.

* * *

Visiting our mother's family in Rockley was usually a high-light of our long school vacation, and was also the time the boys in Lodge Road eased up on beating us. After a visit to Rockley, our arrival back in Lodge Road was an event that all our friends anticipated. We came back with bags full of all sorts of fruit: soursops, sugar apples, Bajan cherries, guavas, and that rarity of them all, sweet tamarinds. All the tamarinds we got in Lodge Road were sour, but Dadah grew a variety that tasted as if they had been dipped in molasses. As long as our supply of the sweet tamarinds lasted, our friends were genuinely friendly.

I looked forward to going to Rockley for other reasons. It gave me the opportunity to spend time with Aunty Ann and for Grand-Grand to tell us stories. She constantly complained that Grandmother wasn't taking good enough care of us and often wondered aloud what Grandmother was doing with all the money my father was sending to support us. She didn't like the idea that Errol spent his evenings picking meat for the sheep, or that Stephen had to carry so many buckets of water on his head every evening. Grand-Grand also wondered why paying Stephen's school fees appeared to be a perennial problem when our father was supposedly sending the money on time. And she particularly did not like the reports of the vicious floggings Grandmother administered to us for discipline.

Being with Grand-Grand was a time to sing songs that I learned in church, and to gorge myself on the guavas, cherries and tamarinds that were readily available. I was always encouraged to eat soursops, especially the heart of the fruit which was supposed to be a cure for bed-wetting. It never worked for me. One trip to Rockley I paid the price for eating too many guavas. On the day we were to return to Lodge Road, I developed a severe bellyache. Grand-Grand rushed me to hospital, where I was apparently diagnosed as suffering from acute appendicitis. The word came that I had to be kept in hospital overnight and prepared for surgery. The next morning, orderlies placed me on a gurney. They took me into an elevator, pulled some iron bars, smiled at me, and that was the last thing I remembered. When I awoke, I expected pain from surgery, but there was nothing. Apparently, some wise surgeon double-checked me before beginning the operation and found that my bellyache was from nothing more than my stool being bound by too many small guava seeds. Grand-Grand must have sighed loudly with relief.

Grandmother was not happy when I arrived home from the hospital. First, she felt hospitalization would not have been necessary if Grand-Grand had taken better care of me; and second, she didn't like the idea of exposing me to hospitals, which she felt practised bad medicine and were noted more for killing than healing people. She trusted none of the surgeons at the hospital. And, she said, to think that I was *delivered* into their hands. What would she write and tell my father if the worst had happened? Grandmother decided to administer her own remedy—a strong dose of castor oil that more than did the trick of cleaning out what was left of the guava seeds, and anything else.

*　　　*　　　*

With few exceptions, the men I encountered in Barbados were bullies. Their claim to fame usually corresponded to how much they hurt people, whether strangers or family. The men virtually lived in a society of their own: few went to church; many gambled heavily, whether playing dice, draughts or dominoes; drank lots of white rum and chased it with water. They worked, if they could find employment. For a growing number of them, finding a job meant leaving the island for months, as agricultural workers in North America or as seamen roaming the globe.

They came home with foreign money in their pockets, but deep anger in their hearts. While their return signalled temporary good times for their families—with new clothes, gramaphones and the latest records, and various toys to show off—the men who came back were terrorists. Most automatically seemed to assume that while they were away their wives or girlfriends fooled around. Many of them resorted to beating their women frequently, sometimes forcing the women to flee their homes in the dark of night, or to somehow silently survive the abuse they received. Too often we heard the noises coming from nearby houses as people crashed into furniture, or the thudding sounds of fists hitting flesh, and children screaming.

Many of my friends were afraid of their fathers, whose main contact with them was to administer sound floggings. Just the distant sight of a father, even if the man did not live at home, sent boys and girls scampering for their houses. The occasion might be nothing more than the father unexpectedly coming by to drop off the financial support for the children.

It seemed that the main duty of the men was to provide discipline. They were adept at using the tamarind rods or the leather straps usually kept in the roof or hanging from a nail. Often, the only words to a child were to "go and get the tamarind rod [or strap] and let me deal with yuh." Part of the discipline was enduring the indignity of bringing your whip to the master.

The men, however, also provided protection for their children, so were expected to be good fighters. If another man harmed their children, the fathers, even those who didn't live in the home, were expected to settle the score. Someone taking a message to a father that his children were being threatened or under physical attack was often enough to bring the man running to their assistance.

The most feared men, and perhaps most respected, too, were those capable of using their fists or knives. Sometimes, they brought out the cutlasses used mainly for cutting canes or specially prepared guava sticks as weapons. For weeks, people talked about a good fight, especially if the combatants ended up in magistrate court. In a perverse way, losing the court battle was a clear sign of having won the fight that really mattered, for the court was expected to side only with the defeated or the weak. It was for this reason Grandmother lamented not having a man in the house to protect us. For this reason, she was always threatening to put some bully in court, indirectly signalling she was so weak and unprotected the *strong and mighty*, as she called them, didn't have to prove anything by taking us on.

Above everything else, the main job for the men was to provide money for child support, and to do it with the most reluctance. Over the years, I overheard conversations on this issue: women whispering about putting a former boyfriend in court for child support; young men boasting, as if it were a rite of passage, about the women forced to resort to the courts to get them to cough up the *cock tax.* If a man disappeared for some time, his return was usually met with friendly taunts from other men that he must have *gone up* for refusing to honour the orders of the court.

This talk made an early impression on me and must have shaped my awareness of the role of fathers in society. One thing I knew when I was growing up: I did not want to be mean and violent like these men. This might have been because I was frail and unlikely to do well in any fight. I did not want to strut around the village looking for fights, or dodge policemen on the lookout for trouble-makers, or recount in male gatherings under the street-lights the vivid and sometimes exaggerated details about the beatings the men *uncorked* on the police. I learned many valuable lessons, which even from an early age made me swear that if I ever had children, I would never be like the fathers I had known. I would not beat them and I would not leave them destitute. Neither would I leave them wards of grandmothers and aunts. I was starting to see my father as no different from the other men around us, although I was willing to believe that England might have changed him the same way Grandmother promised that going to England would reform my brothers and me, making us gentlemen.

*   *   *

Calvin Drakes used to come by our home at night, and he and Princess would go walking or riding on his pretty Raleigh bicycle. Calvin was considered somewhat of a catch. After all, he could afford a bicycle, he worked and he appeared to come from a respectable family who lived about five miles away. Grandmother was always suspicious of him, claiming she would never trust a *short-me-crouch* man like Calvin. He was not a tall man.

Grandmother became more accepting of Calvin when Princess became pregnant. Mrs. Brown had been right: time had shown there was more than food in Princess' belly. Princess and Calvin had a daughter, Joan, and later a son, Whitney. It was about the time of Whitney's arrival that trouble set in and Calvin hardly came around anymore. I overheard some of the conversations: Grandmother asking a distraught Princess if Calvin "ain't giving yuh nuthin' to feed the two children he give yuh," and Calvin telling Princess he wasn't coming, not even to see his children, to the house of "that woman that never did like me." At the same time, Calvin claimed he wasn't so sure it was a good idea for Princess to walk the distance to his house in Enterprise, especially with two children in tow, as he didn't "want people to think the two o' we in anything, any more." He was willing to support his children, but not to bring the money to the house or to encourage Princess to visit him at home. I became the compromise.

One day, Princess took me to Calvin's home, leading me through streets and along long roads I had never travelled before. She cautioned me to take good mental notes of where we were going. Should I forget my way, I was to ask anyone to point me to where Mrs. Drakes lived. Everyone in the area would know who I meant, especially if I told them that Mrs. Drakes' son, Calvin, had a Raleigh bicycle and two children from a young woman in Lodge Road. Princess waited at the side of the road and pointed to the Drakes' house, partially wood and wall, well painted and with electricity—nothing like ours. She was not allowed to visit the house so I did for her and, with the job complete, together we walked home in the evening darkness. It became my task to go to Calvin's home every Friday evening and collect the child support. Even the five or six dollars made a big difference in our lives.

Each time, before I left for Calvin's house in Enterprise, Grandmother and Princess would give me instructions about which child was sick, which had special needs and temporarily needed additional support, what to say in my most polite manner to Calvin's mother, and what remarks to drop, either in conversation or in the presence of his mother. With the money in my pocket, I was to head for Oistins to buy the evening meal of flying fish, if they were in season, or the cheaper pot fish called barbaras. I was to buy a can of baby formula and to make a special stop at Edgehill Pharmacy to buy a bingo card for 25 cents and to copy the numbers that had already been drawn and announced on the radio. (The games started midweek, but we never had a card until Friday.) Most of all I was not to lose the money. To avoid such catastrophe, Grandmother showed me how to hold the money at the bottom of my pocket, roll up the short-pants leg and use a piece of cord to tie a strong and secure knot.

Getting the money from Calvin was never easy. I would visit his home at the appointed time and would be my most respectful to Mrs. Drakes. Then I would wait seemingly for hours outside the house, in the light from the kitchen, as darkness closed in. I would worry about encountering some bully on the way home and losing the money. It seemed Calvin came home later and later with each passing week, to the point where his mother had to intervene, asking him pointedly, "Why yuh don't hurry up and come 'long home on evenings when yuh know you does got the little boy waiting out there for yuh?"

One Friday evening, Princess asked me to be especially attentive and to be on my best behaviour. She had heard that Calvin's brother had returned to Barbados *from over and away* in some country named Canada, a rich country. Princess was hoping he had brought back something special for the children of his brother, maybe even some money. While waiting beside the house, I noticed a man dressed strangely in a multicoloured silk-looking housecoat or bathrobe, and wearing fluffy slippers that looked very different from what people wore in Barbados. He came to the door, looked at me, nodded and mumbled something I didn't hear and disappeared inside the house. I never saw him again, but he left a lasting impression on me.

"Why he dressed so?" I asked Princess, after explaining there was nothing extra for the children.

"Well, you see," she explained, "he is living in a place called Montreal in this place, Canada. It's very cold up there. Lots of a cold, cold, cold thing they does call snow. So that when he comes back to a hot, hot, hot country like

Barbados, he got to be real careful he don't catch a cold going from the cold weather up there straight to the hot down here. He have to acclimatize himself, get back in the swing of things down here real slow, not rushing out and getting sick."

That was why he had to keep himself warmer than usual, wearing the housecoat or robe and protecting his feet, she explained, why he was "not be spending much time outside of the house, not even standing too long at the door."

This was the first time I had heard of Canada, a land of snow, so cold but rich. Still, this place called Montreal sounded intriguing, somewhat like England. I must have learned some lesson back then as I waited for Calvin to show up, although in later years I puzzled over why Calvin's brother needed to acclimatize slowly to the weather in Barbados while planeloads of white people could arrive in Barbados from the same Canada, and only hours later be fully exposed to the hot sun on some beach.

When Calvin got home, he painstakingly went through the same ritual. He took his bath in the backyard. Then he got dressed, readying himself for the weekend. He sat at the table and ate the meal his mother had cooked. It seemed to me that he ate particularly slowly, or it might have been that I was hungry and I still had to rush to Oistins to buy the fish that had to be cooked when I finally got home. When he could not draw the matter out any longer, he would call me and give me the money, all the time grumbling about somebody or the other spending money for which he had to work so hard. Once in a while, a smile broke on his face, and he would give me an extra five cents for myself, or bus fare to Oistins. I hated having to go for this money. Most times when I got home, Grandmother would have started the evening meal, waiting only for the fish.

"You hungry?" she asked.

"Yes, Grandmother."

"Did that short-me-crouch man send anything extra?"

"No, Grandmother."

"Anyway come here. I know yuh hungry and yuh can't wait like the others for the food to done cook." She often took some of the rice from the pot and put it in a container and spread some salted butter over it.

"I hungry, too," she said. "Come, let we eat this morsel here. The others can wait for the fish to done and the rice to dry down." The rice and butter tasted delicious and was our special treat. Often, it was the last thing I remembered before falling asleep, my head in Grandmother's lap and she feeding me and dreaming of winning the weekly bingo.

On nights like this Grandmother mixed telling us what fine things she planned to buy with the bingo winnings with talk about our going to England. But there were ominous signs of things going wrong. The remittances from my father were sporadic and Grandmother was always under pressure to come up with Stephen's school fees. And we found that food and other necessities of life were harder to get. The household was expanding, with Aunty Allison and Aunt Princess each adding two children. One of them was David, who effectively became my little brother and followed me around, just as I did with Errol and Stephen, who were becoming more mature and tired of having a little brother running after them. Grandmother was becoming worried about Stephen, afraid that he wanted to run with the wrong crowd. She often had to resort to giving him a good thrashing, just as if he had a father to deal with him.

*   *   *

One day Grandmother sent me into Oistins to collect money owed to her from some sale. Her instructions were specific in one point: I should walk straight to the home, explain that I was Ermie Goddard's grandson from Lodge Road, ask for the sixty cents owed my grandmother, and come straight back. Instead, I had decided to play on the beach. I was walking on Oistins beach, playing in the afternoon surf, when I came to an older boy. I wasn't quite sure which house to visit, so I asked this friendly-looking stranger if he knew where the woman I was looking for lived.

"What you going there for?" he asked.

"I going to collect money they owe my grandmother," I said.

"Oh," said the boy as he brightened. "Let me show you."

I received the few coins from the woman and returned to where my new-found friend was waiting some distance on. He had deliberately chosen not to accompany me right to the house.

"Why don't I show you another way to where you live?" he offered.

We ended up walking by a cane field, some distance off the main road that Grandmother had specified. My new friend suggested that we should take a short cut through the cane field. I agreed. Once in the field, he grabbed me by the neck from behind and threw me to the ground.

"Give me that fucking money or I'll kill yuh!"

The shock itself was enough to kill me. I couldn't even breathe, far less scream for help. Frantically, I reached into my pocket and gave him the money. "Stay here," he commanded and ran from the field. Minutes later I came out, my heart racing not only from the fright of the choke and theft, but more so at how I was going to explain all this to Grandmother.

By the time I got home, I had concocted a story. I could not admit to Grandmother I was so careless that I had lost the money. That would have resulted in a sound beating. Neither could I admit that I had been playing, or that I had gone into a cane field with a stranger. That would also have resulted in a beating, both for disobeying Grandmother and for being so foolish. I settled for the half-truth that I was robbed but that it had happened behind one of the big walls at the top of Oistins hill, someone grabbing me from behind and dragging me behind the wall.

To my surprise Grandmother bought the story. Worse, she became enraged with all those lawless young men walking around with nothing better to do than to create trouble, all those vagabonds roaming the world only to choke and rob innocent people. "Princess," she ordered, "I want you to take this boy with you down to the police station right now and lay a complaint." By this point I wanted to die, but I was even more fearful to admit the truth.

The policeman who took my statement had great difficulty keeping a straight face. He kept asking questions, changing a word here and there, asking me to demonstrate the choke hold on him, seemingly winking at Princess as I held his head and felt the rough stubble of his beard, wondering if I wasn't a little confused when I said the man was not only choking me but also going through my pockets, asking me to describe the scene behind the wall, if there were other people walking the streets, and could I describe the young man . . . and could I answer these questions all over again. I tried to keep my story straight, improvising as I went along. He wrote my statement in his book, stopping every so often to stare at Princess and smile.

Finally, he said that he had enough, but that he would like to come by our home to complete the investigation. He suggested that some day when he was driving around in the police jeep, he might just drop by and take me and Princess for a ride in the hopes that I might see the suspect as we drove around. I was now petrified of being caught in my lie.

True enough, one afternoon the policeman showed up in the Land Rover, immediately drawing us to the attention of the neighbours and passers-by. As I climbed into the back, I overheard one woman saying to another, "You hear what he do, so that the police carrying him away?" They must have thought I had done some wrong and was likely on my way to Dodds, the centre for junior delinquents.

We drove around the area, seemingly forever. Wherever the van stopped, people gathered round to peer in at me and mutter to themselves. Finally, the policeman brought us home, laughing and joking with Princess. He promised to come back and take us for another drive, but fortunately he never returned. I never told anyone the truth out of fear of what Grandmother would have done to me, and for the same reason I prayed that the robber would never be caught, just in case the truth got out. Still, this incident gave Grandmother much more to talk about when she warned us to be careful dealing with the *bad-minded* people around us and not to trust strangers.

*   *   *

As we sat around the fire, we could hear the piglet squealing. It was tied by a rope around the neck to a stake just behind the paling, beside the pen where Errol tended the sheep. The piglet was a new arrival that Aunty Allison had bought as a way to raise some money. There was something special Aunty Allison was saving for and she would tell us at the appropriate time. Meanwhile, everyone would have to pitch in to raise the pig while Aunty Allison continued working as a domestic.

Aunty Allison's boyfriend had immigrated to some other country. Earl Chase was tall and handsome and Grandmother was extremely proud of her "son-in-law." The neighbours were impressed, too, because they talked constantly about Aunty Allison's good fortune in nabbing this man who lived near the city, but most of all who owned a car. Everyone in the village knew the car, but none more so than we did, who felt a pride of ownership at having this Prefect car parked in front of the house—licence plate number M 555—at a time when it was still a sign of status for people to be identified by the licence plate number. It was an even greater honour when Earl took us driving. Soon after the birth of Aunty Allison's second son, Dalton, Earl had gone overseas, much to the delight of some bad-minded neighbours who felt, or even wished, that Aunty Allison was on her way to becoming yet another woman jilted by her man. It was in this environment that Aunty Allison entered the pig business.

This was a new form of entrepreneurship for us, marked by the obvious fact that we didn't even have the traditional pigpen. More than that, we had to make arrangements for feeding the pig, which meant going around to homes in the area to collect slops, which consisted mainly of the soapless water used to wash dishes, bits of food, and the peelings from yams, potatoes, bananas, sweet potatoes—anything that a pig would eat. After several hours in the sun, the slops were the foulest thing to smell, perhaps topped only by the pig's excrement.

One morning, we awoke to find that the overnight rain had thoroughly soaked the rope around the pig's neck and weakened it. When the pig bolted from us, as usual, the sudden tug broke the rope and the chase was on. We all joined the pursuit, hoping to corner the pig, but not knowing how to catch it. The pig sprinted off with all of us racing behind it, Aunty Allison probably having mental images of her hard-earned money, and the potential profits, escaping from us.

We finally cornered the pig, which by then was backed up to the edge of a pond. To the endearing calls of "here piggy, piggy, here piggy, piggy," we closed in. Suddenly, the pig lunged into the pond. We were convinced that Aunty Allison's money was dead, for none of us knew pigs could swim. But the little piggy kept its head above water. We watched from the banks as it moved deeper and deeper into the pond, its front legs doing a kind of dog paddle. None of us would venture into the depths after the pig because none of us could swim. On the other side the pig emerged and ran promptly across an open field, disappearing into the underbrush. We knew for sure that Aunty Allison's pig business had now gone bust, and returned home, all sad and forlorn, but wiser for knowing that pigs could swim.

But all was not lost. Later that day the woman who Aunty Allison had bought the piglet from came calling to ask why the animal had returned home. We retrieved the runaway and this time used an iron chain to tether it.

Late one evening we made the trek, back and forth repeated times, from the house to the standpipe. Each trip we carried water to fill the big barrels, washtub, and just about any large container that could hold water. Grandmother and her daughters cleaned up the yard, prepared a large slab of wood and retired for the night, earlier than usual. There was an air of expectation. In the previous weeks Grandmother and Aunty Allison had gone around the village, taking orders for meat. It was time for Aunty Allison to make her profit by slaughtering the pig.

Early the next morning two men arrived. Grandmother and Aunty Allison were already up, boiling the water over the fire in the backyard. The men advanced on the pig and bound its feet. Hearing the squealing, I came running, but Grandmother instructed my brothers and me to stay out of the way. I stood by the paling gate and watched the men go about their business. The more senior man took a long, thin knife from a bag, held it up to the flickering light of the fire and tested it for sharpness. The pig squealed even louder as he stooped down beside it and the knife disappeared into its chest and heart. The men caught the spewing blood in a container. They held the pig until it stopped squealing and shaking, and the blood had stopped flowing.

The men put the pig on the slab of wood. They threw boiling water on the carcass and began scraping the skin. After they'd finished scraping, they then gutted the pig, placing the intestines and organs in another container. By the time the sun was fully up the men had the carcass hanging from hooks and were parcelling portions according to the orders listed in a book. People arrived for their orders and eventually nothing was left of the pig except for the stench from where it had once been tied, and a few blood spots in the backyard.

What we didn't sell, we ate. The blood was fried with onions and other seasonings. The intestines were used as the outer skin for a sausage-like Bajan delicacy called black pudding. The ears, head and trotters were pickled into souse, another delicacy.

Aunty Allison had made her profit and obviously her big day had arrived. When Mrs. Brown asked Errol and me where Aunty Allison was going, if it was to another small island or a big country, we genuinely didn't know what she was talking about. Grandmother laughed when we reported our puzzlement at the neighbour's questions. "Good for she," Grandmother remarked. "She's too fast with other people's business."

A few evenings later, Grandmother and Aunty Allison dressed up and opened the front door that was always kept closed. Soon members of the Pilgrim Holiness Church arrived. In no time, the special service was underway, with the women praying for God's blessing for a church member who was taking the chance of travelling to another country. There was much singing, too, with songs such as *God Be With You, 'Til We Meet Again* and *Vaya Con Dios*. This was the kind of celebration we had heard coming from houses the night or so before some boy or girl went off to join his or her parents in England. We didn't know who was travelling, and wondered if our opportunity had finally arrived.

Aunty Allison was the lucky one. She was leaving Barbados to join her intended husband in Nassau, in the Bahamas, where he had gone to work as a prison guard. With much fanfare the next day, we all piled into the rented car parked in front of the house, and headed for Seawell International Airport.

"I am going now," Aunty Allison said to me as she said her final goodbyes at the airport. "Try and be a good boy. Listen to Grandmother and Princess and do what they tell you to do. You be a good boy."

I nodded my head as the tears welled in my eyes.

"And continue to take good care of David for me," she said. Remembering this, I often wondered if she had not seen David when she looked at me, or if she wondered what would become of David. "And Rawle, too," she said, almost as an afterthought. Her second son was Dalton, the toddler we affectionately called Rawle, whose father Aunty Allison would soon marry, and whose last name would be changed to Chase in short order, just before he was reunited with his parents. Did she know something on that day, something personal about her own left-behinds? Then, she walked out to the plane and was gone.

Once again, I cried all the way home and this time David cried with me. He looked forward to joining his mother soon, and to my going to England to join mine. Tragically, neither of us would see our mothers until we were men.

*　　　*　　　*

For days Grandmother had been packing away our possessions in cardboard boxes or tying them up in cloth bundles.
A short time earlier she had come home and announced
that she had found the right place for us to live. By then
she was already running out of time, for Mrs. Ashby had
given notice that she wanted us off her house spot.
Grandmother seemed happy to be moving, for the weekly
rent was onerous, and she was not on speaking terms, as
she called it, with the neighbours on either side of us. We
didn't want to move because we would be leaving our
friends behind, but Grandmother promised that the new
house spot was closer to school and that we would not have
any neighbours around to *gypsy* into our business or war
with us.

Men arrived mid-morning, with the carpenter taking
charge. They dismantled the house side by side and laid it
flat on the back of a truck. Taking apart the house this way
was the most embarrassing part, as the entire inside was bit
by bit exposed to the prying eyes of our neighbours. The
other children from the area were already beginning to
distance themselves from us. We stood by ourselves, off to
one side, and cringed at the remarks from the growing
crowd of onlookers: "Look, ha-ha-ha, they have newspaper
on the sides of the house; look at how black the inside of
the house look; they don't even have a stove." We heard the
laughter and felt the separation.

With everything and everybody crowded into the truck,
we headed to the lower part of Lodge Road. Once again the

men grunted and strained, lifted the sides from the truck and, by evening, had reassembled the house. Except the house wasn't quite its former self. Some sections didn't fit as closely and neatly as before, so the whistling wind was more noticeable and some panes of glass were broken. Grandmother was right. The spot was closer to school but it was on a pasture. More important to Grandmother, the spot was disused land, owned by the Newton Plantation. She felt secure in the knowledge that the plantation owners seldom issued removal notices, even to delinquent rent payers, especially on land that had no real commercial value to them. And, as she had also promised, we didn't have to worry about prying eyes. Only a few houses were on this section of the pasture, with more than enough space between them. However, some noticeable shortcomings were inescapable. There wasn't a paved road leading to the house, just a track through the grass between the fields. The main road with the electrical lights now appeared to be miles away.

For me, there was one more problem. Mrs. King lived in one of the nearby houses. This meant I had to contend with her dog on a daily basis, a dog that somehow seemed to pick on me more than it did anyone else.

*   *   *

Stephen suffered most from the disappointment of the delayed reunion with our parents, maybe because he was older and better understood the taunts we were facing. He must have realized before Errol and I that going to England was a pipe dream. This may have been the reason for his rebelling against the restrictions, the continuing pretence of our parents and grandmother, and against going to school and being singled out before the entire assembly because his school fees were so much in arrears that he could not return until they were paid.

In a tearful confrontation with Grandmother, Stephen blurted out that he didn't want to hear about going to England and that he didn't want to go to England. Errol and I exchanged glances. In our silence, we partially understood what was happening, but we didn't expect Stephen to reject England.

"He's upset and don't know what he is saying," Grandmother later explained to us. "He don't really mean what he's saying." We weren't convinced. A short time later, Stephen officially dropped out of school because of the fees, and left us. He went to visit Grand-Grand one day and never returned to the crowded house in Lodge Road. About this time, the automatic deductions from my father's military pay abruptly ended, too. Plaintive letters from Grandmother, Errol and me went unanswered. Life got even tougher. All talk of our going to England ended.

5

Broken by Hard Times

Early Monday morning, Grandmother woke Errol and me as she had promised, and just as we hoped she had forgotten. Grandmother had sent us to bed the night before with the stern warning that life was about to change.

Beginning the next day, someone else would have to start "contributing to feeding us," as she put it. After all, she argued, she was doing as much as she could providing us with shelter, and washing and ironing our school clothes. She didn't even know if our father was dead or alive, as there were no answers to her letters. The last few times she had heard from our father, the letters were virtually incomprehensible, seemingly a string of polysyllabic words that made no sense to us, except for the ever present admonition for us to vindicate ourselves. Vindicate. Vindicate. Vindicate yourself, he would write, in what must have been some code that we never understood. It would be a long time before the mystery behind these strange letters became clear.

The result was that there was no money to buy food to

feed us. Moreover, Grandmother said, she now had too many mouths to feed. The grandchildren by her daughters had to have priority: because they were from the belly of her daughters, she could swear to God they were her grandchildren.

As much as she loved us, we could not pass this crucial test: she did not have absolute certainty about the authenticity of grandchildren from her son, for no man could ever know for sure if some women wanted to put *ready-made shirts* on him. With the severe shortage of food in her house, and the imagined abundance in the home of Grand-Grand—a grandmother who could vouch for us because we came from the belly of one of her daughters—she said it was time for someone else to feed us.

Grandmother had decided that Errol and I were to turn to Grand-Grand for our meals. She argued that Grand-Grand continued to live well and might even be benefiting from money her daughter in England might be sending her. Once again, we felt caught in the middle. As we went to sleep, we silently hoped this was just an idle threat, one of the many Grandmother was making to deal with her increasing poverty and frustrations.

Unfortunately, it was no threat. Grandmother woke us, telling us to put on our school clothes and go to Grand-Grand's for our morning tea. She also told us to make similar arrangements for our lunch and our food, as we called the main meal of the day, after school. She would continue to give us a place to sleep at night. Errol and I didn't respond. We dressed and set out on our journey, numb from the prospects of what lay ahead. It was a long, long silent walk that hurt us more with every step. We had no idea of how to break the news to Grand-Grand. No matter how we put it, we could expect only another long discussion that would include Grand-Grand's going back to the first mistake our mother had ever made, even to her condescending to talk to our father, and then getting mixed up with his people. But what could we do?

In previous weeks, Grandmother had told Errol that he should join me visiting Grand-Grand on Saturdays. That way he, too, would get at least one good meal a week. I had started visiting Grand-Grand several months earlier. Grand-Grand, perhaps as fate would have it, had moved from Rockley to a government tenantry on a pasture in Kendal Hill, about an hour's walk from Lodge Road. When our grandfather died, his will had stipulated that his land in Rockley was to be sold, and the proceeds distributed among his children. Our mother had already received her inheritance when our grandfather sold a piece of the land to send her to England, so instead of another share of the proceeds going to her, he had willed that a token amount be set in trust for Stephen, Errol and me. It was money we would only receive when we reached twenty-one years of age. As a result of selling the land, Grand-Grand had had to move and ended up living closer to us.

Every Saturday, I visited. Errol, always trying to prove he was not a burden on anyone, even to the point of denying himself, steadfastly refused to accompany me, until Grandmother gave him the ultimatum that he visit his other family on Saturdays, or he didn't eat.

The other reason for me to visit Grand-Grand was to keep in touch with Stephen, who rewarded me with real pocket money every week. Stephen had started work at a supermarket and could afford a bicycle. He appeared to be enjoying life, had new friends and was acting more like a grown-up, even accompanying Aunty Anne and her boyfriend, Mervin, to the movies. Stephen seemed to be happy and fit in well. Every Saturday, he sent me back to Lodge Road with a quarter in my pocket and another quarter for Errol. Grand-Grand didn't like the condition of our clothes, or how every week I appeared to have more cuts and scrapes on my feet. She wondered why Grandmother didn't use the money she was getting from our father to take better care of us. Seeing us once again caught in the middle, Stephen bought us new shirts and underclothes. New clothes! Real pocket money, too! Money that allowed us to treat ourselves to the Barbadian delicacy of black pudding and souse in a bun, called a *salt bread*. We swore that the woman who sold black pudding and souse by the Providence School, the home ground for Lodge Road's cricket team, Hamilton, was the best black puddin'n'souse maker on the whole island. This was our treat of the week, especially when she dipped the bun in the souse pickle made from cucumber, parsley, hot peppers and who knows what host of other spices. The quarters did not stay long in our pockets at the cricket ground.

Although Errol didn't like going to Kendal Hill with me, he always awaited my return. And it was because of Stephen—and the allowance that I did not pass on to Errol one week—that I saw my first movie.

*   *   *

Movies and television were the big craze among boys of our age. Those who could afford the admission spent Saturday evenings at the Plaza Theatre in Oistins. The really fortunate could go to Bridgetown and choose from an array of cinemas. All week, they would talk about the cowboy and war movies they had seen, and about the *cuts* or trailer highlights promoting pictures they were expecting to see in the coming weeks. I could only listen because not only did I not have the admission price, but Grandmother had no time for idle and ungodly talk about *going to pictures.*

Television was new to Barbados. The government, as part of its modernization plans in preparation of political independence, had set up a radio and television station. The few homes in Lodge Road that could afford the black and white sets, which received the only station and operated as a radio receiver during the day, became rallying points for the boys and a few girls at night. Gone were the days when we sat under the moonlight or in the glow from the light in the house and told stories or played games steeped in our culture and history. No longer did the women and older girls meet together and laugh, joke, whisper or shake their heads knowingly until it was time for bed. That era was officially passing, to be replaced by watching television. Most times there were only one or two television sets in the village and they instantly became communal property for us.

The youths of the island were so captivated with this new medium that we were called by a new name—*TV-ticks.* Like the leeches that stuck to cows and other animals, we were glued to the TV. Perhaps, too, we were just as parasitic, sucking from this box the images of different and better lifestyles in foreign countries. There were no bigger TV-ticks than Errol and me. We were always talking about what we saw, sometimes coming home and recounting in minute detail, to the delight of Princess and Grandmother, who both vicariously participated in the craze through us.

The television transmissions began about six o'clock in the evening. Before they started transmitting, we would find a vantage point to watch the TV in the home lucky enough to have one. At times we had to be quite creative just to get a glimpse of the screen. Several of us might climb the tree next to the house and, perched on a limb, watch through the window. If the owner was mean, or we were too noisy, or if there were too many mosquitoes and moths flying around, we might have to watch through the glass of the closed windows, through cracks in the sides of the house, through the jalousie slats of the windows and door, or through the keyhole. Many times we had to be content to see the moving pictures but to do without the sound. A good downpour would send us scattering, but we might endure a slight drizzle, not daring to move for fear that when the rain from the overhead cloud holed up someone would have claimed our position in the tree or by the window. Many times a prolonged shower just defeated us. In drier times, if we were really lucky, the owner might throw open the front door and allow us to sit on the steps with an unimpeded view. The more generous might even invite us to sit on the floor and stare at the TV, as long as we promised to keep quiet. Usually, it only took one boy to break this rule and all of us were ordered out, sent back to finding a hole in the house that we could see through. When the transmission ended, plunging the area into darkness as the few TVs were switched off and people with electricity turned out their lights, we would run all the way home, hoping that in the deep darkness we would not encounter any bad people or bullies—the likes of which we saw on TV—or in my case, Mrs. King's dog. Most nights Errol and I would walk to the edge of the light from the streetlamps and run nonstop through the darkness to our home deep in the pasture.

I wanted to make the step up to movies. During the week, I enquired from a friend about such things as the price of admission, the start times and what he did when he was in the theatre. The next Saturday I found an excuse for leaving Grand-Grand's a bit earlier than usual, and with Errol's and my allowance in my pocket, walked to Oistins for the 4:30 p.m. showing. I watched a double bill of *Kid Galahad,* some boring story about a white boxer who talked and loved a lot, starring someone named Elvis Presley. That I didn't enjoy, but I revelled in the second show, *To Hell and Back,* starring Audie Murphy. This was my type of picture—lots of shooting, loud explosions and not much talking. Then I went home and took the risk of bragging on Errol. All the while I was hoping he wouldn't tell on me for going to the movies, just as I trusted that he had bought my story that Stephen said he had no money so there was no allowance. I think he did.

*   *   *

On any other Monday morning, Errol and I would have had much to talk about from a weekend of watching television and cricket, but on this morning we didn't talk. Not one word was spoken on this trip to Grand-Grand's. I remember how each of us was so deep in our thoughts, so ashamed of what was happening to us, that we could hardly look at each other. I remember walking beside Errol, he and I walking beside each other across fields of grass still wet with dew, the moisture washing our feet as we walked zombie-like under the soft rays of the morning sun. I remember wearing my best school clothes, a striped blue and white shirt and a pair of khaki pants.

We arrived at Grand-Grand's and, without talking, Errol and I entered the backyard. We stood there. The house was quiet and we thought everyone was still sleeping. I followed Errol under the house, which was on a incline and propped on some high beams, the cellar like an open basement. We sat on a rock, me beside my bigger brother, the two of us alone in the world. We sat in the quiet and listened, the calm occasionally broken by the cooing of the pigeons that Grand-Grand kept in a pen behind the house. The house started to come alive. We heard footsteps, but we didn't move. We couldn't bring ourselves to do anything. So we just sat on the rock. When the back door opened, we didn't move. Someone stepped outside for whatever reason, looked under the house and exclaimed.

"Wait, what the two o' wunnuh doing there?" We had been discovered.

Grand-Grand was quickly alerted. We were brought into the house. Stephen was fidgety and concerned. He must have had some understanding of what was happening and probably didn't need any answers except for the confirmation of what he was thinking. Errol and I looked at him and at all the worried faces around us.

"Grandmother send we down here," Errol said. "She say we gotta come here for tea on mornings."

Needless to say, the long discussions started. Grand-Grand provided us with breakfast. Stephen and the others left for work. Errol and I left for school with full stomachs and empty hearts. We had not told Grand-Grand we would be returning for lunch. We did, once again surprising her. Once again, we encountered Stephen, home from his supermarket job. He had to share his lunch with us. Once again, we left with heavy hearts, for how could we tell Grand-Grand to expect us back for the main meal of the day? We couldn't tell her.

After school, when I asked Errol if he was going back, his response was simple: no. Without another word, he turned for home. I followed him. We played around, killing time, to make it appear that we had gone for supper. For the next while that became our secret: we endured having to go for breakfast and lunch, but we never let anyone, not even Stephen, know that we went without supper.

Errol taught me how to get through the nights. He was still responsible for picking meat for the sheep. Every evening after we came home, pretending we had eaten, he would set out with his crocus bag. Fortunately, this was the season when plantations replanted some of the fields that had been allowed to lie fallow. This was known as the *butts* season. The men took the canes and cut them in small pieces for planting. From these pieces sprang the first cane stalk, which would later be cut and allowed to ratoon for several years, before the field was ploughed and the process started again.

For children, butts was another crop season. We looked forward to getting the pieces of cane not needed for planting. Errol would find the fields with the butts. He would load up his bag and later, he, David and I would sit and suck the cane. The butts we didn't use, we stored in a corner of the backyard. Indeed, we liked the old butts, especially those that were tainted after several days in the sun, the juice starting to ferment and the ends turning reddish. The juice seemed sweeter from the tainted cane. I don't think Errol and I ever told anyone of how we got through the nights.

*   *   *

The tension and frustrations were having other effects on us. We were becoming more violent. Or maybe we were internalizing what we saw in the wider society, beating one another in retaliation for the taunts, insults and threats that we received elsewhere. Maybe it was just our way of dealing with the uncertainty and insecurity. But down the line, we were turning violent, the older beating up on the younger, who in turn looked for yet a younger member of the family.

Grandmother's floggings had become more frequent and violent. It seemed that every single thing was an excuse for a flogging: not bringing the sheep home early enough, disobeying the slightest demand. Errol and I suffered from those beatings, and at times Grandmother even threatened to *put her hand on* Princess, who was already a mother of four children. Princess, in turn, flogged us, too. Sometimes she did so just as brutally as Grandmother, and sometimes for no reason.

Errol and I fought more than the usual fights between siblings. Errol seemed to withdraw into his own world. He talked less and occupied himself with various tasks, such as building toy tractors and trucks, making kites, repairing the sheep pen and setting up a swing for us in the tree in front of the house. He also had to look after all of us when Grandmother went to town and Princess wasn't at home.

Errol did not like me to intrude on his space and thoughts. He also got angry with me for trying to run with the bigger boys of his age, preferring that I play with those my own size, or with David. This was also his way of not having to defend me when I got into trouble with the bigger boys, or when I embarrassed him by crying.

But I wanted to act big, and Errol and I argued a lot. We invariably ended up fighting, with me always the loser. One thing about Errol, which I never seemed to learn from all our fights, was that he had a wicked left hand. He was left-handed and, fool that I was, I always watched his right. Then, *bam*, he would unleash that left hand and literally end the fight. He would slam it into my mid-section, dropping me in agony to the ground. It was a wicked punch. "Why do you have to up and cut the boy's wind like that?" Grandmother remonstrated the first time she saw me writhing in pain. And Grandmother, drawing her cue from the wider society and acting like some magistrate entering the fight on the side of the weak and defenceless, would flog Errol. Even that did not stop our fighting. I never learned how to guard against that fight-ending left hook.

The one person I knew who absolutely abhorred violence of any kind was Grand-Grand. Nothing made her angrier than to hear us tell of our floggings, whether at home or at school. She was adamant that corporal punishment of any kind was wrong. She often recounted how she had raised her children without once—well, maybe just a few times—hitting them. In the battle between corporal punishment and a good talking to, she put her money on a good verbal dressing down. "A kind word turneth away wrath," was one of her favourite sayings. "The only thing that people should be beating is balled black pepper, not children."

I found her argument intriguing if somewhat unusual. Imagine living in a house without getting flogged. I would think about this, especially when she became really angry from seeing my bruises and welts. She would take my shirt off and apply her cure-all of mentholated spirits, all the time fretting about the unfair treatments to which we were exposed. It wasn't long before Grand-Grand confronted Grandmother over this unfair treatment, in a move that would close a chapter of my life.

*　　*　　*

I had returned home from school, hungry as usual, and changed my clothes. For some reason Princess was angry with me. I had gone to the section of the backyard where we stored the cane butts and filled my arms. As I walked out, Princess pushed me. The butts went flying among the rocks, and I scampered after them. Princess claimed that I had gone for rocks to stone her and unleashed one of the most severe floggings I had ever received.

So hot was the punishment that I had to run away from her. With her coming after me, still armed with her whip, I decided I had to keep running. I ran and ran and ran. I didn't know where I was going. I kept running, I was so afraid. My feet seemed to take a life of their own. My back was burning from the bruises and stings of the whip. I was bleary eyed and crying. And my feet were just taking me somewhere.

I ended up, of all places, at Grand-Grand's house. Not a smart idea, I told myself when I realized where I was. This could only lead to more trouble. Grandmother would not take kindly to my letting Grand-Grand know about such a beating. I told myself that I'd better not go inside the house, but it was too late. Someone had spotted me and called out to me.

"Boy, what you doing back down here so late in the evening?" asked Aunty Stella. I entered the house and Aunty Stella, her instincts getting the better of her, approached me. "Mama," she shouted. "Look, somebody been beating this boy. Come here, boy, and let me look at you."

She examined me, making me take off my shirt.

"Who's been beating you, boy?" Aunty Stella questioned. I broke down and related the story of the flogging. Then, the worst possible thing happened.

"Well, what Ermie Goddard think she's doing with these children?" Grand-Grand said. To her daughter she said: "Stella, look put two shoes on your foot and come with me. We going up to Lodge Road this very minute and ask Ermie Goddard what she think she's doing. Look at this boy here, she beating him like some animal. And she don't even feed them now. At least you feed the beast of the field if you beat them. Come with me."

I was in so much trouble. I wanted to explain that there was no need to accompany me back to Lodge Road, that I would be fine once I recovered from the blows. Any showdown with Grandmother would make matters worse for me, and possibly Errol, too. But I was at a loss for words. I realized nothing could shake Grand-Grand and Aunty Stella. I took them the longest possible route I could think of back to Lodge Road, doing everything possible to avoid the confrontation. Taking the detour had its disadvantage: Grand-Grand wondered how early we had to get up in order to arrive in Kendal Hill in time for breakfast. "Are you sure this is the right way?" she asked at one point.

Every journey has to end and ours terminated outside the house in Lodge Road, where Grandmother was sitting on a large stone eating her meal from a bowl and catching the last rays of sun. I noticed Errol sitting on the swing.

Grand-Grand and Aunty Stella approached Grandmother. They enquired as to the reason for my beating and why it had to be so severe. Grandmother was explaining how boys tend to get out of hand and have to be treated firmly, when Princess appeared on the scene and instantly resumed her ferocious beating of me. She thrashed me with nettles that really stung.

"Run," I heard Aunty Stella calling to me. "Run, boy. Run."

I couldn't run. Where was I to go? Where would I sleep? Neither Errol nor I wanted to be a burden on anyone. The thought didn't even occur that I might sleep at Grand-Grand's, for in my mind, her having to take care of Stephen was enough of a burden. "Run. Run. Run."

I stood fixed to the spot. Princess flailed away. I could not move. I could only bawl. Finally, self-preservation took over and forced me to run. Too exhausted, Princess could not catch me.

"Look, if this is the way you treat these children," Grand-

Grand said, "let me have them. Give me his clothes right now."

"What you want his clothes for?" Grandmother said. But David, the closest thing I would ever have to a little brother, unexpectedly intervened. He ran into the house and grabbed the shirt and pants I wore to school. Before Princess could intercept him, he handed them to Aunty Stella. She snatched the clothes and David ran back towards where Errol was sitting on the swing.

"Errol, you come, too," Aunty Stella shouted.

"You come, too," Grand-Grand encouraged.

Errol refused. He sat on the swing, not swinging, his feet just hanging down, and his fingers digging into the ropes. Eventually, they gave up trying to get him to join us. With darkness setting, Grand-Grand and Aunty Stella took me away. I looked back and saw Errol still sitting on the swing, transfixed by the ferocity he had witnessed. Perhaps. I really believe that in his mind he was calculating that Stephen and I were enough of a burden for Grand-Grand and he would not add to it. He would continue to be the sacrifice.

*   *   *

Overnight, my life changed. I found myself in a more struc-tured environment and there was always food. Grand-Grand believed in three square meals a day: breakfast, the main meal around midday, and a light evening snack before bed. And there were absolutely no beatings. She wanted me to concentrate on school and to learn to speak well. It annoyed her no end when I used "me" as a possessive pronoun. "What is this me this and me that?" she asked. "It is *my* cup, not me cup. *My* pants, not me pants. Cut out this me this and me that. It makes you sound like the uneducated country people in Lodge Road."

Truthfully, until this time I hadn't thought much about education. Yes, I went to school but that was simply to put in time, not to get anything out of it. In any case, most of the time spent in school was devoted to thinking about such things as the next meal, the long walk from Lodge Road to Kendal Hill, finding butts or hoping that some evenings Grandmother might share the food with us, even if she thought we had already eaten.

While life improved for me, it became worse for Errol and David. Errol still came for breakfast and lunch and occasionally on Saturdays. Then he stopped coming and I didn't see him at school. When I next saw him, he told me that Grandmother had found him a job. He had left school. I did not see Errol for a long time, until one day he casually walked into the house in Kendal Hill carrying a small bag with a few clothes.

"Grandmother told me to go and live down here," he said in a resigned, matter-of-fact way, as if the fight had gone out of him.

Stephen, Errol and I had left Lodge Road after all. But it was not to the land of milk and honey as everyone had once envisioned. Even in our reunion, we knew we were only encountering different problems. Although Grand-Grand's household was financially better off than Grandmother's, it wasn't much better. Grand-Grand didn't work and got by on a government pension only. Our parents were not supporting us. The only people who worked were Aunty

Stella, who had her daughter Jennifer to support, and Aunty Ann. We learned that the bulk of the money used to support the household came from Mervin, who was then only Aunty Ann's boyfriend. We didn't want to be a burden on this stranger. And knowing how men hated their money being spent on other people's children, we didn't want to cause any friction between Mervin and Aunty Ann.

Without complaining, or if he did it wasn't in our presence, Mervin took on the role of being the main provider for a family that had suddenly ballooned on him. He became the closest thing I ever had to a father figure at home, and though he didn't talk much to Errol and me, he was always there for us. He helped to turn our lives around. He showed me that men could be good, kind and selfless. He taught me that men can get angry without beating anyone, especially their loved ones. Years later he would affectionately refer to all of us raised in Grand-Grand's house as his and Aunty Ann's children. And he is so right. Mervin must be an angel, for he is certainly a very special man.

*   *   *

Although I left Lodge Road, I never really cut all ties with Grandmother. There was something that wouldn't allow me to let go. Even though I knew her treatment of us was cruel, I was willing to give her the benefit of the doubt. I believe she was a very strong woman who broke under pressure. Raising a large family in such a cramped house, without a steady income and in a village like Lodge Road was simply too much for her. Soon after I had changed homes, Grandmother reached out to me in a way that left me thinking she had wanted to say she was sorry for what had happened.

Concerned with the brutal thrashings that I had received, Grand-Grand did not want me to come in contact with either Grandmother or Princess. She felt they would hurt me and her instructions were simple: if I saw them in the distance, I was to run away before they got close. She was worried they would attack me on my way to or from school.

One evening on my way home I unexpectedly encountered Grandmother. I suspect that Grand-Grand was right, that she was looking for me. Grandmother was walking along the route I usually took from school, a track that was out of the way for her. She carried a big bamboo basket on her head and called to me.

I went over and stood in front of her. She didn't appear angry, so I didn't feel threatened and I relaxed a bit. Grandmother asked how I was doing and said she hoped that I was doing well. She also hoped that I was continuing to read a lot because she knew I liked to read, and that I was doing well in school.

Standing there with the basket on her head, she told me life was still very hard for her. There was no money. She did not know what had become of our father, and she was having a hard time feeding the children at home. Grandmother said that she never wanted me to leave her home under the conditions I had. After all, she and Princess had raised me from when I was only two years old and there was that attachment. She had always thought that, when I left, it would be to go to England or as a man taking my ship to sea. Still, she said, she had done her *levelest best* to bring up the three of us on the straight and narrow path, and nobody could expect more of her. She wished me God's blessing and suggested that I should visit her from time to time in Lodge Road. She told me that Princess and David missed me, too, especially David, whom she said she had hoped would have gone to join his mother in the Bahamas at the same time Allison and her husband had sent for Rawle. She felt they should have sent for the two boys at the same time, and not have left David behind. She didn't look happy. I listened to her, not talking much, if at all. I didn't feel threatened. When she finished, I ran off to join the group of boys and girls from the Kendal Hill.

Shortly after that encounter, Grandmother started appearing outside the school with her tray at lunch time, trying to sell whatever she had to the students. I couldn't help thinking that her life must have really taken a turn for the worse, for she had always sneered at the idea of hawkers *cheating* students of their pocket money. Moreover, I noticed there was never much on her tray to sell.

My lunch time was easier. I now had money from Stephen to buy lunch from the shop in front the school, saving me from having to make the trek home and back. Having spending money put me in the league of those who could buy the traditional fare of a bottled soft drink, a bread and two fish cakes, coconut turnovers or rock cakes. One day, soon after my encounter with Grandmother, I was eating my lunch in the shadow of the school when David approached me. Minutes earlier, I had seen Grandmother talking to him.

"Grandmother tell me to come and ask you if I could share your lunch," David said. I looked across at Grandmother and she nodded her head, as if silently confirming David's request.

How could I not share my lunch with my little brother? How could I not share with him what was made possible from the generosity of my bigger brother? This was the David who I always felt as responsible for as my brothers did for me; the David whose mother had asked me to take care of him and I had promised I would; the David I had proudly brought to school on his very first day and had kept his cap for him, the same way Stephen had kept mine. From that day on, I shared my lunch with David whenever Grandmother was unable to provide for him. It was not only sharing lunch, it was a celebration. For by eating the standard fare of most of the students—the ice cold soft drink, the turnovers, the bread and fish cakes—David was eating what he could only have dreamt about, which Grandmother could not afford to give him.

Even after I left Christ Church Boys' Elementary School, David sought me out. With time, he started visiting in Kendal Hill on weekends, so much so that he and Aunty Ann became close. He brought me fruits and cane, and I gave him my outgrown clothes and used shoes. Later, when both of us were at high school, he would show me his book list. Books I didn't need, I gave to him. And with time, he got me to start visiting him in Lodge Road, where we would play outside the house just as we had in the past.

David always loved Grandmother. He helped me to understand that Grandmother hadn't been happy when the dreams for all of us had just withered and died; how it was possible for even the best people to be broken by hard times. He taught me how necessary it was to forgive, especially those who sought forgiveness through their actions but could never bring themselves to say the words. And I still believe him.

6

Christ Church High School

Several months later, Grand-Grand and I took another important walk, this time more leisurely and with a more pleasant purpose. Each step gave her a chance to tell me that I was at a turning point in my life. Most important, she told me, was that I must realize times were changing in Barbados and only those with an education would get ahead.

She told me of bright, bright people who came to nothing because they did not get the chance now being offered to me. Even she did not reach her full potential, she said. Neither did my mother who had been a really bright girl at school. She explained that in those times poor people did not stay long in primary school and had far less a chance to excel in high school. To underline her point, she raised her hand in front of me and, with her thumb and index finger holding an imaginary pen, made a writing motion.

"That's how you write an M, right?" she asked. This puzzled me. I knew Grand-Grand could read and write. She read the Bible often and she, perhaps more than we did, enjoyed reading our comic books. Specifically, she liked to follow the exploits of "The Phantom" and "Dr. Kirby" in the Sunday edition of the local *Advocate* newspaper. She also enjoyed listening to the short stories on radio, and she loved to read the stories published in the magazine section of the weekend newspaper. So, why was she asking me how to write an M?

"You write the capital M in the opposite direction to the capital W, right?" she said.

Hmm, I thought. This fact of penmanship had never occurred to me. "Yes, that is how you write an M."

"I just checking to make sure," she said, "so that when I have to *sign* my name on the papers at the school for you. If I did get the education that you're going to get, I won't have to ask you anything."

Crafty, Grand-Grand. It was her way of underlining that she was literally putting herself on the line, especially financially, to ensure an advanced education for me. Minutes later, she was in the headmaster's office, having no difficulty signing Margaret Legall in a firm hand. I was now a high school boy, enrolled at Christ Church High School, and I didn't know of anyone prouder of this achievement than Grand-Grand. Certainly, nobody was as adamant as Grand-Grand that I understood I had arrived at a turning point in my life, a juncture that she also felt coincided with the arrival of better times on the island.

Grand-Grand must have realized the danger of my taking Christ Church High School too lightly. After all, it was then an independent school run by the Anglican parish church, and long considered a refuge for those without too much upstairs. Because it was an independent school, it operated largely outside the purview of the Ministry of Education, and its standards were therefore suspect. This was not one of the posh grammar schools that produced the politicians, lawyers, doctors and top civil servants of the island and region. This was a school where you left after five years with hardly anything to show, but hopefully with enough education to get a job as a clerk, bank teller or low-level civil servant. Still, Grand-Grand warned me, "It is better than nothing."

Only the most brilliant boys, which usually meant those from the moneyed class or children of wealthy foreigners and colonial officials, went to Harrison College or Lodge. The latter was primarily for white students, but the two schools were mainly populated by the cream of this class-conscious society. For the same reasons, the top girls went to Queen's College. Then came the second tier: the boys going to Combermere, Coleridge and Parry or Foundation Boys; the girls to St. Michael's, Alexander's or Foundation Girls. Those who didn't make the cut simply hung around their elementary school for a year or two until the end of their formal education, usually at age fourteen. If their parents had money, they could go to a school like Christ Church High School.

For some time, it had been widely debated whether the Common Entrance Examination, which was open to all eleven-year-olds on the island, was a true test of the ability and knowledge of the average student, or if it was biased towards only the exceptionally educated students, those who had been exposed to more than what was offered in the public schools. People fighting the status quo believed the examination, which qualified those for attendance at grammar school, was not a genuine test for all.

Grand-Grand must have been politically conscious, for the mood was not only changing on the island, but throughout the Caribbean. The broad availability of a good education had become a major issue for the young politicians, the so-called young Turks, who were pushing for political independence. When I was just starting high school, the party in power was the Democratic Labour Party, led by an energetic young lawyer. Errol "Dipper" Barrow had trained as a pilot in Canada during the Second World War and had become the highest ranking black airman in the British Army. He had crowned his achievements by being the personal navigator for Sir Sholto Douglas, the air commander-in-chief of the British Zone of Germany. On the local political scene, Barrow was a brash young man, capturing the imaginations of the poor by arguing that independence was their only salvation. One of his first targets was the reform of the educational system, which meant students like me were his guinea pigs.

The first of these reforms, which helped bring Barrow to power in 1961 (and from where he could formally push for independence), was to abolish the prohibitive fees at the grammar schools. A student needed only to pass the Common Entrance Examination and a place and attendance at a grammar school were guaranteed. Barrow would announce other reforms as the date for independence, set for November 30, 1966, approached. This was the beginning of his educational thrust that guaranteed free education for

Barbadians—from elementary school to university—along with the provision of free textbooks and, in elementary schools, a daily hot lunch at a minimum cost. These were the days when radical-thinking politicians argued that Barbados had to fully develop the only resource it had—its people. As they pointed out, Barbados did not have deposits of bauxite, gold or petroleum like elsewhere in the Caribbean so it had no choice but to develop its human resources.

*   *   *

It was on a Saturday morning that we crowded into a classroom at Christ Church Boys' Elementary School to sit the first part of the 1966 Common Entrance Examination. I arrived early and found my place in a room that seemed unusually dark. After tackling the paper on arithmetic, we broke and went to lunch, returning for the paper on English. Towards the end of session in walked Mrs. Pickering, one of the most loved teachers at the primary school, and the final invigilator for the examination. (According to legend, she was also a great fan of my father's, the musician.)

Something seemed to have upset her. Several students had already handed in their papers and were leaving. Linda Pickering looked at the answers.

"What's this foolishness, here?" she said aloud. One part of the English paper was to spot errors of grammar and word usage and to correct them. She read aloud: "*The sun sets at dust.* Who ever hear people round here talking like that: *the sun sets at dust*? This exam must be set by some Englishman. We don't talk this way, so how they expect the people children of this island to pass this exam? Look, come back here!" she ordered the students.

"How many of you get to that one: *the sun sets at dust*?" she asked the room. "Any of you see the mistake?" Nobody answered because, as she had said, none of us talked that way.

"See what I tell yuh? We don't talk about no dusk down here in the West Indies. It is, *the sun sets at dusk*," she said, spelling out slowly, "D-U-S-K. Now, everybody change it to that."

She didn't stop there. Mrs. Pickering walked us through the paper. Obviously, she must have been part of her social consciousness to lessen the odds against us. She didn't feel this examination was fair, but biased, as so many people suspected, towards the white and upper-class members of society, those who went to private schools and had received special tutoring for the test. Mrs. Pickering was showing her political colours here, for with this thinking she must have been a supporter of independence. That year, an unusually large number of us, including me, passed the first part of the Common Entrance Examination.

To ensure the school and students received similar results in the second part of the examination, the head-master, Mr. Lynch, decided to take responsibility for tutoring us. First, he demoted me and a few others from Class Five to Class Four under the tutelage of a young local man named Covey Carter, who was admired as an exceptionally gifted cricketer even when he was at Foundation High School. Carter was a strict disciplinarian who occasionally

showed a sense of humour. Mr. Lynch wanted all the candidates for the second part of the Common Entrance
Examination in the same class, which turned out to be a
major attack on the pride of those of us he had demoted.
Not only did we have to put up with this indignity of being
dropped back, but when we arrived in the new class, we
quickly realized we were not nearly as smart as some of the
students a year younger than we were who were taking the
examination for the first time.

Mr. Lynch had a plan and he was central to it. We were
to meet with him for private classes after school and on
Saturday mornings. All this extra work, and being
constantly under the watchful eye of a principal, didn't
appeal to me. Worse, Mr. Lynch had said the lessons were
optional. I decided I would rather be playing than staying
for the extra classes. Most of us must have felt that way
because on evenings Mr. Lynch had to physically scout
around the school to find students for his classes. One
evening I was in a classroom when someone shouted
"Lynchie coming." I was among the last to dive under a desk
to hide. From then on my best friend, Ian Nurse, and I hid
under the desks until the path was clear. In part, this was
our way of rebelling against Mr. Lynch for demoting us.

We didn't have invigilators like Mrs. Pickering when we
sat the final part of the examination. The morning of the
results, I left home hoping to bring back the news Grand-
Grand wanted. One by one, Mr. Lynch proudly called out
the names of the passing students and the schools they
were to attend. Mine and Ian's names were not on the list.
Later, Mr. Lynch called me aside. "Let this be a lesson to
you, Foster. You should be going to Lodge or Harrison

College. I know your father. But remember when you and Nurse used to hide under the desk instead of coming to lessons? You thought I didn't see you, nuh?"

But Mr. Lynch had some consolation prizes. In another of its reforms of the educational system, the ruling party had decided to influence the election just months away. It offered scholarships at independent schools to students who had passed the first part of the examination but failed the second part, who had not qualified for the top schools. We got a consolation scholarship. All that was needed was for Grand-Grand to sign the papers promising to pay the five dollars per term for my education. The scholarship covered the remainder of the fees. By the time I left school, the fees had increased to an onerous fifteen dollars a term.

Sending me to high school was a major financial undertaking for Grand-Grand, especially when I had to be equipped without the help of my parents in England. School fees were only part of the problem. A high school student needed to dress properly, in a specified uniform that included a tie and knee-high socks with little flags on the elastic garters. Brown shoes were specified, and there was a list of textbooks for reading and exercise books for writing, a geometry set, a drawing book and crayons or paints, a special hymnal because it was a church school, and a bag for carrying all of it. Grand-Grand rose to the occasion and sent out an S.O.S., of sorts, to just about every member of the family. Aunty Ruth, with her civil service job at the main hospital, was asked to provide the khaki pants for my uniform. Her daughter, Beverley, also a civil servant, provided the matching khaki shirts and some underclothes. Stephen helped with my shoes and money for incidentals. Aunty Ann and Mervin kept me clothed and fed and Grand-Grand even sent out the call for help to her eldest daughter, Aunty Olga, whose relationship with the family had always been strained. Aunty Olga helped with my books, starting by offering those that her children had used at other independent high schools. Even I had to make a financial contribution. Every Saturday, I harvested the half-ripe papayas growing in the backyard and sold them to the hotels and supermarkets on the south coast. This meant walking a few miles with a basket on my head, but I returned home with enough money for the next week's lunches.

*   *   *

On the first day of school, I set off feeling somewhat like a syndicate, like one of those prize fighters entering the ring for the first time who carries the weight of the financial investors' expectations on his shoulders. A collective effort had gotten me this far. Every member of the family shared in the dream and had contributed. As Grand-Grand reminded me, very few members of the family got the opportunity for a secondary education largely at the government's expense, and it was up to me now to deliver, not to disappoint them.

The school was constructed from brick and wood. It backed onto the main cemetery for the parish, with high limestone walls separating our play area from the burial ground, with its towering mahogany trees that sang so sweetly in the trade winds and sheltered so many nesting birds. To the east of the school was the main parish church, itself a majestic whitewashed building, with stained glass windows, rows of polished seats and a balcony at the back. To the other side were the well-manicured playing fields for Foundation Boys' and Girls' schools, but we were not permitted to venture on these premises. The difference between a grammar school like Foundation, even though it was not even elite, and an independent school like ours had to be maintained and policed, especially by the Foundation grounds watchmen and the schools' teachers.

One of the features of our school was the long barn-like windows and doors that gave rise to the name Christ Church High School Stables. They were painted bright green, one of the colours of our school. It was the colour of the girls' uniforms, of the epaulets on our socks, and of our striped yellow and green ties.

The school was made up of two main parts. There was a series of compartments that were form rooms for the senior students, those older males who wore long grey pants and white shirts, and the females who wore white bodices and green skirts. The other part of the school was a big open hall, with a raised platform. The hall was used for school assembly, and special events such as prize day. But for the most part it was reserved for the junior boys in their all-khaki uniform and short pants and the girls with one-piece green uniform dresses and matching green bloomers. This section also boasted a small cafeteria, a play area with a few ping-pong tables and a classroom for the home economics classes.

On our first day, we were grouped into four first forms, each of about forty students seated three to a desk and bench. These forms took up most of the hall. With pride we wrote our form and its number on our exercise books. We had graduated from classes or standards of the primary school to the more prestigious forms. Ian Nurse and I were in Form 1-3, at the foot of the raised platform. One of the pleasures of arriving early at school, or staying late, was to sit on our benches and listen to one of the senior students, Lloyd Wilson, play the piano on the dais. Wilson was the designated school musician. He accompanied us with the hymns and national anthem during school assembly, and absolutely delighted us when he just took to the piano and played, especially the latest hits. Music was obviously the most important thing in his life. For us, even when he was practising, it was like attending a one-man concert. In a short while, there was no doubt among us that Lloyd Wilson was the best pianist we had ever heard and it didn't surprise us when, as a school boy, Wilson formed one of the top bands on the island and eventually went to an American university to study music. I wondered if my father possessed similar talent, but was becoming aware that I might never know.

We loved the excitement at Christ Church High. It was school, but there was still the feeling of maintaining the informality of village life and of not taking ourselves too seriously. We were not like some of the boys and girls who had gone on to fine grammar schools and who, certainly for a while, felt they had to prove they had now put aside the old ways. At our school we enjoyed dominoes, table tennis and improvising various forms of amusements while the principal, Mr. Gilmour Roachford, always complained that he didn't have enough money to run the school and buy us sports equipment. We got by with a few pieces of cricket gear, some basketballs, which we used for soccer balls when the teachers weren't looking, and table tennis. Unless it rained, we sat in the shade of the tall trees to quickly eat our lunch and then played a fast-moving version of cricket called firms, with everyone trying to be the next batter or bowler in a mad scramble for the bat or ball. One afternoon, the group of us first formers who were fast becoming tight friends were under the tall trees having lunch. I stood off to a side, not eating.

"What happen, Foster?" Maurice Quintyn asked. He was sitting on a rock that was part of the escarpment that gradually dropped off to the south coast of the island. "Where's your lunch, man?"

"I forgot it at home."

"And you ain't say nothing, man?" Maurice said. "Here, have some of mine." From that day none of us went without lunch, whether we forgot to bring a meal to school or, as was the case for some of us, we didn't have any on that day. Maurice Quintyn and I spent the next five years sharing the same benches as we moved through Christ Church High School.

*   *   *

Grand-Grand set herself a task. She vigilantly kept watch on my school work, setting a routine for my homework. One of her first orders was that homework had to be completed before I could even think of playing cricket. And she wanted me in bed early so I was rested for the next day.

She demanded nothing short of excellence on any tests or examinations.

Roderick Taylor, no more than a few years older than we were, assembled the members of Form 1-3 on the final day of our first term at Christ Church High School. This was our first day of reckoning, when we were to take home our school reports, the first indication of how we were making the adjustment to high school. A quiet fell on the form as Mr. Taylor sat in front of us, the book containing our fate opened before him.

Mr. Taylor could always be counted on to tell us a joke. He was a teacher who made a difference at Christ Church High School, part of the attempts by administration to improve the quality of teaching. I knew Mr. Taylor, then simply called Roderick, from Sunday School where his father was a superintendent and one of the elders in the Pilgrim Holiness Sunday School. Of course, he was no longer Brother Roderick, who occasionally preached at the church and performed at special events, but Mr. Taylor, a title that he appeared very uncomfortable with in the class-room. For him, teaching was a way of marking time until he had raised enough money to study meteorology at an American university. Some of our teachers, including a few who had come from other Caribbean islands, were working part-time while studying at the Barbados campus of the University of the West Indies.

Mr. Taylor felt the tension in the form room and tried to humour us, just as he had over the past three months. His ritual was to announce each position in form, starting at the bottom and rising to the top. Everybody in the form wanted to be first in class. That was what our parents and guardians expected. Mr. Taylor tried to ease the disappointment.

We were no longer elementary school children, he explained. We had made the transition to high school and, as form master, he was proud of us. Yes, he knew that every one of us wanted to be first in class, but with almost forty students in the form, everybody couldn't come first. Those who found themselves at the bottom this term should view it as an opportunity to improve themselves the next time around. And then he gave us what he suggested should be our speech when we got home with our results.

"You are in high school now," he said, "so the position you place, in the form, should not matter as much as your overall percentage. Look at the percentage, not only at the position." He said, once again, that he was proud of us because the average for the form was almost 60 per cent, further proof that we were making the transition smoothly.

Then, he let the shoe drop, starting with the student at the bottom, who promptly broke into tears. I came sixth in form. Grand-Grand took the report, showed it round to members of the family with an air of authority and suggested there was still room for improvement.

Grand-Grand's reaction was far different the next term. I had slipped to fifteenth.

"You come *fifteenth*?" she said.

"Well, look at my overall percentage," I said, remembering Mr. Taylor's advice. "It's higher than last term."

"Fifteenth," Grandmother repeated. "You mean there are fourteen boys and girls in that form brighter than you? I mean, sixth last term was bad enough. But fifteenth?"

"But the overall percentage . . ."

"Don't tell me about no percentage. If there are fourteen students ahead of you, that means they have a better percentage than you. So, what are you telling me?"

Grand-Grand always said she preferred giving a child a *good talking to* as opposed to corporal punishment. By the time she had finished with me, I was silently wishing for the physical beating. I was reminded of how money was hard to come by and how she had had to spend her widow's mite, as she called it, on my school fees; how the various members of the family had to work hard and contribute to my schooling; how I wasn't studying hard enough or applying myself to the task of learning and how she was not going to stand for such behaviour. I returned to school suitably chastened. Grand-Grand's advice was that I constantly pray to God for wisdom and understanding, but I should also do my part by opening up my head to take in the education that was being offered.

Three months later, I held my breath when Mr. Taylor brought us together for the final time as the first form. This was a crucial meeting, for we were also being informed if we had passed the final examination to be promoted to second form. The third term report was always the best test of how a student performed over the year, for it was based on a series of final examinations covering the entire curriculum for the academic year.

Nobody wanted to be left behind, or to be sent to the remedial form for students not succeeding academically. Part of me worried just about passing, but my other concern was how many students would come in ahead of me and how I could break the news to Grand-Grand. While Mr. Taylor went through the ritual of telling us how well we had performed, how we should focus on our percentages and how we were all being promoted the next term, I thought back to one of my earlier examinations.

*   *   *

I was sitting a short distance away in the semi-darkened hall, writing the English paper. No two students from the same academic year sat together, to prevent cheating. I sat beside Junior Lane, a senior by two years, who lived a short distance from me in Kendal Hill and was considered the brightest boy in the school. But something else stuck out in my mind. I had returned from playing at lunch and was seated in the hall. I could see right across the escarpment to Oistins below, and beyond that to the aquamarine and various blues of the Atlantic Ocean. It was a most beautiful day, with hardly a cloud in the sky. I looked at the examination paper and found out that I had to choose from several essay topics. I wrote on what I wanted to become when I grew up. Looking out over the ocean, as the examination room fell calm with only the occasional fidgeting and rustling of papers, I started to dream. And I wrote that one day I wanted to be what I called a communicator, maybe someone working on radio, like Buddy Boy Vic Brewster, who hosted a midday show on the local radio station, perhaps a reporter bringing news from overseas or maybe just someone who wrote.

In this essay, I must have been tapping a vein that had first appeared when I was about seven years old. I was in Class I-C at Christ Church Boys' Elementary and Mr. Allen had asked us to write a composition on our dreams in life. Just prior to that day, we had received a parcel from my parents in England and it had contained two things for me: a pair of heavy brownish tweed pants that were far too big for me, and a long brown exercise book. This book was unusual, for it was the size of legal paper and not the regular and smaller exercise book. It stood out. I wrote my essay and handed in my book.

Some days later, I glanced across the school hall and, to my horror, saw this big brown exercise book moving from class to class. A teacher took the book from a student, read it, pondered, then chose another boy to take the book to the teacher in the next class. On and on it went. I knew it had to be my book. There was none other like it in the school or, for all I knew, on the island. Finally, the book ended up with Mr. Daniel, a senior teacher and one of the strictest disciplinarians. His strap or bamboo was always close at hand and he seldom hesitated to use it. I was petrified.

With the book open, Mr. Daniel started walking across the room in the direction of our class. He stopped in front of the class and spoke in hushed tones to Mr. Allen. They smiled. Mr. Daniel came over to me, and with the book still open, placed the essay in front of me.

"Anyone help you with what you wrote here?" he asked.

"No, sir."

"Good essay. You, like you, have the makings of a writer," he said. My essay was something about how I wanted peace on earth, for the strong to stop bullying the weak, for the hungry to have enough food and for the police to catch all the *man-outs*—literally men out of prison on the lam and considered dangerous to the general population—so the world could live in peace.

Now, Mr. Taylor was telling us how well we had done in our first year as high school students. I kept focused on the positions, wondered what I was going to tell Grand-Grand, not wanting to take another *good talking to* from her. The fifteenth position came up and went to some other student. So did the sixth position. I held my breath. Finally, Mr. Taylor announced, "First . . . Cecil Foster." From then on, the results would be the same for every term during my stay at Christ Church High. "And first," the form master or mistress would always announce, "Cecil Foster." I had found my niche. It was in the books.

*   *   *

Ian Nurse had everything to live for. Of all of us in the group of young boys going into our teenage years, he was the most naturally talented. This was the case in Kendal Hill where we lived and at Christ Church High School, where we were in the same forms and were members of the scout troupe. Ian was my best friend; perhaps the fact that our birthdays were eighteen days apart had something to do with this bond. Ian always believed September people were special. There was something magical about Ian, in his winning smile and in his natural ability to perform well in sports, particularly at cricket, the ultimate test of our emerging prowess.

We dreamt of becoming great cricketers like Gary Sobers, Wes Hall, Rohan Kanhai or Lance Gibbs, and of one day achieving the ultimate goal of playing for our island or even the West Indies. To this end, every one of us had a nickname, taken from some famous cricketer. Ian's name was Thomas Veivers, after an Australian all-round cricketer, someone equally talented with the bat and with the ball; because I was tall and lanky, mine was Ian Greig, after a South African all-rounder who was almost seven feet tall. At least, that was the argument of our friend, Merton Mayers, a budding boxer, cricket fanatic and the informal leader of our group, who went by the name Chev, named for, of all people, the Soviet Union leader Nikita Khrushchev. He chose our nicknames and they usually stuck. (Somehow it did not appear ironic that Merton had pinned on me the name of a cricketer from a country banned from international competition because of its racist policy of apartheid. Even in an era of political independence and black pride, when it came to dreaming about sports, these things didn't really matter. Nor did it stop us from arguing whether a West Indian cricket team of primarily players of African and Indian ancestry would soundly beat an all-white team from South Africa. Many times, we played the game in our minds, even if we knew that as long as apartheid lived, the real game was merely a dream. Still, Merton Mayers pinned the names of the brothers Graham and Peter Pollock, supposedly the top South African players of the day, on any of our friends who best demonstrated the skills of these white South Africans.)

I learnt many things from Ian, starting with hiding under the desks to escape from the principal of our elementary school and his after-school lessons. But there were other things, such as girls. With his curly hair and baby face, Ian was the first boy of our age to actually have girls running after him. After school, I often waited for Ian as he sat in some darkened corner at Christ Church High School with one of his girlfriends who was waiting for her bus to come and take her home. Or he would be in a crowd of girls, having his hair combed and brushed, the young ladies applying makeup to his face and taking the ribbons from their hair and putting them in his. Ian laughing and enjoying the attention, being so pliable, later telling me it is easier to get your way with females by giving in to them, by letting them comb and style your hair the way they did their dolls. And these were girls from, of all places, *town*. Listening to the bigger boys, we knew it was nothing short of an achievement for country boys like us to get the attention of town girls—so sophisticated and beyond our age in knowledge of the real world. Ian was a natural.

When the buses pulled out, he and I would grab our school bags and walk home, he telling the great stories of what had happened, me envious, but learning. The only area where I was better than Ian was at things academic. And yes, with my longer legs, I ran faster and probably outpaced him when we walked to and from school. But at that age, especially when girls were coming into our lives, who would not give up this easy affinity with books, school work and higher grades, just for a few stolen moments with a favourite girl?

The books were not even all mine. Individually, Ian and I could not afford all the books required every school year. Ian's mother was a single parent who worked as a domestic servant, but was absolutely devoted to this son who came late in her life. So, he would ask his friends and family for hand-me-down books. I did the same, selling the books from the previous year to buy the needed replacements. In the weeks leading up to the first class, we consulted and saw which books were missing from our combined lists. Those we purchased together. We shared all our books.

Ian really stood out on the cricket field, where his confidence and ego were as strong as in a social environment. Because he was left-handed, he developed the natural swing of a good fast bowler and the special touch of all those great left-handed batsmen. I know, because I was usually no match for him when we played cricket on the pasture near our homes or in the road. I always had great difficulty getting him out when he batted, and when it was my turn at the wicket, he made short work of me with one of his balls that deceived with its speed, bounce and swing.

We played cricket virtually all day on Sundays. Early in the morning, especially those of us old enough not to go to morning church and Sunday school, we met in a pasture that was once a sugar cane field. We called it Wanderers, borrowing the name of one of the famous cricketing grounds near Bridgetown. In reality, it was nothing like the real Wanderers with its lush and well-watered lawns and hardly a stone in sight. Instead, we had to put up with cane holes, *pimplers* or thorns, broken glass bottles and rocks of various sizes. In the morning, we picked opposing teams. We sat around, informally decided the captains and then allowed them to pick players alternately. Usually, the best players were chosen first, followed by the mediocre and lastly by those making up the numbers, which usually included young boys earning their spurs and still learning the game. Ian was different. Often, he was among the early picks. He batted high in the order, instead of bringing up the tail end like those of us still proving ourselves. Occasionally, we engaged a team from another village or we went *touring*. Invariably, Ian Nurse made the eleven-man team, sometimes beating out older and established players. Or he was definitely the first among the reserves or substitutes.

The first game would finish around noon. We would head home for our traditional Sunday lunch and rest while the hot sun lost some of its fury. About three o'clock, we again met at Wanderers and played another game, which usually ended when the sun disappeared. Then, we sat on the mounds of dirt near the cricket pitch *skylarking*, simply fooling around, rough sporting, teasing one another, telling long stories and sometimes fighting.

So we had spent the weeks of our vacation playing cricket and road tennis, which was a combination of ping pong and lawn tennis, played with paddles and a tennis ball. I was better than Ian at road tennis, for I had learned how to master the top spin, so that the ball hit in his court and spun back sharply into mine before he reached it. On this particular evening, we disagreed over the game and we fought, going to our homes angry with each other. Tragically, we never spoke again.

The following Sunday evening, Grand-Grand stopped me when I was leaving for Wanderers for the final game before going back to school. She had a chore for me: go to the neighbour's shop and buy a half gallon of kerosene oil for the lamps. Then, she instructed me to take care of my school clothes, to polish my shoes and prepare for my return to school. When the sun went down, she asked me to fill the lamps with oil and light them.

At that moment something strange happened. I filled a lamp with the oil, turned up the wick and applied the lighted match. Nothing happened. The wick would not catch fire. I tried several times with the same result. I was becoming frustrated, because I still hoped to join the boys sitting on the mounds and skylarking. Finally, the wick took the fire, but instead of burning evenly, it sputtered, giving off small sparks. I knew something was wrong. I called into the house for help, shouting that the neighbour must have added water to the kerosene to stretch it, something that we always suspected but could never prove. Just then, Stephen came home with the news.

"You hear that Ian just got hit with a rock and got cut real bad so that they have to take him to hospital," he said. With that news, the lamp started burning brightly, no sputters.

I later found out Ian had been struck in the face while on the mound. Two boys were fooling around or fighting, one threw a stone, and Ian was in the way. The next day, I went to school and told everybody that Ian was in hospital. That evening, Ian's mother asked me and another friend, Alister, to accompany her to the hospital, to be on standby in case blood donors were needed for Ian. We went to the hospital, but were not allowed to see our friend.

In the still of the next morning I was awakened by the piercing wail of Ian's mother. It came from across village, over the cane fields. Nobody needed to tell us what had happened. The black hospital van in front of Ian's home told the story. My best friend had died. And we had not talked since our fight.

It was a long and slow walk for me to school that morning. I told the news to members of our form and then went to tell the headmaster, Mr. Roachford.

"Ian Nurse dead," I said, stumbling for words.

"What? Another one?" Mr. Roachford said in disbelief. "That two. Rawle Applewhite died in a car accident." Rawle Applewhite was a senior student. Minutes later, the headmaster announced the sad news at the morning assembly. Throughout the prayers came the sounds of crying, especially from the girls who wept openly for Ian and Rawle. Most of the day came a string of questions for which I had no answers. The next day, school ended at lunch to allow us to attend the two funerals. The senior students went to Rawle's funeral, while the juniors attended Ian's. I was among the guard of honour provided by the Scout troop and I was asked to lift the head of my friend as we carried the casket from the church to the burial plot. It was a heavy coffin, and at one point, we almost dropped it. The steadying hand of the Scoutmaster and several adults helped.

Since then, hardly a day has passed that I have not remembered Ian Nurse. I was walking to school one day when an older woman said, "You really miss your friend, don't you? He would be walking with you now." I mouthed something to her and continued on my way. I guess I must have looked rather lost. Worse was when Ian's mother called me to her home to offer me Ian's textbooks and other school paraphernalia. She was badly distraught. "Take all of them," she sobbed. "They ain't any use to me or Ian any more." And she began crying, switching from demanding justice against the man whom she claimed had murdered her son, to angrily questioning why Ian had to be on the pasture that evening, how she had wanted him to stay home and prepare for school. Mrs. Nurse never recovered from this loss, and watching her disintegrate, body and mind, was a painful experience.

I have never forgotten my friend. I remember him on special occasions such as birthdays, because we always celebrated birthdays together. Whenever I have a special achievement, I wonder if he would have had the same accomplishments, or if he would have been better, as I suspected. He was so talented. And to this day I wonder why two stones that inadvertently struck both of us on two different occasions, both accidentally, had such different results. Ian's killed him; mine knocked me down and left me with a bandaged head. Grandmother and the neighbours must have realized that an outcome, similar to what happened to Ian, was possible when I was struck with that stone, and that was why they were so frightened back then. And maybe it was fate that decided the different outcome.

I'll always remember Ian Nurse.

7

Little England No More

In the life of a people, there is hardly a more defining point than the birth of their nation. That unique time when they are at the same time the parent and the newborn. November 30, 1966, was that moment for the people of Barbados, when we created a new country, the fourth Caribbean nation to be carved out of the dying British Empire.

The signal of this successful birth was a new flag waving in the cool tropical wind. Raised at a minute past midnight, it was a blue and gold flag with a symbolic broken trident in the middle. With each flap, the flag represented survival, arrogant defiance and *feistiness,* pure and simple. How else to describe so bold a step taken by such a poor and isolated island—a new nation no bigger than the smallest city in some countries?

Perhaps hoisting the flag was no more than an expression of naive faith in the belief that size really didn't matter internationally. This childish expectation that ideas and dreams in even the smallest collection of people were the true test of what constitutes a nation. Or maybe it was simply a well-entrenched sense of self-importance and collective egotism: the unquestioning expectation that powerful inspirational talk eagerly consumed by oppressed colonial peoples elsewhere also applied to us. For like the older men running their mouths with seemingly idle talk in the rum shops at night, their tongues lubricated with too much rum so that unattainable dreams pour forth along with inspirational lies that took form only in philosophical discourses, all this talk about such things as asserting freedom, claiming sovereignty and taking control of destiny had galvanized some oppressed people around the world to fight to the death. Could it really be said that anyone on the international stage seriously expected a quarter million people living on this tiny island in the Atlantic Ocean to buy into this dream? Were we to wake up, like the old men the morning after a good discussion-and-drinking binge, only to discover by the light of a new day the headaches of actually having what we said we desired?

Not only did we believe we were included in this international debate for a new world order, but we accepted among ourselves the conviction that our puny size and lack of natural resources did not automatically exclude us from aiming for the same things as other colonial people. In a perverse way, we argued that our tiny size was indeed an asset: nobody felt threatened by us, and we could prove a point or two by simply going about our business methodically—becoming something like a garden of tranquillity for the world, a small plot that flowered for the admiration of everyone.

Whatever it was that inspired us, the result was now on display for the world to see. Thousands of Barbadians at home and thousands more abroad believed that the statement this flag made was of some international importance. We had started out on the same road as such great nations as India, Ghana, Kenya and, closer at home, our three neighbours in the Caribbean. And we were achieving our goal without having to resort to bloodshed as in countries like Algeria, Angola or Mozambique.

Winds of change were indeed wrecking the British Empire, starting in India and Africa. Like the famed trade winds that brought the original Arawaks and Caribs, who gave the region its name, the Europeans, then Africans and later Indians and Chinese to the New World, these winds were also sweeping the Caribbean. And like hurricanes that rush through the region destroying and making anew at the same time, these winds of change were arriving whether or not we were ready and prepared. Time for delivery—or was it deliverance, as some claimed?—had arrived.

The flag also had special domestic significance. It signalled a new beginning and limitless potential. Our pride was in keeping the world's newest flag aloft, bringing forth a brand new country with the enthusiasm of a first-time parent. Instead of baby pictures, we showed the flag with a pride we hoped would impress and win over the non-believers, both at home and abroad. We were now our own nation, *"we is people, too,"* according to local parlance; no longer the possession of some mother country thousands of miles away.

Realistically, we knew the lowering of the British flag was symbolic of an empire collapsing under its own weight. The pressure and demands of looking after people on the periphery were now too onerous, quite frankly too expensive, for rulers in London and Westminster.

For 339 years the trident was the symbol of our colonial ties with England. This bond was so deep that at times our island had been referred to as Little England, a title bestowed on an island long considered to be a gem in the colonial realm. This distinction was at the same time the ultimate insult or highest compliment. It was derogatory because even among Caribbean people the title was meant to indicate how compliant the sons and daughters of former African slaves had become, how accepting we were of things white, colonial and English, how respectful we were, how much we acted like and wanted to be English. It was a signature of how comfortable we were supposed to be as a loyal colonial outpost, why we were considered by the British as a favourite child of sorts among their Caribbean possessions.

Even in our classroom we had heard stories of how fellow West Indians made jokes of Barbadians. We cringed at how they loved to remind us of the time, supposedly of misdirected self-importance—or was it colonial kowtowing?—when the political leaders of our dear island dispatched an urgent message to London. The cable supposedly read, "Carry on Britain. Barbados behind you." Fortified with this knowledge, Britain marched into war against Hitler's Nazis, and won. We became the butt of a regional joke.

For others, it was a compliment, for the nickname suggested a kind of fastidious attention to detail and organization, of Barbardos' having become the source for administrators in foreign countries, and of having built educational and health systems that were the envy of most developing countries. It was a big commendation to us for having established a reliable political system, respect for the rule of law and order, deference for justice and a rational way for settling differences without resorting to rioting or violence, in essence shepherding and applying those rights and privileges flowing from that auspicious treaty signed in Oistins in 1652. Like the Big England that exported the original institutions, Little England in turn repackaged them and re-exported them to other places in the western hemisphere. Indeed, for a time Barbados had provided some of the best police and colonial administrators in the Caribbean, saving England the task and expense of sending out its own.

In Little England we had internalized how to be rational. Supposedly, we had learned so well from our colonial masters that we were not given to open displays of emotion, certainly not in political matters, not like some of our *brethren and sistren* on other Caribbean islands. In the main, we were devout Anglicans, imposing on this island the mores and social conditioning from the Church of England, for there was no more powerful institution for maintaining the old social patterns than the established church. Obviously, this point was not lost on the young political leaders. After independence, they promptly disestablished the Anglican Church as the state religion and set about trying to limit the control of the church on the lives of the people.

In many ways, the broken trident captured the ambivalence that was still strong in some quarters. In breaking the trident, but not totally discarding it, Barbadians were at the same time hoping to hold on to what was good from the past while looking to chart an independent future. In our classrooms, we were strongly urged to dedicate ourselves to lawfulness and respect for law and order and the new political system. If we didn't like what a government was doing, we would endure and wait patiently for the next election, but we would never resort to violence. This was the foundation on which to build, on the retention of this all-important image of political stability and rationality. This was the message read to us at special functions; the theme of speeches by local dignitaries; the gist of everything we had learned while preparing to celebrate the arrival of nationhood.

At the same time, the clean break was recognition that the future could only be what we made of it. For this reason we were told to venerate a long list of firsts, the people who set benchmarks of attainment for a new nation, such as the first prime minister, governor-general, chief justice, or even the first baby to be born in post-colonial Barbados. There was a deep-felt pride to be the first standard bearer, to be the person to hold high a flame lit from the original fire.

Still, there was also a realism to go with this purpose and international bravado. We knew that we were collectively cutting free, like adolescents setting out on our own, carrying only our pride and dreams, and, in this case, the seemingly worthless gift of a glass bowl from the former mother country. Someone must have felt a glass bowl was the appropriate gift for the Queen of England to send us, along with her regrets for not making it to the biggest party in our history.

The regrets and the bowl were presented at the same time by Her Majesty's representatives, the Duke and Duchess of Kent. How interesting, some of us thought: the symbolic mother not on hand when one of her supposedly favourite children left home. And for that child's inheritance, as it made its way into the world—a glass bowl. A glass bowl that shines if polished and handled gently; a fragile bowl that could so easily shatter if allowed to slip from the grasp that until now had been so steady and confident. Only an assured mother would send a gift of glass—or perhaps only a mother so far away that she didn't really care, a mother who had long ceased to be a nurturer.

The pride and confidence of the people taking this step made the occasion memorable, even on a wet and soggy night. It was a moment recorded on the front page of the local newspaper, a picture of a victorious premier raising his hand in a V for victory salute, at that symbolic moment when he was instantly transformed from the last premier into the first prime minister. It was a picture indicating the fulfilment of a promise and a rendezvous with destiny, a picture of a new flag fighting back the strong wind and asserting itself.

"We gotta pray that God bless Buhbaydus," Grand-Grand had commented in the days leading up to the attainment of independence, lapsing into the Buhbaydus that, like Bim, was a name of endearment for this island. She, too, was uncertain but hopeful about the future. As were the neighbours and the men who came home with Mervin to fire a drink, usually of rum, at the end of the working day. Mervin was a carpenter, essentially an independent contractor as was the case for most tradespeople. He had men working with him on jobs, and they, too, would be praying for Buhbaydus, although some of them cussed the government of the day for leading the *foolish* people on the island into a proverbial blind alley.

Waving this new flag must have been seen as either the height of arrogance or the quaint exoticism of foreign lands, especially those countries with cities several times the size and population of Barbados. Could a little island like Barbados really expect to be treated as an equal to these bigger nations? Could it really expect admittance to certain clubs, where countries with military might and standing armies set the standards? Certainly, we could not forget that the Caribbean was a playground for the Cold War rival, and before that for just about every international conflict, going back to the days the European powers started sizing up the region. Only a few years earlier, the world had tottered on the brink of a potential Third World War and an all-out nuclear annihilation over a Caribbean island, when the United States and the Soviet Union had flexed their muscles over Cuba, stopping just short of firing the first missile. This was the environment into which our new nation was born.

And should a vote in international forums by such a tiny island have any real merit? These questions arose in our debates and at sobering moments during the celebrations. We were familiar with the argument of those who referred to all of us in the Caribbean as simply mimic men and women. By this they meant there was nothing intrinsic and indigenous to an island like Barbados that needed saving or preserving. It was the argument that our societies were held together through the strong disciplinary arm of a foreign power. What would become of us, what would we do to ourselves, when that colonial stabilizing power was removed, when our society and tolerance for one another broke down under the weight of our own meanness and political immaturity?

These were academic debates because they did not speak to the intent and desires of the people. Our statement to the world was not supposed to come from military might, but from a developing community of successful people, a real home for those who had previously considered going elsewhere. Land mass or population did not decide morality, we argued. Why should anyone deny us the chance to make of the little rock in the Atlantic Ocean what we wanted, and to declare to all that strong belief in one's ability was just as relevant in the smallest child as in the biggest adult, as much in tiny countries as in those with huge populations and armies?

Sitting at home, we listened to the commentaries on radio. By the time the big day came around, I was fully primed and wished that I could attend the official ceremony, but I was too young and it was still too late in the night for me. Stephen got to witness the making of history. At home, we heard the internationally famous Royal Barbados Police Force band play the national anthem of our new country, and we took the words of our national song to heart.

We write our names on history's page
With expectations great
Strict guardians of our heritage
Firm craftsmen of our fate.

CECIL FOSTER

Our ears pricked up when the commentators excitedly prepared us for the raising of the new flag. We listened to the colourful description of the fireworks that were illuminating the sky and to the roar of the people witnessing the event. Earlier in the night, even as we sat up listening to the countdown to the raising of our new flag and to the rain showers in our part of the island, we wondered if the event would be completed as planned. A heavy downpour had threatened the open-air official ceremony and had left a pronounced chill in the air. The Garrison Savannah, noted mainly for horse racing, but on this night the focus of the island's attention, was waterlogged.

When the commentaries finished, we went to bed not knowing exactly what to expect when we awoke later that day. Sunlight promised the only certainty of the first day in the life of our nation, and the realization that there was no turning back now. The die had been cast and this awareness frightened some people, especially those afraid of the unknown, some of whom were members of my family. There were some who really believed we were mimic men and women and that three hundred years of social and political development was about to unravel. Wasn't this the case in so many African countries so soon after attaining nationhood? Didn't they plunge straight way into military coups and dictatorships?

Two things we knew for sure on this first day of independence: first, that the famous African-American singing group, Diana Ross and The Supremes, was to give a free public performance at the main square in the city—a stone's throw from the wharf where generations of Barbadians, like my mother and father, had slipped out to sea. This parking lot had been the scene for many of the battles leading up to independence, where politicians angrily and loudly debated the issues while calling on the people of the island to make their choice. The wharf and its immediate environs were still where ideas clashed, where the past and the future collided. Not everyone supported independence. Many people still remembered 1958, when a new flag was raised in the winds across the Caribbean, the flag of the West Indies Federation—a flag of blue background divided by four equally spaced wavy lines, with a gold disk over the middle two lines. This was the flag of the British colonies in the Caribbean, a nation in the making, the blue background and the gold disk representing the region's sea and its sunshine.

The federation was the latest in a series of attempts by Britain to bring one central administration to its Caribbean possessions. In 1956 leaders from the Caribbean islands met with British officials in London and agreed to set up a federation, but the new nation was virtually stillborn, the result of inter-island jealousies. Some still longed for a political federation of the English-speaking Caribbean islands— especially the Little Eight that were left after Jamaica and Trinidad and Tobago bolted confederation in 1962. Why not have a federation of the remaining eight islands and Guyana? That idea became a non-starter when Guyana also became independent. And, indeed, there were some people content with remaining a British colony, for that was the only life they knew and they feared any change.

Perhaps it was intended that the sweet voices of these American singers drown out the ghost of this long debate. This battleground was officially renamed Independence

Square. Unfortunately, the bad weather continued into the night, causing the barge on which The Supremes performed to collapse, resulting in a near riot among the thousands of fans. And what would the world have thought? some people asked. Imagine the indignity from the international press's reporting that so-called peace-loving and respectful Barbadians marked the attainment of independence by rioting! This thought was even more frightening to those still holding reservations about political independence.

The other thing we knew was that the cricket players of our new nation were going to make the rest of the world sit up and take notice. In a fit of pre-independence bravado, our nation had challenged the entire world to battle. Choose the eleven top cricketers throughout the world and match them against our top eleven and see which team wins. After all, what other nation on earth could boast of having a Garfield Sobers, then acknowledged as the greatest cricketer ever, and with him the fastest bowlers and best opening batsman? Who had as many talented cricketers as Barbados? Over the years, didn't Barbados contribute more than its fair share of players to the West Indies cricket team, and didn't international teams touring the Caribbean always claim that a match against Barbados was as tough as any against the entire West Indian team? We were going to take our place among the nations of the world, starting with dominance in cricket. On the battlefield, we may not have been in the same league as Cold War rivals, the United States of America, the Soviet Union or any of their satellites. But on the cricket field, we knew we were more than equal and were quite capable of beating them. Unfortunately, our cricket heroes faltered, losing to the international forces.

Still, we had great moments to celebrate: when we watched via television the raising of our new flag at the United Nations and at the Organization of American States. With the same pride we listened to our nation's maiden speeches from these bodies; when world powers sent ambassadors among us and accepted our diplomats with full aplomb, when Barbadians arrived at foreign airports and presented their brand new passports. There was also the pride of choosing our friends. Small as we were, it was supposedly our sole discretion to decide the nations with which to have diplomatic relations. We were friends of all and enemies of none, our leaders claimed, and in the battles between the superpowers, we clung as firmly as possible to a non-aligned position.

This ability to choose our friends also brought the possibility of discovering long lost relatives, prompting us into some wild dreaming that the time was ripe to redis-cover our African roots. By reaching back across the Atlantic to Africa, we were planning to achieve the symbolic return that had eluded our ancestors. The same way that, perhaps in choosing The Supremes to serenade us on our big day, we were also reaching out to other deprived brothers and sisters in the Americas. This was the era of the civil rights movement in the United States. We followed the developments and we knew of those born in Barbados and the Caribbean contributing to this important crusade. We also knew that political indepen-dence was our own act of civil rights, for which we showed the flag: a symbol of what fully freed black people could do and achieve; our testimony of how people of all races could live unrestricted together and prosper.

*   *   *

I was among those deemed fortunate to be young at the moment of political independence. First, I was chosen by my school to attend a gala dance performance by a Senegalese dance troupe at the main sports ground on the island. This was another of my nation's gifts to me, an introduction to authentic African dancing, a link between black people living on both sides of the Atlantic. The second token was an independence pin. These specially minted gold pins with a small flag were handed out at schools across the young nation to deserving students. My pin was a reward for showing academic potential. This was the only time these pins were available. I lost this pin; perhaps I was not careful enough to appreciate the uniqueness of this gift.

Independence was supposed to be a gift to the young. By the time our flag was hoisted, we had heard the arguments for political independence: that this step was really for the future of the people of the island, starting with the boys and girls of my age. We were special because at the point of transformation for the country we were young and full of potential.

Everyone called us the future of the new nation. We were fated to be the first generation on the island to be prepared for adulthood with the certain knowledge that our future was defined by only our dreams, determination and commitment to the development of a new country. At the same time, this was to be our honour and purpose, our price and reward for being young and full of promise at such a crucial juncture. From that point on, not only were we to accept that we were free of colonial bondage, but we were supposed to act free—to succeed or fail without the fallback of blaming some external power for holding us down or proscribing our hopes and expectations. We were to be the prototype of the new Caribbean men and women, for even in independence we were told that our future was still intertwined with that of other Caribbean people; even if we might flirt with the notion of fielding a team against the world that it was only cricket for us as part of a West Indian squad. Independence was supposed to lead to a deepening of regional integration called a Caribbean Community of Nations. Our islands were to succeed as free and independent nations where they had failed as colonial outposts hurriedly thrown together in a federation by a departing mother country.

During the day, our schools had been battlegrounds for our young minds, as much as the all-night political meetings in the renamed Independence Square and on street corners everywhere else had been for the adults. We had learned the words to the new national anthem and practised drawing the new flag and the new coat of arms. We had started to learn about Barbadian and Caribbean heroes and to sing nationalistic songs, such as the regional classic, *Island in the Sun.*

For months the excitement had been building, leading up to our classroom discussion that coincided with the sustained debate in the island's House of Assembly and, subsequently, in the final general election before independence. No one could have avoided the debate. Like the majority of adults across the island, we in the classroom were pro-independence. We boldly echoed the arguments of the supporters. And we believed what we were saying and hearing.

Perhaps this defining moment was supposed to have added meaning for another group of us: those reared in the belief that our future and accomplishments could only materialize by leaving our home. I was in this group, still hoping to follow in the footsteps of my mother and father, and before them the various members of the family who had immigrated to the United States. Barbadians had always been an immigrant people, whether as temporary agricultural workers in North America, seamen on merchant ships, or domestic workers in England and Canada. Ours was an island that sent an estimated 60,000 young men—a full one-third of the population—to build the Panama Canal. This made us the largest contributor of foreign labour to the building of what was one of the world's Seven Wonders.

We knew from what we had been told in school that immigration was a social safety valve. It drained off the excess population before all the financial and social resources were used up, causing harmful explosions when nothing was left.

These long-held truths were up for re-examination. Now, all around us, people were suggesting that immigration was an option, but only that, an option. As I listened to the speeches of politicians, teachers and even frightened voters debating on street corners and in rum shops on what the future held, I heard many things. I heard the promises that political independence was a message and an honour in itself. The almost yearlong buildup to the great day had prepared us for the moment: the lectures of teachers reminding us that the island was achieving peacefully what others in foreign lands had fought and died for; the opposition politicians arguing that our biggest task in the early days of nationhood was to ensure we did not stumble into a dictatorship or one-man rule, as had happened elsewhere; the government of the day responding with the slogan, Now we have a country, and suggesting that all things were possible.

We now had choices. One of them was to stay at home and grow. The government of the day said it was planning to spend significantly on social development, specifically on education. Coincidentally, this was about the time I realized living in England was not part of my future. I still hoped to live with my parents, but by then it was obvious that this wouldn't happen in England. Stephen and Errol had long arrived at this same position. Our parents must have, too, for we rarely, if ever, heard from them. Their letters had stopped coming a long time ago.

To be part of the generation, as I was, for whom the brand new country was called into being, was not only flattering but exhilarating. How else to explain the propitiousness and excitement of being present at such a moment of demarcation? This was an event for the history books, a time that could never be repeated, a phenomenon that could only be experienced by those fortunate enough to be crossing the threshold at that very moment.

Later, there were bound to be achievements of national import when the people rallied around the flag or institutions, but that sentiment could only be a restatement of the initial pride that came with the first flutter of our new flag.

For all the boys and girls in Barbados at the time of independence, we had to be blessed. The long legacy of colonialism, the scars from a history that included penal exile of Europeans and forced exile of Africans through slavery, had come to an end. We were not only entering a new era but taking a new country with all its hopes and expectations with us.

This sense of discovery fuelled our anticipation and gripped our lives in public and private. Almost overnight, it appeared that everyone was adjusting to something or the other, somewhat like a young child holding on to a piece of furniture and struggling with that irresistible urge to take a first step. We had to know the truth by testing our limits. Not only did we have to make that step away from whatever had been holding us up, but we also had to stand on our own feet, be independent. And we knew there were no guarantees of success.

This was what political independence had brought us: the feeling of discovery, of venturing into the unknown without a road map; of flying after dreams without a parachute or safety net; of feeling somewhat like the tiny baby unsure of its true strength. Discovery came splendidly dressed with expectations and pride of achievement. But just as easily we knew it came with hardships and obstacles. As the strong breezes would fray the flags that were flying across the nation for the first time that morning, these challenges were capable of causing us to wear ourselves out, and this time we would have nobody but ourselves to blame.

For me, this sense of discovery came together in the classroom. Grand-Grand and the government had taught me that a good education was a ticket to the future and I was up to the challenge. Going to England was receding from my mind, but not the longing to join my mother and father, who were living in what was now just another foreign country.

8

New Roads and Politics

Final minutes of the periods with Glenroy Straughn were always the most interesting. This was when he broke off his regular teaching and lapsed into discussing events of the day. We eagerly looked forward to the next tangent where he would take us. The one thing we knew for sure was that the digression was going to be exhilarating and educational, even if the theme of the discussion was unpredictable. Usually, it was some item in the daily newspapers, maybe some juicy rumour that had set tongues wagging. For this reason, he encouraged us to read the newspapers. Or it might be an international event, heard during the local shortwave rebroadcast of the news from the BBC in England or the CBC in Canada.

These sessions were important for other reasons. Mr. Straughn became the stand-in and illuminator of all we were grappling with intellectually. Through him the world came into our classroom. Not only did he make us feel that we mattered on this stage, but he got us to believe that we were main actors in training.

"But *Straughnie,* you really did think that you would have won that by-election?" Maybe it was Maurice Quintyn asking, or it could have been Anthony Alleyne or Winston Thomas, Karl Holder, Lloyd Blades, Wayne Barrow or any of us in the group that formed the nucleus of my five years at Christ Church High School. "For even your family didn't vote for you, man. You have to have more than eight people in your family, and you only got eight votes. Man, you even lost your deposit."

The form laughed and Glenroy Straughn smiled, too. And yes, he said, he really expected to win the by-election in the city. In any case, in the bigger picture, it didn't really matter whether he won or lost. Someone should always be challenging the system as a guard against complacency. (Here he told us of countries, specifically in the Eastern Bloc at that time, where citizens were penalized for not voting. Not a bad idea, he offered.) Someone should hold the system and the politicians of the day accountable to ensure they remained humble and in tune with the wishes of the people. All of which meant, he suggested, that *that* someone might have to be a sacrificial lamb, although he didn't use this term. What he said was that anyone with political vision must recognize the risk of being ahead of his or her time. Maybe, one day, the people would catch up, but there was no guarantee. More than that, the excuse of I-didn't-know could not apply if, *later on down the road,* people woke up and found themselves living under strange conditions.

Officially, Mr. Straughn taught us English literature and English language, but he really exposed us to life beyond our form room and textbooks. During these sessions, Mr. Straughn veered far and wide, seemingly jumping in an erratic fashion from issue to issue, example to example, like a tour guide entertaining and informing us on a long ride. On these journeys I first learned about something called West Indian literature, reflecting a growing body of works written primarily by English-speaking Caribbean expatriates in London. Our introduction came through a slim anthology of writers such as V.S. Naipaul, George Lamming, Jan Carew, Edgar Mittelholzer and Roger Mais. It gave Mr. Straughn the chance to talk about realistic writing, of the importance and joy to be gained from recording and documenting our everyday experiences. Of recognizing that Caribbean people, too, can produce good writing that reflects a proud and unique culture.

In this vein, he also told us about the powerful works of the *émigré* writers in France. Among them was someone called Franz Fanon from the neighbouring French territories of Martinique and Guadeloupe. French colonies really, he explained. Another was Aime Caesar. Here again, Mr. Straughn taught that we should be careful not to fall into the trap of thinking we were different from the people on other Caribbean islands, just because we spoke English and they might speak French, Spanish or Dutch; nor should we fall into the Little England smugness of thinking that as Barbadians we were superior to other Caribbean people, regardless of what language they spoke. Such thinking was a colonial legacy, from when we were forced to adopt the *fire-rage* of our European masters who, down through history, had fought some of the most brutal wars over language and religion, and for the possession of other people's property. The people of the Caribbean were essentially of the same stock. They had had the same or similar experiences. The majority of them faced the same problems, regardless of what language they used to express their woes and dreams. We could learn about the experiences in these countries and islands by reading the great writers from the region. Other brilliant writers came from Africa, such as Chinua Achebe and Leopold Senegal.

Into our classroom came, if only fleetingly, African-American writers like James Baldwin, Richard Wright and Langston Hughes. We fought the battles of the U.S. civil rights movements in our discussions about Malcolm X, the Black Panthers and Martin Luther King, Jr., and we knew about the Black Power militancy sweeping the region as part of an awakening among black and Third World people.

Our government, even though essentially black, had reacted draconically to the Black Power scare. A number of prominent activists had been born in the Caribbean. One of them was Kwame Toure, then known as Stokley Carmichael, who became a minister with the Black Panther movement after earning his spurs in the youth arm of the civil rights movement. They were banned from entering the island, or were not allowed to speak freely or to give public speeches. Fear that these militants would whip up violence or sedition was strongest in Jamaica, Trinidad and Tobago and Barbados, coincidentally the islands with the three campuses of the University of the West Indies. Apparently, there was a social cost to be paid for opening the eye, politically speaking, of so many people in the region. One of our people to suffer at the hands of the government was the brilliant academic Dr. Walter Rodney, whose seminal book, *How Europe Underdeveloped Africa*, was as high on our unofficial reading list as *The Autobiography of Malcolm X* and *Soul on Ice* by Elridge Cleaver of the Black Panthers. Rodney, a Guyanese, was kicked out of Jamaica, sparking protests across the region. Another deportee from Jamaica, Mr. Jake Degia, big afro and all, taught us industrial arts while coaching us to be mindful of The Man.

Various militants were banned from entering Jamaica, and an extended state of emergency was declared on Trinidad and Tobago. Was this emergency an attempt to prevent Black Power militants and some elements in the military from overthrowing the government, as the prime minister claimed, or was it a cynical attempt by the government of the day to retain power? This, coincidentally, was happening when the government of Trinidad was introducing voting reforms in the face of mounting opposition. During the election, we noted that the ruling Peoples' National Movement won all thirty-six seats in the Trinidad and Tobago House of Representatives when the opposition parties boycotted an election during a state of emergency. Who was going to hold the government accountable and responsible, and could this happen in Barbados, too?

In Barbados, the ruling party, which had come to power through all-night political meetings and supposedly impromptu gatherings, had brought in new legislation. Police permits were required for public demonstrations and stipulated that, except during an election campaign, all political meetings had to end by midnight. It was now a crime under this legislation to preach hate against identifiable groups, a move intended to tone down the fiery rhetoric of the Black Power militants.

These nontraditional works from around the world that Mr. Straughn introduced, even if they were not on the approved syllabus, competed for recognition with the accepted fare of William Shakespeare, Jane Austen, George Orwell and Charles Dickens. But they also helped us to understand what was happening to us while, as the children of independence, we found our wobbly feet, all the time marvelling at the world unfurling around us.

Mr. Straughn instilled in us the idea of studying real or meaningful history, such as West Indian history to replace the tired, stale and foreign English, British or European history that was on the curriculum. He made us memorize Abraham Lincoln's *Gettysburg Address.* This, he said, was for us to better understand the importance of African slavery not only on our island and in our region, but throughout the entire western hemisphere. And he told us how the American states fought a bloody war to end slavery, several decades after slavery was officially ended in the British possessions, but how slavery continued almost into the twentieth century in Cuba and Brazil. On the subject of Gettysburg, as in politics, we discovered that things don't always appear as they are. It seems that Lincoln was very disappointed when he gave this address. There was no applause or visible reaction in his audience, so Lincoln thought the speech had bombed. Except that it had touched the listeners so deeply, the audience had been reduced to stunned silence. Only later did Lincoln see the results of this inspirational and insightful speech and be venerated. Similarly, the initial disappointment and even feeling of rejection should be no different for the lone voices in the political wilderness in Barbados. At some later date, these visionaries, too, were bound to be rewarded when the people, still stunned by the vastness of the dream and what they were hearing, finally stirred and rewarded those voices.

Mr. Straughn appeared to be a combination of the greatest dreamer and the biggest cynic. It seemed to be his goal to make us just as critical in our thinking. He supported political independence and the ending of British and European colonialism in the Caribbean, yet he fretted that we might be replacing European colonialism with an American version. He feared what could happen in an independent country where the elected government went unchecked. While he praised Abraham Lincoln, and talked at length about the U.S. stars in baseball and boxing, even helping us to form a square-dance club, he openly admired Fidel Castro in Cuba for standing up to the Americans. A pet peeve was when we referred to the United States of America simply as America. "We are all Americans," he said. "We live in the Americas and it really makes our brothers and sisters in South and Central America very angry when we suggest that only the people in the *United States* of America are Americans."

He strongly supported the goals of the Cuban revolution, and even suggested that we in the rest of the Caribbean could learn a few good lessons from the Cubans. However, his ideal system included regularly held elections with campaign agendas set by the individual and not some homogenizing party. This was why he presented himself as a candidate in every election or by-election, why he ran as an independent and not under some party banner.

Mr. Straughn taught us history as literature and literature as history. He keenly encouraged us to write the way
we spoke. While in English language classes we studied the
rudiments of the Queen's language, we also digressed into
long discussions on the local Bajan and Caribbean dialects.
Sitting in front of the class, sometimes looking over his
wire-rimmed glasses as he marked a test, Mr. Straughn
often became the object lesson for us.

In second form, my first year under his influence, I
must have impressed him with my ability to bring together
all we discussed in the class. We were studying in the
English grammar text about some Europeans trekking
through the Amazon rainforest. It provided Mr. Straughn
with the opportunity to tell us about the exploitation of
the indigenous people in the rainforest and of their
natural resources, an abuse of man and land that was no
different from what had happened elsewhere in the
region. Apparently, these explorers drank out of a tin
utensil with a handle. One of the comprehension questions posed to us was to explain what this tin utensil could
be. Bearing in mind what Mr. Straughn had said about
local dialect, I suggested that the utensil was really a cup,
but that in Barbados it was called a *tot*. The exercise book
came back with three little red check marks above the
word *tot* and one big tick mark at the end of the explanation. Many of us in the form would have had our individual tot, usually a solid tin can that had been recycled for
further use after the original contents of maybe dried
milk, Ovaltine or Milo mixture were used up, to which the
blacksmith had added a tin handle. Or they might have
had enamelled cups, which with each fall or bounce were

soon no different in appearance from the traditional tot.

Other times, Straughn stood by the blackboard, some-times drawing stick men to illuminate a point. It was always exciting when Mr. Straughn abandoned the textbooks and called upon his experiences, especially those about his exploits and understandings of the inner workings of local politics.

Glenroy Straughn was pleasantly eccentric. At heart, he appeared to be everything he should not. First, he didn't mind when we called him Straughnie, unlike other teach-ers who demanded the honorific Mister or Mistress, Sir, Madam or Miss. Straughn dressed casually, usually in a khaki uniform and short pants. This was at a time when other men teachers wore jackets and ties, when there was a full-scale debate over whether the traditional jacket and tie should not be jettisoned. For the cultural purist, the jacket and tie, as with the gown, wigs and robes of the legal courts, were trappings from a colonial past. They were unsuited to a hot climate like the Caribbean's, so why not drop them for more comfortable clothing? Some of the region's political leaders even adopted the so-called *shirt-jac*, similar to a bush jacket. If independence gave India the distinctive and stylish Nehru jacket as the ulti-mate nationalist statement, we could settle for our own combination of a shirt and jacket, just as suited for formal and informal wear.

Mr. Straughn obviously did not support retaining any colonial trappings, although he seemed to choose his clothes more for comfort than for style or politics. His short pants stood out in a school with a mandatory dress code for boys to wear ties, and—as a sign of maturity—long pants. These trousers were usually made of dark cotton, but we managed to work in the latest fashion, which during our time at school was bell bottoms that swept the floor. They went smashingly with our big unisex afro hairstyles, symbols of solidarity with the international black conscious-ness movement. Occasionally, for non-school events, we wore brightly coloured African print shirts. Every one of us had an afro pick, usually a piece of wood with wire bicycle spokes. The most fanciful picks were made in the shape of Africa or a Caribbean island and the wood would be heav-ily stained or varnished. The picks had to fit into our shirt pockets. And, every night, we had one last chore before going to bed: having our hair plaited, so that it created the big, fluffy afro that we kept shaping with our afro pick all day long. Straughan's hair was too wavy and straight for an afro, but in our books he more than compensated with a full-face salt-and-pepper beard.

Straughnie identified with the poor and black people on the island. This, too, was different, for Straughn could pass for white, curly hair and all. In a society where social status came with different shades of skin, his thinking seemed to be refreshingly out of line. We liked Mr. Straughn because he was radical.

"You boys and girls don't know anything," Mr. Straughn always explained, a broad smile on his face. Often, he used the palm of his hand to brush his full face of beard. The beard, the khaki fatigues and the colour of his skin reminded us of none other than Fidel Castro. "But we have to be careful. We got to be so careful. Who will provide the checks and balances?" Then he would be off, telling us some story about Ché Guevara, Simeon Bolivar, Mahatma

Gandhi, Julius Nyerre or Nikita Khrushchev and his shoes at the United Nations.

Opposite in approach was the headmaster, Gilmour Roachford, also a politician. Unlike with Mr. Straughn, we virtually had to push Mr. Roachford into talking openly about politics. It was almost as if he had decided that his lives as politician and educator needed to be totally separate. Or it could be that he wanted to play the political game as straight as possible, without running the risk of appearing to recruit for his party from among his students. Maybe it was because he was a headmaster and therefore had to keep more distance from us. Still, we occasionally got Mr. Roachford to drop his mask. Even more infrequently, we got Mr. Roachford and Mr. Straughn in the same debate.

They were in agreement on one thing: their opposition to the ruling Democratic Labour Party. Both Mr. Straughn and Mr. Roachford had been members of the opposition Barbados Labour Party, which had been instrumental in bringing party politics to the island about three decades earlier. In its founding days, the BLP was supposedly one of the most radical groups in the region, and like many labour parties in the Caribbean was patterned after the socialist British Labour Party in England. The party was founded in 1938 and was at the forefront of the struggle for universal adult suffrage, especially for the 80 per cent of the population that was African and mainly poor. The right to vote came in 1951, and ten years later the island marked another milestone when it graduated to internal autonomy. It was the BLP that produced the only prime minister of the West Indies Federation, Sir Grantley Adams, a former premier of

Barbados. Most progressive black politicians had flocked to
the BLP, including the current prime minister, Errol
Barrow, who eventually split from the BLP and formed his
own Democratic Labour Party. The DLP came to power
against a weakened BLP in 1961, when Sir Grantley was in
Port of Spain, Trinidad, the federal capital, trying unsuc-
cessfully to save the federation.

The DLP had its supporters in the school, some of
them teachers, but mainly students, especially those
receiving a high school education largely at the expense of
the government. Something else attracted us to the ruling
party: with much fanfare it had announced it was a full-
fledged socialist party, code words to mean that it was
progressive and not as easily manipulated by the small but
powerful moneyed class on the island. Socialism was
supposedly sweeping the world, or so *Time* magazine told
us in one of its much trumpeted cover stories. As far as
we could tell, the progressive parties in the Caribbean,
particularly the Peoples' National Party of Michael Manley
in Jamaica, and the ruling Peoples' National Congress and
the opposition Peoples' Progressive Party in Guyana, were
also socialist. It didn't matter much that Socialist
International, the group intent on helping socialist parties
win elections, already had a Bajan representative—the
Barbados Labour Party. The DLP's response was that it
was more socialist than the BLP and, in any case, its brand
was more updated and specific to local conditions. When
we addressed one another it was either as "brothers and
sisters" to show our Black Power stock or as "Comrade" to
display our socialist pedigree.

*   *   *

We were sitting on the bed when Errol outlined his bold plan. He had decided to let me in on his strategy because it affected me in a real way. Of late, Errol had taken over sending me to school. He was working at the Queen Elizabeth Hospital in Bridgetown and the money he made provided me with lunch, uniform and books. He even contributed to the weekly groceries. By then Stephen had left home, going off to live in the city, acting *mannish*, as Grand-Grand said disapprovingly.

"There ain't no future in working at the hospital," Errol explained. "I know Grand-Grand is going to be vexed with me. She thinks the hospital is a good job because it is a government job. But Grand-Grand got to realize there ain't no future in this job."

I listened in silence. Errol said he had quit his job at the hospital and had decided to enrol in the Barbados Hotel Training School. This was the result of another educational reform by the government, this time to train and produce skilled workers for the tourism industry that was coming into vogue. The government had decided the only way to ensure a strong financial future for this independent nation was to drastically overhaul the economy. No longer could it rely on the boom and bust cycles of the sugar industry, where this year's high prices were followed by next year's rock bottom receipts. With the massive sugar production in Cuba, the threat of sugar beet production in the United States and Europe, and the realization that England was no longer a protected market for imports from the former colonies, the sugar cane industry had become too uncertain. In addition, England was trying to get into the European Common Market and with that went the protection it offered to Caribbean sugar producers.

Tourism was booming. Our school was in the direct path to the Seawell International Airport. Sitting in our form rooms, it seemed that hardly an hour passed without the discussion being interrupted by a jet screaming overhead. And looking out into the Atlantic, we saw the cruise ships making their way to the new Bridgetown Harbour, which had been another development coup for the ruling party. A deep water harbour in Barbados allowed the ocean-going liners to pull right up at our doorsteps, unloading thousands of sun worshippers, and essentially replaced the wharf as the centre of shipping commerce. For a while, we took Sunday trips to the harbour to look at this technological marvel. The expansion of Seawell, the main international airport for the Eastern Caribbean, and the deep water harbour gave a fillip to the tourist industry. More and more we were witnessing the invasion of our beaches by white bodies, the building of large hotels and the sight of visitors touring the island in the mini-moke cars. With the development of international sea and air ports, the wharf was relegated to handling the odd schooner from a neighbouring island—essentially marking the passing of an era for Barbadians.

The tourist industry had started to bring significant money into the island, and created jobs and the need for well-trained people to staff and manage the hotels and restaurants. Errol said he had heard some of the young men at the hospital talking of going to the Hotel Training School. He had decided to follow them.

This decision affected me because Errol no longer had a guaranteed salary. "But it will be all right for us," he promised. "I will be practising at hotels and part of the training is working on weekends. When I get good, I'll also be working during the week. I don't know how much money I'll make that way, but we'll get by."

With that, Errol enrolled in the training school, an institution that would later be attached to the hotel management faculty of the University of the West Indies. Each morning he set off for school in his uniform of a white shirt, black pants and a black tie. Errol was very soon coming home and mesmerizing me with the names of the various drinks he was learning, the different glasses, and offering me bits of trivia such as why the traditional eight-ounce wine glass is shaped like a woman's breast. Apparently, Henry VIII of England wanted his wine glass moulded after this part of the female anatomy, or so Errol told me.

And we never had a money problem. I was usually sleeping by the time Errol came home at night, but the sound of Errol emptying his pockets of tips onto the bureau often woke me. When I got up in the morning, he would still be sleeping. Every morning, I picked out a quarter or two from among the coins scattered on the bureau top to pay for my lunch. If I needed money for books or other expenses, I simply took it from this loose change. Errol never seemed to notice.

Suddenly, money was no problem for Errol. In his billfold, he showed me all sorts of different currencies: British pounds, Canadian and U.S. dollars, German and French notes. And when the school fees were due, I told him in advance and he provided the money.

Perhaps spurred on by what we were learning in the classroom, my form decided to visit another Caribbean island. We chose St. Lucia and for a year we worked hard raising most of the money. We held hot dog sales, concerts and raffles. But we could not raise the full cost of the trip. How was I going to get the extra money I had to provide?

"Here, take my bank book," Errol said. "Go and take the money out of the bank."

He gave me his bank book. When I opened it, I was amazed at the sum of money Errol had saved.

"I will have to sign for the money," I said.

"No big thing," he answered nonchalantly. "Just sign my name the best you can."

I got the money without any difficulty and went with the rest of the form to St. Lucia, my first trip off the island and the first time most of us had entered an airplane. We now, indeed, were world travellers.

Errol was also beginning to make his mark in other ways. He became a master at mixing drinks, one of the *wickedest* barmen around. Not only was he talking about them, but he was bringing them home. His liquor collection boasted such exotic things as Tia Maria, Crème de Menthe, Crème de This and Crème de That, various brandies, vodka, gin, rum. And he could now afford a good record player, which we used to blast the entire village. From this portable gramophone we were introduced to the revolutionary and sensuous music of someone named Bob Marley of Jamaica, and to the emerging reggae beat that was storming the world. We listened to the likes of Bunny Wailer, Isaac Hayes, Swamp Dog, Alice Cooper, Percy Sledge, Otis Redding and a host of other entertainers. We gathered in the shade of the house and played the music, the boys from the village gathering round, some of them smoking some very funny smelling cigarettes and claiming to be feeling *real Irie*. Somehow, they always excluded me from this inner group. "My little brother," Errol said, "got lot of book sense, but no street sense. So leave him alone."

Errol was working at some of swankiest hotels and nightclubs in Barbados, including the internationally known Club Alexandra. Often he came home and told me of some big international star, Mick Jagger, Princess Margaret or some actor, who blew through the club. To top it all off, Errol bought himself a big red souped-up Vauxhall car. It was only a matter of time before he had his own apartment.

"Could you imagine what would have happened if I had remained working at the hospital?" Errol said often enough. He was really proud of his achievements. I always remember his saying that of the three of us, he was the one with the street smarts. Yes, indeed. I often wondered what would have become of him if, like Stephen and me, he had been given a fair chance at high school education and had not essentially had to educate himself.

*　　*　　*

Stephen and I were sitting on a carpenter's workbench in front of the house. He had returned home, much to the delight of Grand-Grand, who didn't like the idea of his running off to live with some town woman. But Stephen was bored. He had been unemployed for some time and, with me on vacation, we often sat on the bench, talked and

whiled away the day. In a real sense the tables had turned.
Once it had been Stephen giving Errol and me pocket
money. Now it was Errol giving Stephen spending money.

"I can't find a job," Stephen said.

"Oh, I forgot to tell you," I said. "I was reading the newspaper in Lane's shop and I saw an advertisement that the
government is looking for health inspectors. The qualifica-
tion is a high school education."

"Yeah," Stephen said.

It was partly for school work, but I had grown into the
habit of reading the newspaper daily. We didn't buy them,
so this meant going to Mrs. Lane's shop some houses away
and borrowing the one she kept under the counter. I always
made sure that I timed my request after her husband, Fitz
Lane, had had a first chance at the paper. I read it front to
back, made mental notes for classroom discussions,
listened to the news on the Rediffusion and, if I had any
extra money, bought the occasional *cheese-cutter*. This was
a salt bread with a hunk of salted cheese in it. The cheese
was on display on a big plate in a glass case, swimming in
its oils because of the heat.

Stephen got the information from the newspaper. He
came home and, in his fine penmanship, wrote a letter of
application and read it back to me. He got the job, which
started his career as a public health inspector and, more
importantly, gave him the security of a civil service job.
Grand-Grand couldn't have been more pleased.
Unexpectedly, I had two brothers working at the same time.
Money for school was not such a problem. My only task
was to make sure that the money spent on me was well
invested, that I provided the best possible return.

*   *   *

Grand-Grand and I were sitting in the house when Mervin and some men pulled up in a truck. With some straining, they managed to get the big white box-like item into the house. Mervin plugged it in and the machine started to hum.

"See, it works!" he shouted. "She's working!" Life was improving for us. We now had our first refrigerator, even if it was second-hand. Only a short while earlier we had received electricity.

One day, a government truck had come through the village dropping off long poles, and men came to lay down big pipes. Within a short while the poles were in the ground and wires bringing electricity and telephone wires were strung from them. Mervin, a carpenter, had started rebuilding the house, adding rooms and bedrooms. We already had running water and electricity followed. Now, we also had a fridge and shortly after a new way of cooking by natural gas.

Grand-Grand seemed a bit overwhelmed by the sudden changes. She reluctantly lit the gas stove, always fearing an explosion, feeling more certain about the kerosene stove. And she absolutely did not eat refrigerated food or leftovers. As for electricity, it was well and good, but she had to have her kerosene lamp lit while she slept. She appeared much more accepting of the telephone when it arrived.

About this time something else happened on our streets. For years, the residents of our area had protested and lobbied for an extension of basic facilities. The unpaved road that ran in front of our house and terminated in a pasture about a hundred yards beyond us was usually water-logged after a downpour, making it impassable for vehicular traffic. The lack of drainage created a virulent breeding ground for mosquitoes, adding to the woes of Stephen and his fellow health inspectors who were spreading across the island in a concerted, government-sponsored effort to eradicate the *aedes aegypti* mosquito and dengue fever. Big government bulldozers turned up and started to dig up the pasture near us. Up went low-cost housing, another government project to improve the housing conditions of the nation. Almost overnight, the number of my friends had skyrocketed. The road was relaid, paved over and extended.

In light of these developments, we had something new to discuss in the classroom, rum shops, homes and at political meetings: had independence transformed Barbados from what had essentially been a backward plantation, as some claimed, into a developing nation with modern amenities and an improved quality of life?

This question formed the basis for the 1971 general election in Barbados, the first since independence and the first in which I took an active interest, though I was a mere sixteen-year-old and too young to vote. This election was supposed to be a test on many fronts. Would the people reward the ruling party for the marked social and economic improvements effected on the island in its first five years as a nation? But there was a more personal question for many of us—had Barbados really been transformed into a country where class or station in life no longer was of primary importance, but one where a person's willingness to serve the people and to dream of higher goals could make a difference in the standard of living? These issues were settled in a personal sense for me. And they decided the outcome of the general election.

My parish of Christ Church appeared to be the main battleground of the election. The opposition, the Barbados Labour Party, was mounting a sustained campaign, with four Aces or top candidates running in the parish. One of these constituencies had captured the intensity and excitement of the entire election. It was in Christ Church East, where the leader of the opposition, and the man seeking to form the next government, was up against none other than a civil servant named Anderson (Peanuts) Morrison. The same Peanuts with whom my father had left the papers of his three sons for safekeeping.

Anderson Morrison had worked his way up in the civil service and he had now decided to enter electoral politics. To succeed would be nothing short of a rags-to-riches story, and proof that in the new Barbados anyone could dream and attain the highest positions in life.

Except that, to many of us, Morrison was a sacrificial lamb. He was up against Bernard (Bree) St. John, a long-time parliamentarian and a brilliant local lawyer, with the best contacts and credentials. Few expected that Peanuts Morrison would knock off such a high-profile candidate. Socially, there was no contest if their resumes, bank accounts, education, achievements and following were compared. Indeed, people were already talking about St. John in prime ministerial terms.

Yet this was the race we all talked about. Primarily because of Peanuts Morrison, I took a keen interest in this contest, but also because nobody had any real passion for the contest in my constituency, where the choice was between two white men: one, a naturalized Englishman running for the ruling party, and the other an old stock Barbadian running for the Barbados Labour Party. Those people remembering the Black Power discussions didn't like the choices and turned the attention elsewhere. Morrison, someone I had seen on streets and who came from the same social conditions as me, was more exciting. And from what we heard, the race was unexpectedly very close. According to the buzz, St. John had either *gone through the eddoes*—Bajan parlance for losing the campaign—or he had ensured that fate for his opponents by having Morrison *caught in the slips*.

This election was fought with passion, with clearly demarcated lines. St. John and his BLP were strongest in Oistins. They held large meetings and draped a banner across the main street, clearly signalling this was their town. Morrison and his ragtag team of dreamers held many of their meetings a short distance away, but closer to Lodge Road where we had lived. Late into the night, Morrison railed against St. John, resorting to the constant refrain, *"Bree, let my people go."* In typical Caribbean fashion, Morrison touted himself as a saviour coming from among his people. St. John appeared dismissive of this upstart who didn't appear capable of making a telling speech beyond the refrain of his campaign. Unfortunately, when St. John and his people pointed out this shortcoming in their opponent, they saw their remarks coming back at them as an example of how snobbish they were; how they represented the old Barbados and the party that had fought against independence and all it offered for the development of the poor, for people like Peanuts Morrison and the thousands of voters.

Errol, Stephen and I disagreed openly on the campaign. Errol supported the BLP and passionately wanted them to win. Stephen and I supported the DLP. Late at night I came home from the political meetings with the various speeches, retorts and singing ringing in my ears. Errol and Mervin brought news of what they heard at BLP meetings. We argued, joked and staked out our positions.

Finally, the election night came. It was soon apparent that the people of Barbados had agreed to reward the DLP for its stewardship. But late in the night it was still unclear who was winning the seesaw battle between the underdog Peanuts Morrison and St. John. Live reports on the radio told of crowds gathering at Foundation School for the vote counting. I bolted out of the house and didn't stop running until I, too, was standing outside the gates of the school waiting for the final result. Somebody was snapping pictures with a flash camera.

Suddenly, a cheer went up and Peanuts Morrison emerged on the shoulders of his supporters. *"Bree, let my people go,"* he shouted. My father's friend was now an elected member of parliament. Briefly, I wondered what my father in England would think of this news. Did he still care about what happened in Barbados, about those dreams born in his village, among his friends?

Apparently, Errol was also outside the counting centre, his disappointment heavy. Later, he would hotly dispute my claim that it was the poor people who had defeated St. John. Not so at all, Errol reported. He had irrefutable evidence. On their way home after the counting, Errol and two friends were offered a ride. The lone driver in the car was a politician and he claimed that the deciding polls in the election came unexpectedly from the white and rich areas. The driver was Tom Adams, the son of the former premier, Sir Grantley Adams. Within days, Tom Adams was the new leader of the opposition, continuing a political career that eventually made him prime minister. This would not be the first time Tom Adams and I would be on opposing sides. Except as I found out later, despite what Glenroy Straughn and others taught us, and perhaps what I still believe instinctively, sometimes the risk is simply too high for running afoul of those with political power. When that happens, there is usually no choice but to run.

The week following the election, a man came through the village selling copies of *The Democrat*, the official organ of the victorious ruling party. I bought a copy and there on the front page was the picture of the crowd standing outside Foundation School to witness the upset. In the very front of the picture, as clear as day, was . . . me. My picture. This had to be a keepsake. I tore off the front page and decided I had to show everyone, before eventually taking it to school, before keeping it forever.

"Look, look," I said to Errol, the first person to whom I showed the picture. "That's me there. That's me in the picture."

But Errol was still smarting from the election loss. "Stupid people," he said. "And why would you want to keep that picture?" I watched helplessly as Errol ripped the page, with my picture, into tiny pieces, scattered them on the floor and walked away. Perhaps I should have learned how destructive politics could become. However, by then I had learned one thing: not to mess with Errol's left hook. I kept my distance.

*   *   *

With the long vacation drawing to an end, I knew my day of reckoning might only be days away. Still, I didn't know what to expect beyond looking forward to starting another year at school, my final year when I probably had a good chance of becoming head boy. The results of the examination for the General Certificate of Education were the last thing I wanted to think about. After all, Christ Church High School was not known for producing students with stellar GCE performances.

By my own standards, I knew that my results could not be too great, for I might have overextended myself by taking six subjects. Some teachers had suggested six was too ambitious. I disagreed. There were two good reasons: in the trial examination I had done well enough to qualify for maybe eight or nine subjects, but I had settled for six after weeding out mathematics, science and technical courses. I planned to concentrate on these courses in my second year of preparation for GCE's, while repeating those I failed. The second reason was Jennifer Clarke, the young woman I loved, whose presence in my form over the past four years had been the very incentive for me to do well. Typically, I had come first each term and Jennifer second. Jennifer, too, against the odds, had taken six subjects. And even though our relationship had effectively petered out in the last year, with her appearing to have other interests, I knew I had to continue outperforming her. That was what men were supposed to do—outperform their women.

Going back to school meant finding out if this was still the case when it came to this all-important ordinary level examination. It also meant that if I passed any of the subjects, I would have money to pay for additional subjects. In yet another education reform, the government had decided to reimburse the cost of every subject for passing students from independent schools. Grammar school students paid nothing, probably because of the government's mistaken assumption that they were more likely to pass than fail.

And I wondered about the success of my friends. Over the years, we had worked hard and long for these examinations. We knew so much of our future rested on the results, yet we also knew that the odds against us were heavy. Still, I had high hopes for my best friends, Maurice Quintyn and Anthony Alleyne. The three of us had formed a team—the three musketeers—from our second form. In every class, we had sat in the same position: in the second row of the middle aisle of the class, Anthony in the middle. We studied like this, shared books, checked homework, gossiped and planned our future.

Maurice Q had the sense of humour and was probably the best-loved boy in the class, one of the most popular in the school. It was Maurice who encouraged us to come to town, who showed us around and who was one of the biggest horse racing ticks or fans in the world. Maurice was pretty good in most subjects.

Anthony was the richest student in the form. His family owned a grocery store and Anthony always came to school well provided for. Early in the morning, Maurice and I would polish off Anthony's sandwiches, their edges neatly trimmed. We loved them but Anthony was bored by such fare. He seemed more interested in the typical lunch sold in the school cafeteria: coconut turnovers and a sweetened fizzy drink. Many times, Anthony simply sponsored our lunch, shared his books with us, and invited Maurice and me to his home on Saturday evenings. Anthony was stronger than Maurice and I in mathematics and perhaps some science subjects. But we also knew that for much of our final years at Christ Church High School, Anthony was hurting. Anthony always spoke about his oldest brother, Clinton, and occasionally Clinton drove him to or from school. One Saturday, Maurice and I had visited Anthony and we missed the last bus back to the city, perhaps deliberately because we were playing; both Maurice and Anthony had girlfriends in the area. We jumped into the car and Clinton tried to catch up to the bus. By the time he caught up he was almost in the city, so he decided he may as well complete the trip. It was an exhilarating ride along the darkened roads with the cane fields on both sides, with just the bright beams from the car headlights piercing the blackness, a drive that magically topped off our day of studying and then playing in the countryside. A short while afterwards, Clinton drowned while swimming near his home. Anthony never got over this loss.

But we were the team that moved together. Every week, one of us was responsible for buying our lunch. That person collected the money, headed to the cafeteria, waited in the line and then came back with his hands brimming with the drinks and turnovers. We either waited in the classroom, studied or more than likely chatted up some girl or played cricket. In the year leading up to the examination, we had all elected to study West Indian history. Collis Morris, our teacher, came up with the idea of putting us in teams, sending us off to the main library in Bridgetown and making us submit a team report. Maurice, Anthony and I were, naturally, one such team. We met on Saturdays in the library, searched for relevant texts, met with other students and talked and talked. At the end of the session, Maurice and Anthony usually looked at me and said, "Fost, you writing the report, right?" Which I did and which brought us a stream of top marks. I really liked West Indian history. This was one of the subjects I had hoped to pass, perhaps the only one I felt any confidence about.

Now, here I was on the final day before returning to start a new school year. I assumed that the results of the examination were going to be available within the first week or two of resuming class. I had spent the summer vacation in typical fashion, playing cricket, running around with my friends Volney and Brian Welch, two brothers, visiting the beach, even though I never learned to swim, and watching the political campaign unfold. This was the time to see how Mr. Straughn and Mr. Roachford were doing on the hustings. Neither had been elected.

We had spent much of the vacation in Graham Hall swamp, about an hour's walk from our home. We fished, picked and drank coconuts, and kept an eye out for an eccentric man known as Chicken Bladder. He virtually lived in the swamp and frequently we heard the sound of his shotgun firing at the birds nesting in the trees and long grass. On the final day of our vacation, we decided to go fishing in the swamp one last time. I was more interested in the coconut water.

Walking down the road, I ran into a school friend, Junior Layne, long considered one of the brightest students at Christ Church High School. If anyone was going to do well in the GCE's, it was Junior. He had taken his second try at the examination and was awaiting the results before deciding his future. Junior got off the bus and walked towards me, his head down.

"Hi, Junior," I shouted to him. "How you're doing, man?"

"I didn't do too good," Junior said. I didn't really take note of what he was saying.

"You ready for school tomorrow? You decided if you're going back or what you'll do?"

"No, I ain't going back. But you did really good, nuh?"

Suddenly, my heart was pounding. Volney, Brian, David (Hopper) Blackman and other friends wanted to move on. The swamp was waiting. But what Junior had said wasn't in keeping with our light-hearted conversation.

"What you mean?" I asked.

"The GCE exams came back today. We were up at the school to get them." My heart stopped beating, my throat went dry. I started to think of how I could break the bad news to Grand-Grand. After all, nobody had ever done well at Christ Church High and if Junior Layne couldn't break that jinx, then how could anyone else? The teachers had advised me not to overextend myself by taking six subjects. Who did I think I was, a student at Harrison College, Lodge, Combermere or Foundation? This was Christ Church High, man. What would I tell Errol and Stephen? This was going to be just as big a disappointment for them, for I knew how badly Errol and Stephen wanted me to succeed. My mind flashed to the time I was walking home from school and I passed Stephen and a group of his inspector colleagues while they were working. "Hey, you're Fost brother?" one of them shouted to me. "Man, he says that you bright as *shite* when it comes to school work." I had smiled and walked on. And wasn't Errol always boasting that his little brother had a lot of book sense, even if he didn't have street sense? I had to know the truth.

"So how did I do? You hear how I do?"

"You did really good, man. You got back the most certificates. Nobody at Christ Church High never get as many passes as you and Jennifer."

"What you mean, Junior?"

"You got back five passes, the same as Jennifer. The most certificate at Christ Church High. People can't believe it."

I felt Junior was joking. He had to be! Then, I looked at his face and found he was serious. He was also very disappointed with his results, which he said would be available to the entire school the next day, the first day of the start of the new school. Later, they would be published in the local newspaper.

Volney and the others were calling for me to go to the swamp and fish.

"All o' *wunnuh* go ahead," I said. "I got to go home."

I ran home and told Grand-Grand the good news, stressing that this was only what Junior had told me and that I had to verify it myself. I telephoned the school. Only Mr. Roachford could give out the results and he had already left for the day. I would have to wait until tomorrow.

As I walked into the school, I knew Junior had told me the truth. My classmates were waiting, many of them having heard the news. I walked between them into the headmaster's office to get my slip of paper and his congratulations. The teachers were standing and watching, among them Mr. Straughn. Jennifer and I exchanged our good news, and talked about spending the next year concentrating on science subjects before thinking of anything else.

I was on top of the world. This was information I should send to my parents in England. And *ohmygod*, not only did I have as many passes as Jennifer, but I could look forward to a cheque from the government. More than that, at a minimum, I could leave school and find a civil service job. Five passes would start me almost at the top of the entry level scale.

Later in the day, Mr. Roachford called Jennifer and me separately to his office. He wanted to talk to us about our future. I told him I wanted to spend the year concentrating on science and mathematics, but he seemed to be of another mind.

"Maybe you should hit the iron while it's hot," he said. "Have you thought of going on, doing your 'A' levels now and in two years or so going to university?"

"No, I was thinking of science . . ."

"I think you and Jennifer should. I have spoken to her. Did you apply to the Barbados Community College to do 'A' levels?"

I had not, simply because it did not even figure in my plans. The community college, another government reform, was built so that students like me and Jennifer, who did well at independent school, could get our pre-university schooling, putting us somewhat on par with the finishing grades at the established grammar schools. Except the community college didn't have the social standing of, say, a Harrison College.

"I tell you what. I'll make a few phone calls and see where I can place you and Jennifer. I'll try to see if I can get Jennifer into Queen's College and you into Harrison College. Now, you should go home and wait until you hear from me."

Befuddled, I went back to the classroom, collected my books and left Christ Church High School. So did Jennifer. It took many years before I understood the reason for this abrupt ending. Apparently, Jennifer and I were now far more qualified than many of the teachers who would have tutored us. Yes, individual teachers might have had a pass in physics, chemistry, biology or mathematics and other subjects, but few of them had as many passes as we did. So to make the teachers feel at ease, we had to move on.

With great ambivalence, I went home. I did not want to move on without my friends, primarily Maurice, Anthony, Lloyd, Winston, Wayne and Karl—all of whom would spend another year at Christ Church High, with Karl and Lloyd eventually immigrating to Canada, Wayne to the United States and the others remaining in Barbados.

9

Harrison College

Sitting behind his big imperial desk that straddled the social divide, the headmaster looked yet again at the slip of paper with my passes. He scowled yet again. "The Barbados Community College was established for people like *ah, um*, you," he said in a deep distinctive voice. "You should be attending the community college, not coming here to Harrison."

As he spoke, he continued to gaze steadfastly at the official document with my passes. He appeared to be double-checking them. "You do have the passes to get into the college, *ah, um*." When he talked, he did not lift his eyes, but spoke to the piece of paper, as if under his steely gaze he was daring it to reveal the truth, causing all the passes on the paper to transform into failures, confirming his belief that this kind of performance was not to be expected from a school boy who attended Christ Church High.

Everything about the headmaster showed that he really did not like having to deal with this situation. Dressed in his blazer and tie, his bald head pointing towards us, he was decidedly unenthusiastic, the big desk forming a barrier between us, a social gulf that separated this all-powerful headmaster and the two of us awaiting his judgement.

"You were not supposed to be coming to Harrison College. And the new school year has already begun, *ah um*," he said. Later, I would learn, like all the students, to *ah um* like the headmaster when we mimicked him. Stephen and I exchanged glances. We had not expected such a chilly response, a coolness that left us speechless.

This was the first time either of us had entered Harrison College, this hallowed school that educated the upper crust of the male population in Barbados, the sons of visiting dignitaries and top officials in the East Caribbean looking for a finishing school. We were overawed by the surroundings, by the paintings of old white men in gowns, by the musty smells. My fate was in the hands of the headmaster of Harrison College, Mr. "Tank" Williams, his bald head sweating, either from the early morning heat or from having to make such a socially sensitive decision.

The telephone call had come from Mr. Roachford the previous day. I was to take a guardian with me to Harrison College to make arrangements for my continued schooling. Mr. Roachford said he had made the arrangements for me, but casually commented that he had not had the same success getting Jennifer into Queen's College, the equivalent school for females. Jennifer would enter Barbados Community College.

My going to Harrison College was great news in the family, especially for me. I had not yet come down from the high of my performance in the General Certificate of

Education examination. Here was my chance to get to Harrison College, to make up for the missed opportunity when I had failed the Common Entrance Examination six years earlier; here was my opportunity to finally live up to the high expectations of Mr. Lynch, the elementary school headmaster who had scolded me for not attaining my potential, even back then. His words that I could have gone to Harrison College or Lodge School, but for my hiding from his classes, had always remained with me. Now was my chance to make everything right. And, as Grand-Grand always said, better late than never.

Stephen, five years older than me, accompanied me to meet with Mr. Williams. We arrived at the school, walked around the impressive old buildings and grounds that contained lots of trees with birds chirping, immaculate lawns and playing fields—all of them behind high limestone walls with big iron gates. It looked like something out of a foreign book, a part of the island still secret to us. Even though it was a school day, with the classes underway when we arrived, the schoolyard was quiet, with no sign of a straggler or student going from one form to another. A very disciplined silence, unlike what I had come to expect at Christ Church High, or ever noticed at Foundation, the grammar school next door.

"But I promised Mr. Roachford," the headmaster said, finally putting down the paper and looking at us. "You'll be in Modern Arts sixth form. I think your best subjects are English, history and geography." He gave Stephen some forms to sign and impressed on him that Harrison College was strict about its uniform and behaviour code. In sixth form, I was expected to wear white shirts with the school's distinctive red and white epaulets, grey long pants and black shoes. On my first day, I was to come to his office for the papers to take to my form master.

"Boy, he really don't want you here," Stephen whispered under his breath as we left the headmaster's office. "Now you know it's up to you to prove him wrong, 'cause anybody should be able to come to Harrison College. And if he knew he was going to let you in, he shouldn't keep saying you don't belong at Harrison College." For years after, Stephen recalled this experience. Over time, it became a fond memory of our beating the odds. "Remember when that headmaster at Harrison College said you weren't good enough for his school? I wonder if he'd say so now." But so had begun the two worst years of my life.

The headmaster was right when he said Harrison College was not really for me. Indeed, sixth form at Harrison College was not really for the average black boy on the island, even if the opportunity was technically available. I learned of the mindset among most of the poor students. Even though they were guaranteed five years of schooling for passing the Common Entrance Examination, many of them were not really expected to go on to sixth form. Some of the students thought it strange that I wanted to continue studying, most of all at Harrison College, when they were in a hurry to get out. They hoped to do well enough to get a good crop of ordinary-level certificates. With the good name of Harrison College behind them, this was enough to get them a well-paying job. Advanced level at Harrison College was for a different class of people.

Over the years, it was a practice for exceptionally bright boys, or those with parents who could pull strings, to end up at Harrison College for their final two or three years. I was not the only transferee in 1971, but because of my newness, the school I had come from and my family's lack of political or social clout, I immediately found myself at the bottom of a well-established pecking order, one surprisingly reinforced by some of the black teachers, who in an age of independence might have been expected to act differently. Two students came from other schools, confirming that all grammar schools were not equal, even if they were fully supported by the government treasury. Whitfield Andy Knight transferred from the Boy's Foundation School. Tyrone (Taipei) Griffith came from Coleridge and Parry School in the northern part of the island. I knew Whitfield, as I used to worship at the church where his father was the pastor, so I started out with one friend in the class. As far as I can tell, Whitfield, now a lecturer in political science at the University of Alberta in Edmonton, is the only member of the class to complete a doctorate and is now an expert on technology transfer and development in Third World countries. Griffith later became a policeman and worked his way up in the Royal Barbados Police Force. Griffith probably had as many problems adapting to Harrison College as I did.

Other black students in attendance were preparing for university, but in the form room it was obvious who dominated everything: the white and mixed students. Only the blacks from élite families, whose fathers were senior civil servants or business people on the island, had any social standing. Everyone found his place in the pecking order. It was interesting listening to the privileged students on Monday mornings, their clothes and lunches prepared by black domestic servants, people more like me. They talked about the fun times on weekends, such as playing tennis, sometimes at the Garrison Savannah Tennis Club, or of Sunday lunches at the Barbados Yacht Club. Both facilities were until recently the exclusive domain of the white and planter class on the island.

They played tennis, talking about their chances of qualifying to represent Barbados in various tournaments in the Caribbean and elsewhere, perhaps even dreaming of representing the region in the Davis Cup. The regional competition was among themselves and a small group of friends. In Barbados very few black people played tennis. Sitting in the classroom, we heard them talking about their chances, often deciding among themselves who would be successful. They also swam competitively, played polo, rugby and bowled—élite games that once again gave them the chance to represent the island in some international sporting events.

And they discussed the high-class garden party, or playing for cricket teams like Carlton and Wanderers, which were white enclaves in a sport largely dominated by blacks. These were the children of an entrenched and privileged group that was just beginning to recognize the changing mood in the country. In a planned exodus, many of the families eventually left Barbados for New Zealand and Australia. Before going, they gave long interviews to the local newspapers about how their lifestyles had become cramped, how the good times had ended for them since Barbados had become independent.

I heard them talking about their exciting lives: from driving their own cars and dating girls from Queen's

College, to travelling the world meeting high-level government officials and foreign dignitaries. I heard them sharing inside information about some event we'd heard on the news but that their family, friends or coterie knew intimately. They seemed to not even have a passing interest in local politics, acting as if what happened on the political hustings was of little significance to everyday life. Often they pulled rank on some of the black teachers by talking about experiences they had had in London, New York, Geneva and places that were as foreign to the teachers as they were to me. Gloria Yard, a young teacher, suffered at the hands of the class, primarily because she was a woman and black. She taught English literature, but the attitude was to undermine her achievements as a graduate from the University of the West Indies. Miss Yard was stoic, seldom smiling. She conducted her lectures and got out. I felt that she hated the class snobbery in the classroom, but that even she, a teacher, was powerless to do anything. Tragically, some of the black boys, taking a cue from the more privileged, were just as condescending to her.

Within weeks of arriving at Harrison College, I learned my place. Classes began at 8:30 a.m. and that was when everyone in the form was friends. At lunch, we scattered into private groups, as happened at any school, with me heading towards those students playing softball cricket. This was where I showed my prowess, usually by batting for most of the lunch period, hitting the ball to various parts of the well-manicured lawns, and bowling so hard and fast that I often returned to class tired and sweaty. When the school bell rang at 2:30 p.m., a social transformation took place as we headed in different directions, many of us friends no more. One Saturday I was walking on Broad Street, the main commercial thoroughfare in Bridgetown, when I came upon two of my white colleagues. We were walking towards one another. I called to them. They walked on as if I were invisible. Back at school Monday morning, it was almost as if the experience had never happened. Other black students who had become inured to such behaviour from years at the college were willing to put up with this treatment, but I found it disconcerting and I felt powerless. I was learning some very hard and bitter lessons.

Perhaps nobody taught me as much as my friend Ian Walcott. To me, he represented what the social pressure at Harrison College was doing to us, how institutions steeped in the old ways of life were desperately trying to hold on to a society that, elsewhere, the people of Barbados and the Caribbean were trying to destroy. Ian had the misfortune of having a famous father. Clyde Walcott, later Sir Clyde and an international cricket administrator, was one of the world's best cricketers in his day. He was a natural, a batsman whose mastery was exquisite to watch. Walcott's arrival on the international cricketing scene coincided with Caribbean people's using cricket as a metaphor for independence, when a team of mainly black cricketers had started to show the colonial mother country and her white dominions throughout the world that we were as good as they were.

"*Cricket lovely Cricket / At Lord's where I saw it*" were the immortal words to the calypso that told the story of how people like Walcott helped to storm cricket's citadel. This was a defining point in our history. Walcott gained his fame as one of the Three W's—Worrell, Walcott and

Weekes—all Barbadian batsmen, who, in their era, were the bane of opposing bowlers. Everybody everywhere knew of the Three W's.

Ian felt the pressure of being the son of a famous man. Occasionally, we sat together and talked about life and his dreams, or he told me about the pressures when we walked to the bus stand after school, which in itself was a form of rebellion for him. Ian could have driven home or got someone to give him a lift. The pressure on Ian was for him to play cricket. Whenever a team was picked, whether a house team for interschool play or for trials for the school team, Ian was automatically included. Teachers, team captains—practically everyone encouraged him to come out to practice. For he was a Walcott and cricket had to be in his genes. And he hated it. More than that, like so many rich children in modern six, he didn't even want to be in school. He scarcely did any homework and was bored every day. And because, even at seventeen, he already had a full beard, he was constantly flouting regulations by seeing how many days' growth he could get away with before getting a call from the headmaster. Still, he knew the headmaster would never suspend him.

"Oh, my old man, or my uncle [who had social status by being a selector for the Barbados Cricket Association] would simply call Tank and put him in his place." This seemed to be the only time he enjoyed his social status. "But you know, Fost, you know, all of this is foolishness. Foolishness, man. I don't want to play no cricket. I don't want to have to shave every damn day and I don't want to study, to worry my head about winning no Barbados scholarship and all that foolishness. All me want to do," he said emphatically, lapsing into the accent he had acquired in

Guyana when he'd lived there some years earlier, "is to do me art. To paint and do me thing. But . . ."

But others had plans and hopes for him. And he could not escape those expectations. Ian wanted to paint, perhaps go to art school overseas, with plans to eventually return home and teach art. The last time I saw Ian, we had a good laugh. His father was in charge of hiring at the Barbados Shipping and Trading, one of the wealthiest business groups on the island. Mr. Walcott had interviewed me for some clerking job, which I did not get. I told Ian that I didn't think I'd helped my chances by arriving for the interview in jeans, and that I could not help noticing the disapproving frown on his father's face when he saw how I was dressed.

The last I heard of him, Ian had left Barbados soon after Harrison College in search of his quest, and perhaps to escape the pressures of living in his father's shadow.

*   *   *

We were sitting in the form room in Ralph Jemmott's European history class. West Indian history was not yet a subject worthy of study at the advanced level, certainly not at a prestigious school like Harrison. I was having difficulty catching up with the dates and significance of European history, although on reflection I seemed to be doing no worse than my fellow students, all of whom seemed extremely bored studying the European Renaissance. Mr. Jemmott was frustrated with us, too. He had come through Harrison College and one of the marks of that experience was obviously the reminder that he was a poor black boy.

When he went to university, it was to the University of the West Indies in Jamaica, where he studied economics and history. I got the feeling he was not particularly proud of having gone to the UWI, although he would have been one of the first of a crop of home-grown scholars, but wished he had gone to Cambridge or Oxford or the London School of Economics. Certainly, this was the impression he left with me when I heard him talking about the reputations of various universities and what level of academic excellence was needed for admittance.

"For example," he said, "did any one of you in this form pass history with a grade one?"

"See what I mean?" he said, emphasizing that we would all have to work harder if we wanted to get into a reputable university. We should all be trying for grade ones in our examinations. As he spoke, he surveyed the class, starting at his right side where the white students sat. His eyes swept through the centre of the class to the mixed and richer blacks and barely glanced at the left-hand side.

"See what I mean?" he said again. "None of you had a grade one in history. You all got to start taking this thing seriously."

"But Foster, sir," shouted Phillip Bannister, the son of one of the leading doctors on the island and who, too, would rather have been off painting than studying in school. Like Ian, art was his favourite subject. "Foster had his hand up."

Mr. Jemmott swung around to look at the left side of the class. "Foster, *you* had a grade one pass?" he asked incredulously.

"Yes, sir." I was on top of the world. The social status was going to change. Maybe I didn't have money, pedigree, maybe I still wasn't a fully accepted Harrisonian because I didn't come through the junior school, but I had brains, at least in history.

"In European or British history?" he asked.

"No, sir. In West Indian history," I said, the pride breaking out in a wide grin.

"Oh," he said. "I knew it had to be something like that. In West Indian history. And we got to remember not to get fooled by grades. Sometimes flukes happen. Sometimes a grade doesn't fully reflect ability." He was laughing. Perhaps I didn't get the joke, but everyone must have heard the drop of my heart. I pulled my hand down and remained silent for the rest of the period, and forever after in that class.

Geography classes were less scarring on the soul. Once again, a teacher made the difference. This time it was a gentle woman named Lady Grace Adams. She was the wife of Sir Grantley, the longtime Barbadian and West Indian politician. Essentially, she was the equivalent of the only First Lady ever produced in the English-speaking Caribbean. With her husband as prime minister of the West Indies, she had witnessed the high points and the low points at attempts to integrate the Caribbean. Lady Grace was also the mother of Tom Adams, then the leader of the opposition in the Barbados House of Assembly, who was making his move on the prime ministership of the island.

In many respects, Lady Grace and Glenroy Straughn were alike. They intellectually roamed the world and took us with them. She told us behind-the-scenes stories of events that happened on state visits when she and her husband had travelled to various countries, especially England and African countries. She told us of the hunger she saw on the faces of poor people and of humanitarian efforts to help. Lady Grace spoke almost in whispers with a huskiness that was probably the result of years of smoking. One thing she hated was students talking more than she did, as she told me early in the year. "Mr. Foster, I notice that you are talking as much as I am and I am the teacher. You are talking nonstop. I do not appreciate that as a habit in my class." I took the hint. I don't recall Lady Grace's discussing local politics, although she was very aware of whatever was happening on the island.

*   *   *

Arriving late for school meant a visit to the headmaster's office for a slip of paper. It was very difficult getting into Bridgetown on time. The narrow roads were constantly clogged with traffic, as more people now had cars. The road builders could never have expected such a development. The slow-moving school bus came in a circuitous route, picking up as many students for as many different schools as possible. None of them started as early as Harrison College, and many times I was late.

The other option was to take a minibus, a private-sector initiative intended to complement the government-run bus system. But taking the minibus meant paying full fare, as the government only subsidized school fares on its buses. When I was lucky, I got a ride to school with Tyrone Mosely in the big Cambridge car his civil servant father owned.

One morning I was running to get to the form before the register was taken and to avoid having to visit the headmaster. I decided to take a short-cut across a lawn when I heard a very distinct voice.

"Young man, you know it is, *ah um*, forbidden to, *ah um*, run on the lawns here at Harrison College." It was Mr. Williams. It appeared to me that I would never learn the correct behaviour at this place.

*   *   *

Glenroy Straughn put his arm on my shoulder. "I understand. It is not easy at Harrison College."

On this day I had returned to Christ Church High School for athletics day. I was missing the old school and its warmth. Friends I had made here over the past five years were largely out of my life, and I had not really replaced them with new ones at Harrison College. Sometimes, I ran into my old friends in the bus stand, but conversation was often forced. They looked at me differently, as if they expected me to pull rank on them because I was a Harrison College boy.

"I remember how strange Harrison College can be," Straughnie said. "All those stupid rules and regulations. I remember sitting in my class writing and the ink from my pen spilt on my hands. So I wiped the ink in my hair, just like any one of us would do when the ink spills. Then I heard this voice, an expatriate teacher, saying, 'Hey, you, we don't do things like that here at Harrison College.' I looked at him. I mean, this was *my* ink, *my* hands, *my* hair. I should be able to do with them whatever I wished."

We had arrived at the domestic science kitchen. The

senior female students were selling hotdogs and other treats to raise money for another trip abroad.

"But don't mind. You'll do well at Harrison College," Mr. Straughn said. Turning to some of the students, he said, "Give me and *my friend* something to eat." Talking to Mr. Straughn made life more understandable, if not easier, at Harrison College. And my old friends at Christ Church showed me that I was still one of them. Even though I didn't contribute as much as they and was no longer a member of the French club, I was invited to join them in Martinique for the Easter holidays, ostensibly to practise our French. What a wonderful time we had, experiencing the subtle difference in foods and religion on the French, Roman Catholic island. Every night, we sat on our cots and joked. Mr. Taylor would bring out his guitar and improvise calypsos and ballads that were absolutely hilarious. We ragged one another. Mr. Roachford brought local education officials to meet us. We visited the beautiful white beaches and practised our fractured French. And, even though Mr. Straughn didn't make the trip, I remembered him every time I passed some bench or wall painted with graffiti saying *Martinique libre* and other slogans from the nascent pro-independent movement on the island.

*　　*　　*

"How many of you have chosen your university?" Mr. Jemmott asked. "You should all be applying to your universities of choice now. Don't wait until too late. How many of you have decided what you want to study?"

Once again, his eye began moving around the form. I hadn't even thought about university. One by one, my fellow students reported. Someone had applied to Oxford, Cambridge, Harvard, MIT. Then, they started to mention names like McGill, McMaster, U.B.C., U. of T.—institutions I didn't even know existed. In any case, it was mainly the white or rich black students with these plans. Most of the poor students were applying to the University of the West Indies, where their education would be free if they studied in Barbados. They applied to the big-name foreign universities, just in case they lucked out and won the prestigious Barbados scholarship. The local campus in Barbados housed the law faculty that was mandated to produce future lawyers for the region. My turn to announce my decision was approaching. Geoffrey Toppin, Canadian by birth, who studied the same subjects as I did, announced he wanted to study law at the University of the West Indies.

"Foster?" Mr. Jemmott asked.

"Law at the U-Wee, sir."

Until then the thought had not occurred to me. With Mr. Jemmott's reminder to get cracking, I sent off to the admission department of the local university for my application forms. Grand-Grand watched as I sat at the table and filled them out. Then I put them in a box under the bed and went out to play. When I returned, I saw Grand-Grand showing the forms around, to Mervin and even to the next-door neighbour.

"Look, he's applying to become a lawyer," she said. "A lawyer. Imagine, a lawyer in the family."

Seeing me approaching, she pretended she was talking about something more mundane. I slipped outside again to give her the opportunity to return the forms to the box under the bed.

I was accepted to study law. Then fate intervened. All my life, I had benefited from reforms to the educational system in Barbados. Finally, the reforms caught up with me. The year I was accepted to study law, the government of Barbados decided it would no longer pay to educate lawyers. Prime Minister Errol Barrow, a lawyer himself, but perhaps noting most of his opponents were lawyers, a profession that produced more than its share of politicians, arbitrarily decided there were too many lawyers on the island. From time to time, and even from the floor of the House of Assembly, he warned the general population not to trust lawyers, even though he was one. And we should stay out of the law courts, he lectured us. The government was not going to contribute to the oversupply of lawyers by educating more of them, and so ended my chances of entering law school. (Years later, I returned to Barbados and picked up a copy of the *Nation* newspaper. Prominently displayed was a story about a sleazy lawyer disbarred for misappropriation of trust funds. The lawyer was Geoffrey Toppin. Maybe it was a good idea I didn't follow him into law.)

*　　*　　*

For hours at night, in a more familiar setting, my neighbourhood friends and I met under the streetlamp and argued. Most times it was about cricket, but boxing was also on our minds. We argued about the exploits of

Muhammad Ali, Joe Frazier, George Foreman, Sugar Ray Leonard, with some of us dreaming of becoming as great as any of the well-known prize fighters. This was certainly the case for Merton Mayers, or Chev, one of my friends in Kendal Hill, the very one who always found nicknames for us. Chev had become a professional fighter with big dreams. It had been a tradition for his family to producer boxers, and Merton had decided to follow his brother and uncles into the ring. He became known as the Kendal Hill Mauler, choosing to go by the name of our village, unlike others, who took the ring name of some famous boxer and tried to mimic his style in the ring. When we argued about boxing, we listened carefully to good old Chev, who spoke from experience. When he had a fight at the YMCA in Bridgetown, we piled into several minivans and went off to support him. Merton and I took the same bus mornings when I went to school and Merton to the odd jobs he got as an unskilled construction worker or labourer. We would talk about boxing, with Merton boasting of his ability, talking loud enough for everyone in the bus to hear him.

In the days leading up to a fight, we would see our friend doing his roadwork, running and shadow-boxing. During serious training he seldom had time for cricket after work or for our usual all-day cricket matches on Sundays. Boxing was serious business, especially for the two or three weeks between signing for the fight, getting into peak physical form and entering the ring. Merton made $300 Barbadian (about $150 U.S.) per fight and sometimes had to settle for less than the agreed-to amount when the promoter claimed the gate didn't live up to expectations. But with experience came big dreams: of fighting elsewhere in the Caribbean, winning a British Commonwealth title, or even fighting in the United States. But there were many risks.

One day, Merton received an urgent telephone call from a well-known Barbadian promoting a fight in Guyana. He was looking for someone to fight the middleweight champion of Guyana in a couple of days. Merton was a lightweight, of slim build, with long hands and not much of a knock-out punch. He also did not have a passport. Over the phone the promoter gave Merton the number on his passport and told Merton to tell the immigration officials in Guyana that he had lost his passport and he could only remember the number. Merton got into Guyana.

However, an even bigger challenge was awaiting Merton in the ring. It was in the form of a scowling giant of a man, who was also well trained and extremely serious about making an international career as a boxer.

At the start of the fight, Merton opted to dazzle the crowd with his speed and fancy footwork—in essence to run from his much heavier opponent. "I would hear the wind from those big punches passing by my ear," Merton told us. "I decided that he ain't hitting me tonight."

Merton realized it was only a matter of time before the crowd demanded a real fight for its money. He would have to mix it up. He was relying on his fancy footwork until he was backed into a corner. There were some punches, then some clutching, and when the referee moved away, Merton was on his knees clutching his private parts, grimacing and apparently in great pain. The Guyanese boxer protested vehemently that he hadn't really landed any blows on Merton, far less a low one. Merton held on to his crotch and then something unexpected happened. He heard people at ringside taking on the hometown boxer, saying how it was unfair for this giant to be fighting such a small opponent and that he was a dirty boxer for hitting his younger opponent below the belt. "I heard one man saying: 'You ain't no use at all, man. You had to go and hit that young fellow below the belt, otherwise that Bajan guy would put some good licks in you tonight. You ain't see how good he was looking, right? But you had to go and hit him in the balls because you couldn't catch him.' When I heard that, I decided to stay down on my knees, holding my balls. They could've preached like Peter and Paul, I wasn't getting up." The Guyanese was disqualified.

The big night for our Kendal Hill Mauler was when he challenged the Barbados welterweight champion, Young Cassius Clay. The buildup to the fight had us all talking. The Kendal Hill Mauler encountered Young Cassius in the city, and quickly drew a crowd by boldly predicting to knock him out. Chev mimicked the antics of Muhammad Ali, screaming at Young Cassius, pushing him around and pretending to want to settle the issue on the spot rather than waiting for the night in question. We had seen Muhammad Ali in action. We loved him.

Young Cassius was not only a part-time boxer, but a part-time entertainer, singing and performing at nightclubs with a comedic act of fire eating, limbo dancing and balancing, aimed mainly at the tourists. Of late, part of his act was to dress up like a vampire and move around with a coffin.

The night of the fight, I accompanied the Kendal Hill Mauler to the YMCA. I went with him into the training room, saw him get his hands bandaged and watched him warm up to a good sweat. His corner people (usually anyone with a smattering of boxing knowledge, but also willing to accompany Chev to the ring) told him it was time to go. They took a big bucket, some petroleum jelly and the peppermint water he planned on drinking between rounds, which Merton told me was very good for numbing the pain of a blow and for reviving him when he was tired, and set out for the open-air ring. I went to my ringside seat and crossed my fingers. In previous fights, the Mauler had occasionally looked down at me and winked.

This night was different. Merton started with his trademark jabbing and fancy footwork. Then we saw it coming: the massive fist of Young Cassius that knocked the Kendal Hill Mauler through the ropes. The crowd roared, not at the ending of the fight as the referee counted ten, but at the presence in the ring of the coffin. I could not stick around to see Young Cassius and his supporters put my punch-drunk friend in the coffin. Later, Merton and I talked about many things in boxing, but we never touched on the night of the coffin. Merton continued to play cricket with us, to box a bit and eventually to become a wayside preacher.

*   *   *

"So what are you planning to do?" Errol asked. This was the same question Mr. Jemmott and the other teachers at Harrison College were asking me. I had completed two years at the college and apparently my stock had risen in the last year, even among my teachers. I had sat the general paper, like everyone trying for the Barbados scholarship, and English, geography and history at advanced level. I had passed the general paper and "A" level English. For geography and history I passed at ordinary/advance level, an indication that I had moved beyond ordinary level, but had fallen short of the higher level. Mr. Jemmott and Miss Yard were suggesting that I return for my final year at Harrison College, using the previous year as a base.

"So what you're going to do?" Errol said.

"I'm not going back to Harrison College," I said.

"Is that what you want, because you still have a year and . . ."

"No. I think it is time I take my own ship to sea. It's time to free you and Stephen from my responsibilities. You two have done enough. I'm going to go and find a job."

"If that's what you want," Errol said.

I went to the Ministry of Education and signed up to become a teacher. The woman who took my application was impressed. She liked my qualifications; told me I was starting at the top of the salary scale for beginning teachers—a whopping $210 Barbadian or the equivalent of $105 U.S. per month—and that I should go into teacher training at the famed Erdison Teacher Training School as soon as possible. The next week, only eighteen years old, I reported to St. Leonard's Comprehensive School for boys, still hoping that once I saved enough money, I would pay my way through law school. But I found my true vocation and I soon learned the power—and the pain—of the pen.

10

The Night the Power
Went Out

Three months after entering the classroom at St.
Leonard's Comprehensive School for the first time, I
realized I was unhappy as a teacher. I came across an advertisement in the local newspaper. The Caribbean service of
Reuters News Agency, the London-based news service, was
looking for a cub reporter and editor. I applied for the job,
and a few days later I walked the short distance from my
home to the news agency's offices in Oistins.

There was a reason for my quick exit from teaching. I felt
I was not cut out for teaching, not in the method exhibited at
this school. Perhaps Grand-Grand still had too big an influence on me. She had shown me in so many different ways
that corporal punishment was abusive and achieved very little,
so from an early age I had sworn off this notion of beating
students—or possibly children of my own—to get them in line.

This, however, put me out of step with most of my colleagues at St. Leonard's. Teachers were expected to beat the students often and ruthlessly, usually for the slightest infraction. I saw teachers my own age—some of us were only three or four years older than our students—adeptly wheeling long straps and canes, and later bragging about their skills in this regard, boasting about the verbal traps they had set to ensnare a specific student.

Several times, I saw parents arriving at school to complain to the headmaster about a severe beating inflicted on their son, a thrashing that had left the student's back bruised. In one instance I saw a very angry father complaining about the swollen lip inflicted on his boy. The teacher later explained to us in the staff room that the swollen lip was caused by an accident, when the student had tried to move away and the rod became deflected. I wondered about the amount of force needed to cause such a welt that would make a parent take the highly unusual step of complaining about a beating. Teachers were generally expected to resort to corporal punishment, and parents were only expected to intervene when matters got out of hand. On that morning it took all the calming powers of the headmaster to appease the father, who was threatening real damage to the teacher in retaliation.

I decided to use a different tactic—to try talking to the students of my Form 3C, about thirty fourteen-year-old boys technically getting their last year of formal education, but going nowhere academically. They knew that the students in Form 3A were the cream of the crop and were likely to go on to take their General Certificate of Education. Next in status were those in Form 3B, who would finish with a certificate that might open the door to them if they planned on entering a polytechnic or a vocational school. My form—having been relegated to the "C" stream from an early age and abandoned there to mark time—was resigned to not amounting to much. It also puzzled me why the greenest teachers, like myself, rather than the better trained and seasoned teachers, were made form masters and mistresses in the "C" stream, where students needed the most help.

My students thought my approach somewhat strange. They set out to change me, and I set out to motivate them. They were very disruptive, talking loudly, refusing to stand in line before filing into the classroom, arriving late—seeming to deliberately do all the things that normally drew a flogging. I would not bite.

One day, with rising frustration, I asked why nobody in the form seemed motived, why so few of them could read properly and why they made no effort to improve their lot. By then I had started to attend evening classes at Erdison Teacher Training College, an institution with Caribbean and worldwide respect, and I was looking for ways to apply what I was learning, especially this notion of motivating students. That afternoon we had the showdown. The students told me I was wasting their time and mine. They knew nobody had high expectations for them. Even if they wanted to continue their education, they knew that by the end of the current school year, they would be out on the streets. I would have none of this. I made a pact with them that if they applied themselves, worked hard and improved their grades, I would see if the top students could be promoted into the "B" stream. The deputy headmaster said he liked my idea, but on reflection I realize he was probably trying not to rob a young teacher of enthusiasm. But I thought I had an agreement. Some of the students buckled down and began working hard. I would meet them on the streets and they would proudly introduce their mothers and fathers. And in my street clothes, I could easily pass for their bigger brother.

Except they would not stop trying to get me to conform to their expectations. The dare was still on, even a contest among the students over who would break me. I resisted flogging anyone for as long as I could.

One day, some of the most troublesome students were extremely disruptive while I was taking afternoon attendance. After the lunch hour, when they had been playing hard, some of them still sweating profusely, they did not want to settle down. In frustration, I ordered two of them to the front of the class. I had a flat ruler in my hand which I used as a pointer on the chalkboard. The form held its collective breath. This was the decisive moment. I had challenged the boys. What would I do now? If I just sent them back, what would be the message? So I bent over and gave the two boys a few taps on their bottoms with the ruler. Suddenly, I heard the noise and looked up to see the entire form standing and clapping. The punished boys—obviously conditioned by more painful beatings—jokingly dismissed my *licks* as mere "fly bites." But they knew they had psychologically won. What they were applauding me for I wasn't sure, but they were claiming a victory of their own. I was utterly embarrassed, and angry at myself for resorting to violence.

With this test out of the way, I didn't really have much reason to use corporal punishment. When students got out of hand, I passed the buck by sending them to the head-master. By the end of the term some of the boys were show-ing a marked improvement in both work and attitude. I asked the deputy headmaster about keeping our promise and transferring some of them to a higher stream. He laughed and said it was not possible, not so far into the school year. On the first day back after the Christmas holi-days, I told my students I was leaving teaching because I didn't think I had what was required to help them—and more so because I could not keep my promise. They looked genuinely disappointed when we met for the last time. One boy, appearing to voice the sentiments of his colleagues, lamented that they always lost the teachers they liked but had to put up with those they didn't appreciate. A few days earlier I had gone to Reuters for my interview.

"Have you done any writing?" asked Harry Mayers, a Barbadian, who was second in command at the news agency. Actually, Harry ran the agency's news gathering department, but he was junior to Bruce Cobb, an Englishman posted to the region as the agency's primary correspondent. Bruce wrote the news for international consumption. The local contingent mostly wrote about or supplied international news to the regional market.

Even as I contemplated making the switch to journalism, I was coming to terms with some aspects of Barbadian soci-ety that still bothered me. We were in the early years of political independence, yet change had not come for many, or it had not happened fast enough. This was best demon-strated by the predicament suffered by my students at St. Leonard's Comprehensive School. I tried to put myself in their position and wondered what would have become of me if I had been encouraged to while away my last years at school. I had developed through the nurturing of dedicated teachers, those who thought they saw something in all of us late-bloomers at a lowly school like Christ Church High School. They never gave up on us. This was supposed to be the spirit, the reason the prime minister of this newly independent country was saying that for Barbados to progress it had to develop its human resources, as the island had few natural resources of commercial value. Education was supposed to be the ticket to greater things. Yet this was still not the case for many of us, even though the government was devoting a disproportionately large amount of its budget to education.

In my mind, switching to journalism would not mean I was through with teaching. I had always looked on journalism as a form of education, not in the formal sense of a curriculum and a classroom, but in terms of helping people become better citizens and aware of their circumstances, offering them timely and useful information and analysis.

My interview with Harry Mayers was on the verandah of a big limestone house, the courtyard filled with various trees such as coconut and mammy apple; crotons in the gardens. As we talked, I heard the teletype machines clicking away, the typewriters going and the constant ringing of telephones. Excitement. There was something magnetic about news. The magic of information and entertainment, of transmitting thoughts and ideas and getting a rise out of people—reasons why I had long dreamed of becoming a communicator. Teaching and news reporting—didn't they have the same intent and purpose of trying to pass on information and knowledge? I thought so.

"Yes, I've done some writing," I responded to Harry's query. "I've written some short stories and some poems, including one or two that were published in the school newspaper at Harrison College."

"Well, that's not exactly what I was thinking," Harry said, and broke into his traditional loud laugh. Harry had a full beard and as he talked he pulled on it. It must have been my naiveness or my wide-eyed enthusiasm. Or it was my knowledge of West Indian history and geography, two subjects I had mastered in school. Whatever it was, Harry offered me the job of cub reporter and editor. Taking me under his wing, he taught me just about everything I needed to learn about news reporting and feature writing. I would meet many famous writers and journalists, but few of them had as deep an influence on me as Harry Mayers. Few of them were as good as he was.

By the time I joined Reuters, the newspapers and broadcasters of the region were complaining that the Caribbean services were inadequate. In an era of political independence, the reports sold to them still seemed to have a colonial bias—nothing was really important unless it mattered to some news editor in London or New York. News about the region had to be rather exotic by international standards to merit attention on its own. When our leaders went abroad, international news services hardly paid attention. And when the international press wrote about events in the Caribbean, the reports appeared superficial. It was as though the writers felt compelled to over-explain, as if working on the assumption that Caribbean people did not have a clue what was happening elsewhere in the region. This may have been the case for readers and listeners consuming the news elsewhere in the world, but not in the Caribbean.

Such coverage was not suited for an independent people interested in such issues as development assistance. This was not the way to highlight our efforts in making international contacts and in keeping us abreast of what was happening in the other islands and territories in the region, nations now linked in meaningful economic integration. Talks were already underway for the subscribers to buy the news agency's assets and set up a service of their own. One evening, dignitaries from around the Caribbean showed up at Reuters' head office in Oistins. There was much discussion about the importance of news being reported by Caribbean people for the Caribbean. Thus, the Caribbean News Agency was born. Harry Mayers was chosen to guide CANA in its formative years. Those of us on the staff felt we had an important mission.

In the first months, Harry brought me along slowly, essentially assigning me to tape editing, which meant that I manned the machines spewing out the Reuters international service. I selected what I felt was of interest to the Caribbean subscribers and discarded the rest. This did two significant things for me: it made me understand the importance of writing news with a specific audience in mind and it offered me the opportunity to learn and copy the styles of writers around the world.

With time, I graduated to writing a few short stories, editing the reports of correspondents and even rewriting reports from the Reuters international service to give them a Caribbean twist. CANA deepened my knowledge of the Caribbean. On any given day we had to know what was happening on every island and land mass, from Guyana in the south, to Jamaica in the north, who the main players were and even what the editorial writers on the local news-papers were complaining about. We followed the latest developments in the parliaments, in the courts and on the streets in every country. We wrote about the importance of bauxite in Jamaica and Guyana, petroleum in Trinidad, bananas in most of the Windward and Leeward islands, sugar and tourism in Barbados and Jamaica, and about fishing and coconuts in Belize. And joy of joys, Harry Mayers trusted me to handle all reporting and editing of the quintessential Caribbean institution—cricket. For days on end, I monitored radio commentaries, provided running scores and analyses, interviewed and wrote about the various heroes. On a given day I could be writing about Trinidad and Tobago vs. Barbados, Jamaica against the Windward Islands, Guyana and the Leewards, or even one of the really big games, when the West Indies played some visiting team in an international test series. Occasionally, Reuters' international news services picked up my cricket reports. I was genuinely submerged in things Caribbean, becoming what we hoped to encourage in all citizens of the region—Caribbean men and women living in proud, independent countries.

*   *   *

I was sitting in the newsroom of the Caribbean News Agency in Oistins when the telephone rang. "Fost, this is

Maurice Bishop," the familiar deep voice said. "Look, I think some of you guys in the international press should consider coming to Grenada to cover this election."

Maurice Bishop was the leader of the New Jewel Movement fighting against the corrupt government of Sir Eric Gairy, a megalomaniac then ruling Grenada. Of late, I had had frequent contact with Bishop. A short report had come in late one night that Sir Eric had called an election. This election in late 1976 was the first since independence had been achieved.

Even in the Caribbean, we viewed the election with less than complete seriousness, wondering how the Grenadian government was going to embarrass the region yet again, how it was likely to cause the international community to laugh at us, the same way adults howl at the antics of children playing house or grown-up games. With political independence still new to the region, what the international community thought of us still mattered. It went to the heart of our pride and the sense of who we were. Especially in the case of Grenada where the opposition and the government had been locked in a titanic struggle, with the opposition leading a crippling strike that virtually shut down the island just before the newest Caribbean flag was hoisted. Grenada struggled into independence with a crippled economy, the result of the strike that closed down the nutmeg industry—the main money earner.

When the report came in, I had located a telephone number for Bishop and called to get a comment from him to balance the government propaganda. Bishop was effusive, for he had long learned the power of the foreign media as the antidote to operating in official political silence at home. The local Grenadian radio station was run by the government. As far as it was concerned, the opposition in Grenada did not exist. It devoted entire newscasts to praising Sir Eric and encouraging Grenadians to vote for him. Nary a mention of the opposition.

My calling Bishop was deliberate. Our correspondents in Grenada knew the personal dangers of quoting the opposition, so they didn't, leaving that job to us in Barbados. They knew that when their original reports showed up on the prime minister's desk, as they inevitably did, the reporters could honestly say it was those fellows in Barbados who had embellished the story.

Talking to us was important to Bishop. It gave him a chance to speak over the heads of the local broadcasters and to break the government control. Radio stations on neighbouring Caribbean islands, particularly the powerful Radio Antilles in nearby Montserrat, picked up his comments from our reports and beamed them into Grenada. This was the case with the story I wrote on the election call. Bishop regularly phoned to provide updates on the election campaign.

It was the final week of the election and Bishop wanted more. He feared the government was planning to rig the election. He said his group was detecting dangerous signs that not only was the government planning to steal the election, but that it might even liquidate leading opponents. This was the government's way of reacting to the growing crowds attending Bishop's all-night political meetings, so typical in the Caribbean. Bishop reported that, judging from the size of the crowds at the meetings, especially the large number of young people, the political momentum was with him and his supporters.

In many countries, even by Caribbean standards, such talk might have been a typical mixture of paranoia and exaggeration by an opposition demonizing its opponents and building up its own chances. But everyone in the Caribbean knew there might be some truth in Bishop's warning. He and his followers were constantly putting their lives on the line. Some of them had been killed for opposing Sir Eric.

Bishop and his New Jewel Movement, an offshoot of the Black Power movement in the region, had good reason to be concerned about their safety. The Grenadian leader could not forget—and certainly he could never forgive—how these young radicals had shamed his government. He could not understand why they had called the strikes, why they had whipped up international attention with their antics. It was irresponsible behaviour in his eyes. And he claimed the strikes and international condemnation were based on lies from possible communists. The result of all this was the crippling of the local economy, causing Grenada to start life as an independent country virtually broke and with reduced expectations. This, Sir Eric claimed, was the legacy of Hurricane Jewel.

Several of the leaders were arrested and severely beaten and mutilated. Bishop was singled out for special treatment. A handsome and articulate lawyer, he was a fiery speaker, patterning himself after Michael Manley in Jamaica, a socialist and orator *par excellence*, bent on creating a new order at home and abroad in the region.

Bishop's trademark was his African-print shirts and big Afro hairstyle. The government arrested him, heaped indignity on him by shaving his head and beat him so badly he had to flee to Barbados for medical attention. So did many of his followers who suffered the same fate. Bishop's father was not so lucky. He was shot and killed by the police. Once again it was the outside media that told Grenadians what was going on in their island. Elsewhere in the Caribbean, we viewed Grenada as a pariah state with an unpredictable leader.

Suddenly, there was a new phrase in Caribbean parlance— the Mongoose Gang. This was Grenada's version of the dreaded tontons macoutes of the Papa Doc regime in Haiti. The Mongoose Gang was made up of government-sponsored thugs, some of them beefy policemen or party supporters. These were the mongoose to rid the island of the snakes—all those opposing a prime minister who claimed to have God's divine blessing, a charismatic labour leader to whom God spoke directly and a man who repeatedly embarrassed not only educated Grenadians like Bishop, but the entire region.

Given the opportunity, for example, to speak to the United Nations on behalf of the member states of the Caribbean Community, Sir Eric amused everyone. Dressed in his trademark white suit and white shoes, a red rose in his lapel, Sir Eric—in the name of all Caribbean people— called on the United Nations to investigate reported sightings of UFO's. He wanted an agency set up to study extraterrestrial beings. Sir Eric also claimed mystic powers that protected him, showing he had learned quite a bit from Papa Doc in Haiti, who used the same strategy to frighten potential opponents into submission. And he had erected a big cross in the mountains overlooking the capital, St. George's. He had the cross lit every night so that it could be seen miles around, on land and out to sea.

All of which might not have been so bad if Grenada didn't always appear to be one cheque away from bankruptcy. At a

British Commonwealth meeting in Jamaica, when the Caribbean nations revelled in the role they were playing on the international stage, Sir Eric grabbed the opportunity to present the region in a different light, that of an international beggar. Sir Eric managed to get the then Nigerian military dictator General Yakuba Gowan to write a cheque for $5 million U.S., arguing he needed the money to pay his civil servants. Money, he said, that was needed because Bishop and his supporters had ruined the economy with irresponsible strikes, an independence gift to Grenadians. Gowan, a dashing figure in his military uniform, made a brief swing through the eastern Caribbean, and he and Gairy both cut quite the figure being as impeccably dressed as they were. Not only did Gowan hand over the promised cheque, but he talked about using his trip to the region for the development of trade and cultural links between the long-lost African brothers and sisters in the Caribbean and our ancestors in Africa. Unfortunately for Gairy, Gowan was overthrown in a coup before he could cement the ties between the two countries, relations that were based obviously on Gairy's hitting it off with the Nigerian head of state, a relationship that might have given him access to Nigeria's burgeoning oil wealth. Feeling very full of himself, Gairy made one of his first acts as Grenada's prime minister to ask Queen Elizabeth II to knight him Sir Eric. Unfortunately, other Caribbean leaders suffering from the same disease followed his lead and further cheapened these honorific titles by nominating themselves.

The embarrassment over Sir Eric's erratic behaviour was felt deeply, even outside Grenada. In an outburst during a televised news conference, Barbados prime minister Errol

Barrow angrily dismissed some of the political leaders in the East Caribbean as bandits. It was widely assumed the Barbados leader was speaking specifically of Sir Eric, even if, in a bow to diplomatic language, he fell just short of naming him. Straightaway Bishop and his followers took to printing headlines in their New Jewel newspaper that Barrow had called Gairy a bandit.

"Fost, man, I think you should come in to Grenada to cover the election. We are trying to get other international media and human rights groups to come in and monitor what's going on. We think this madman won't risk doing anything with the world looking on," Bishop argued. "And we think the Caribbean people would be very concerned about the image that would come out of Grenada during this election."

The turboprop plane flown by LIAT—the airline owned by the regional governments to support regional integration—touched down at Pearls Airport in St. George's. I made my way through immigration and customs and took a taxi to the Holiday Inn hotel on Grand Anse Beach—arguably the most beautiful beach in the Caribbean. Harry Mayers had agreed immediately when I proposed that I go to Grenada to report on the actual voting. As usual, he seemed to find the whole episode funny, but warned me to be careful.

The afternoon on the eve of the election, I received a telephone call at the hotel. "We are sending someone in a car to get you," Bishop said.

The driver took me into a mountainous area just outside the city and parked on a desolate side street. Bishop and some of his men were waiting. He introduced them to me, one of them, I remember, was Bernard Coard, Bishop's deputy, a man in whom he said he had full confidence.

"This is your last chance to ask us any questions," Bishop said. "We don't plan to hold any more political meetings. When we leave here, we're going underground. You won't be able to reach us for comments until after the election. We'll be moving among a number of safe houses. We don't plan to sit around and be sitting ducks for anybody."

We talked about the election and the various elements of the campaigns. At that time, Bishop appeared resigned to having the election stolen from him. "We know the people will vote for us but we'll have to wait and see if they'll allow us to win." We agreed that whatever the outcome of the election, he would call with a statement.

I returned to the hotel, tried to reach officials of the government, who had decided not to talk to the media, and filed my report to Barbados. For the remainder of the day and well into the next, while Grenadians were going to the polls, the local radio station continued a stream of reports praising Sir Eric for his magnificent and wise leadership, and encouraging Grenadians to do the Christian thing of voting for this leader that God had blessed. Nothing was mentioned of the opposition.

Fifteen constituencies were at stake. The night of the election, we assembled at a central counting station. Reports were to come in from the field, the numbers tallied and the winners announced. When I turned up at the station, I discovered there were few opposition supporters on hand. I located a phone and placed a call to the overseas operator.

"I want to book sixteen collect calls to Barbados," I said, calculating that I would need at least an extra call for a wrap up on the outcome of the general election.

"Sixteen?" she asked. "When you'll be making them?"

"I want to make them as soon as the winner for each constituency is announced."

"Okay, Mr. Foster," she said. Bishop had told me everyone on the island knew I was reporting on the election. I didn't recall telling the overseas operator my name.

The early results started trickling in. I made my calls, reporting that, surprise, surprise, the New Jewel Movement was actually winning seats. Then panic seemed to take hold. The election was neatly poised, with Sir Eric's Grenada United Labour Party and the New Jewel Movement tied for seats and Bishop's riding and a few other opposition strongholds not yet declared, but enough to give Bishop a slim victory if the vote broke as he expected.

Suddenly, the power went out. Radio Grenada was off the air. Someone found candles and the counting of votes resumed. In the darkness, I located the telephone and before I could announce who I was, I was talking to Barbados. The overseas operators were extremely efficient as they, too, must have been affected by the power outage. After almost three hours, the lights came back on across the island. The results of the election were in. Sir Eric had won by a margin of nine to six. I filed my reports and went back to the hotel.

The next morning Bishop, the new leader of the opposition, called. "Thanks for letting me know that I won my seat," he said. "We only know the outcome of the election by listening to Radio Antilles. They were reading out your reports constituency by constituency. That's how I know I won my own seat." Even as we spoke, Bishop had not been officially notified of his victory.

I left Grenada with no doubt that the sudden power outage was not a coincidence. And I had a greater appreciation for Bishop and the frustrations of fighting a corrupt government.

*   *   *

Two years later, Maurice Bishop called to tell me he was coming to Barbados to attend a meeting of regional opposition parties and we should get together for a drink.

"Are you preparing for the next election?" I asked. "Planning strategy?"

"We've given up on elections and this madman. Look at what he is doing in parliament." Yes, parliamentary life had become somewhat of a farce in Grenada, where the government ruled as if there were no opposition.

The meeting Bishop was attending was at Sam Lord's Castle on the southeast coast of Barbados. I drove up to the hotel to meet with him during one of the luncheon adjournments. Bishop seemed to be smoking more heavily than usual. We walked back to his hotel room. Inside the room, no matter how I tried, I could not strike up a conversation with Bishop. When he went outside on the balcony, he was somewhat more like his usual effusive self.

When we returned inside, I noticed the red light was still lit on his phone.

"Maurice—someone is trying to reach you."

"How you know that?" he snapped.

"There's a message for you. On the phone." I said. Now Bishop was really looking concerned.

"How you know that?" he asked again.

"The red light. That's the hotel's front desk telling you there's a message for you."

Bishop started to laugh. "Is that what that light is for?" he asked. "You know, I saw that light since I checked into this room a few days ago and I thought that was some bug or something. You know you can't trust anybody. The CIA might be working for Gairy and bugging my conversations."

So that was why Bishop would not talk in his hotel room. Neither would he use the telephone until he confirmed with the front desk that there were indeed messages for him and the light went out. As I left him, I wondered why Bishop was so nervous, almost paranoid. I dismissed it as his unfamiliarity with modern technology. Even after he found out about the light on the phone, he was still jumpy and very circumspect.

*   *   *

The news bulletin came early in the morning on the radio station in Barbados. There had been a coup d'état in Grenada. Armed men had stormed the main police station and were claiming to be in charge of what they were calling Free Grenada. They had grabbed their chance when Sir Eric was out of the country and were now declaring him a criminal and *persona non grata*.

Later that day came a broadcast from the coup's leader on Radio Grenada, which was now called Radio Free Grenada. The voice sounded familiar but I couldn't quite place it. The voice was calling on the people of Grenada to show their support for the coup by taking to the streets. It told all police officers to run up white flags outside their stations as a sign of surrender. And it was claiming that the dictator Eric Gairy had been overthrown and banished from the island for good. It was promising free and fair elections as soon as possible.

By the end of the day, English-speaking Caribbean had had its first coup d'état and there was much to discuss. Grenada, which had been the laughing stock of the region was, at last, to be taken seriously. Was this the beginning of chaos and lawlessness in the Caribbean, where we were going to discard parliamentary tradition and replace it with the barrel of the gun? Or was this a sign of what could happen if Caribbean politicians drove their people to desperate measures? Was this what opponents meant when they said political independence would lead to the destruction of our political institutions and was the region now poised for an extended period of social and political uncertainty?

While this debate heated up, the coup leader went public. I was then able to put a face to the voice announcing the coup. It was Maurice Bishop.

Later, it was disclosed that the weapons for the bloodless coup were smuggled into Grenada from sources in New York. The transshipment point was Barbados. I suspect this was why Maurice Bishop was so nervous when he attended that meeting in Barbados several months before the coup. I never got to ask him about this for, with his new role as prime minister, he became distant. Also, he seldom travelled to Barbados because of strained personal relations with the new Barbados prime minister. I met with Bishop one last time in Toronto when I wrote a story on him for *The Toronto Star*. In his suite at the downtown Holiday Inn, we joked about my reasons for leaving Barbados and promised to chat again the next time he was passing through.

The next time I wrote about Bishop was when his friends, including Bernard Coard whom he had introduced me to as his most trusted lieutenant, brutally murdered him and set up a new government. I wrote about the events for Toronto's *Globe and Mail*, reporting on the Maurice Bishop I knew, calling friends and contacts in Barbados and elsewhere for information about what was going down in Grenada. The sordid issue came to an ignominious end when U.S. President Ronald Reagan—using Barbados as his military base and its politicians as his fronts—invaded Grenada in October 1983, supposedly to rid the island of a Cuban threat and to remove the revolutionaries who had killed Bishop. Grenadians welcomed the invading Americans with open arms, which struck me as strange. For even though I thought very highly of Bishop, I wondered what independence and sovereignty could mean to Grenadians and Caribbean people if they welcomed an invasion by a foreign superpower. Is this the consequence of independence?

What occurred in Grenada is one option of what can happen when we do not question and stand up on issues of principle. I believe that most of what transpired in the subsequent years after 1976 had its genesis in those two or three hours when the power went out in Grenada on election night. Bishop had no more reason to believe in a parliamentary system, as Mr. Straughn had told us, without checks and balances. Sir Eric Gairy stole the election from Maurice Bishop and in turn created a Marxist dictator, driving him so far to the extreme left for support that he got caught up in the bitter East–West rivalry, where he became a proxy and was then unable to extricate himself from the mess into which he had fallen. When he tried to retreat, his trusted friends murdered him, even as Sir Eric and his thugs had killed him psychologically years earlier.

11

Twenty-One Years

I was finally arriving in England, or so the flight attendant
said as she gently woke me from my transatlantic sleep,
in preparation for landing at Heathrow Airport. I had
wondered so many times what my first sight of England
would be, what my first feelings would be on seeing this
country, this so-called fair isle that had already intrigued me
from a great distance, this island that held my parents.

With bleary eyes I looked through the thin morning
mist on the land below and experienced my first disappointment. At eye level was the watery blue of the early
morning sky. Below me were ugly red brick buildings and
green fields in a pock-scarred landscape—not the pastoral
images in my mind or those I had seen in books or tourist
brochures.

So this was England. Ah, well. So much for that. I wasn't
coming to England as a tourist, I was on a mission of the
heart. I was going to finally set eyes on my mother and, hopefully, my father—if we could find him. My circle would now

be complete. The hunger and longing to know these people would be satisfied. The heavy burden of loneliness would be lifted off my back. I would be able to get on with my life.

For over a year I had worked and saved for this trip. I had become restless and had begun looking for my fulfillment beyond Barbados. One day Errol came to the house to have a chat with me. He was living on his own, renting one of the units in a new housing *scheme* that the government had built. This was party central: everyone in the area had a hi-fi and blasted music. From miles around everyone could hear the music: the latest reggae and calypso, and the oldies from bygone eras. We listened to the music as we played cricket or tennis in the street or dominoes under the streetlamp. Errol, too, had his gramophone and a somewhat different collection of records, which introduced us to a steady musical diet of rock with the screeching guitars and their fuzzes, music that I found in part tasteless and too jarring to the ears. Stephen and his girlfriend, Icilma, had also rented one of the *scheme* houses, almost right across from Errol. Of the three of us, I was the only one at home with Grand-Grand.

"Barbados doesn't hold much for me," Errol said, "so I've decided to leave the country."

"Where are you going?"

"Well, it's either New York or Toronto. I prefer Toronto as I have some friends up there," he explained, "but I'll first try Toronto and then decide if I want to go to New York." The tourist industry had opened Errol's eyes to the world, and he had met a number of Canadians at his bars at the various hotels and night clubs. "You are going to be all right, right?"

"Yes," I said. By then, I was working at the Caribbean News Agency and coming into my own, but it was still not enough. "When are you planning to leave?"

"Next week," he said.

I was working an afternoon shift on the day Errol left. I walked over to his house and saw the packed suitcases and the friends gathered for one final party. Errol had given Stephen his prized collection of records and the stereo system. The car to take him to the airport was waiting. We said our goodbyes, even as we saw the BWIA plane flying low into Barbados, the plane that would take him to Toronto. This was the first time any of the three of us was leaving the island for an extended period, perhaps the surest sign that we were men, having to act independently, to be responsible for our own futures. Not even Errol knew what to expect. As the car pulled off, I started to miss him. I walked slowly to CANA, taking my time to pray and wish that all went well for Errol, that we would be together again soon. The tears flowed down my cheeks. I was so thankful for all Errol had done for me and I knew it was time for him to worry only about himself.

On reaching CANA, I dried my eyes and set to work. From that day, I kept an eye out for the international weather reports, which I sent over the wires. They now had real meaning for me. Toronto, minus 15 and sunny was typical. I wondered if my brother was warm and if he missed the warmth of Barbados.

I, too, was getting the urge to travel beyond the Caribbean. First, I followed my heart to Montreal, where Glenys, the high school sweetheart who would become my wife, was studying. That was the blissful summer of 1976, the year of the Montreal Olympics. I spent six weeks in Montreal and Toronto, by which time Errol had returned home to work on his immigration papers to live permanently in Canada. It was fun, enjoying the French culture of Montreal, travelling to Toronto and across the harbour to the islands, and being amazed by the beauty of the flowers in the public parks.

I returned from Canada in time to watch the last week of an amazing general election, in which the ruling party was justifiably tossed from power. Barbadians had decided that, after fifteen years, the ruling party was tired, and may have been bordering on corruption. The people imposed their own checks, their own attempts at reinvigorating public life, by voting in a new team. Tom Adams, the son of my former teacher, the man who had given Errol and his friends a ride on the night of the last election, was the new prime minister. Tom Adams, who was going to be central to the decision I was to later make to leave Barbados permanently.

About this time, I also felt a compelling urge to close a deep wound before I did anything else. I started writing to my mother. Life was not easy for her, she said in the letters. My father had disappeared somewhere in London and she didn't know where he lived. They had been divorced for some time, supposedly a messy separation that had left everyone bitter. Could I come and spend some time with her? I asked.

Sure, she wrote back. She would love nothing better. She would like me to think that I could come "home" anytime I wanted, for no matter what, she still told herself that the house in which she lived was "home" for *all* her children. I did not need an invitation to come home, she said.

But my restlessness was showing up in other ways as well. There was pressure to make a decision on whether or not I wanted to go to university. Mr. Roachford and Mr. Straughn reminded me that university should be an option in my life. Just as important, a number of old school friends from Christ Church High School were going to university. Jennifer and I may have helped to open a floodgate, for in the next two to three years, Christ Church High School had a bumper crop of passes. Several of our friends had more passes than we had; some had gone to the Barbados Community College and were excelling, others had gone straight into university.

"Foster," Mr. Roachford had said to me when we met on the streets in Bridgetown, "you must go to university. And you must do it soon. I know you are working and enjoying the life. But don't let the money you are making sweeten you or entice you. Go to university before it is too late."

My first problem was that I wasn't sure what I would study at university. I was not interested in law, so there was no chance of resurrecting that application. I liked writing, period. Still, with Mr. Roachford's words ringing in my ear, I decided to write to the University of the West Indies for application forms to a diploma program in mass communications. This was a course aimed at blending academic study with hands-on training of journalists and other communicators in the region. In concept, it fitted well with the kind of journalism we were supposed to be practising at CANA, a journalism in which the Caribbean and its people were the centre of the universe. I was accepted into the program. This created problem number two, the same as the one that had stopped me from studying law—money.

The mass communications program was in Jamaica. Once again, I felt stymied. No way would I have the money to get to Jamaica, pay fees and living expenses, and certainly not after spending all my money to get to England. So, I decided to put off university yet again.

The plane was flying low over the land on its final approach. It had been a long trip with eight hours of flying time, but psychologically it had been a lifetime. My bags were loaded with all sorts of tropical goodies: rum, special "black" or "great" cakes, fruits; letters to my mother from just about everyone, pictures. My heart was full: this was the reunion Stephen, Errol and I had always dreamt of, and I was the fortunate one to meet my mother first. I wished Stephen and Errol were with me and I made a promise to make as many mental notes as possible to report back to them. Indeed, this was what Stephen had instructed me to do: he wanted to know everything that happened. I couldn't wait for the plane to land and for my new journey across time to begin. There had to be so much to explain, so many blanks to fill. Then, after our catharsis and cleansing, we were bound to emerge with a stronger bond, every fault in our lives corrected and at peace with ourselves. I was going to find the mother for whom I had always cried.

In our letters, my mother and I had joked about how we were to recognize each other. I wrote that I was going to be the tall skinny young man wearing a *shirt-jac* and with a big afro. She promised to be the nervous woman falling to pieces with anticipation, wearing steel-rimmed glasses and holding a red rose; the one person so kinetically drawn to me, and I to her, that nature would bring us together without our knowing, just as soon as we were in the same area.

I floated through immigration, having received my visa in Barbados, collected my luggage and loaded it onto a trolley. As I left the luggage room, I looked up and there she was. My mother. The rose in her hand. The glasses. But more than that, a great big smile. We hugged and clung to each other. It had been at least twenty-one years since we had last touched, touches that I couldn't remember. And just then I began to feel the disappointment. I had never fully relinquished the bigger-than-life childhood dreams of my mother and father. The woman holding me was no different from any of my aunts at home. She, too, was only human. This was what I had waited for all these years? Somebody must have fooled me when I was younger. This was just an ordinary woman, a stranger.

More and bigger disappointments were to come. My mother lived not in palatial surroundings, but in a government-subsidized flat in London. Life was obviously very hard for her. At "home," I met my two brothers, Tony and Roger, and three sisters, Julie, Sandra and Annette. There was some joking about how they now had a big brother—a gentle ribbing of Tony who had always played the role—a part Tony said he was now quite happy to pass on to me, so that he could just be another brother. Despite our jokes, something was missing; the chemistry wasn't right. The day wore on with fragments of conversation, a groping question here and there, and my brothers and sisters trying to carry on with life as usual, but remembering the presence of this stranger who shouldn't really be treated as a stranger among them. Somehow, they seemed on their best behaviour, not showing me the real life in what was supposedly our "home."

When my brothers and sisters finally went to bed, my mother pulled the shades and turned off the television. She offered me coffee, telling me she drank a lot of coffee, that everybody in England did, coffee and tea. She asked me about people in Barbados, about members of the family, about people I didn't know. She sat in a chair across from me and held a big cushion in her lap, occasionally clutching it to her breast and bending at the waist. I kept watching her, trying to match her with all my preconceived images. Somehow, nothing seemed to fit. No mental picture of her conformed with what I was seeing and hearing. There was no instant magic, no real bond between us. We were just two people, who ought to be friends, who ought not to hide secrets, exploring each other's past and hoping to stumble on something that was going to light a spark illuminating everything, correcting every mistake, explaining every disappointment.

The conversation gradually became less forced and urgent. While we wanted to catch up immediately, we realized it could not happen in an hour or two. So we made that adjustment, just letting the conversation flow, letting the information we wanted to give or share come out naturally, with only a prompt here and there. Most of the time, my mother asked the questions and I provided the answers. This was very different from what I had expected, from my getting all those answers from her that were going to explain everything, that were going to correct every wrong and every oversight. She wanted to know everything about me, to hear in my own words what life had been like for Stephen, Errol and me. She confided that she had never felt she could fully believe all the various reports she had heard about us, even those from her family. She wanted to hear everything from my mouth.

Several times in the early moments, I tried to shift the conversation to hear her side of the story, but she always brought it back to Stephen, Errol and me and how we had survived. Some things I told her, like how Errol and Stephen had to leave school before their time, she didn't like. Others made her happy, particularly when I told her how Stephen and Errol took care of me and put me through high school.

"The social workers up here should hear this story," she said. "They are the ones who are always saying brothers and sisters can't help other brothers and sisters. They don't know the people of the West Indies, how we do things."

When she was ready, she started to let me catch up with her experiences, starting from what life had been like for her as a young unmarried woman with three children in Barbados. It had been very lonely and she had despaired about the future. "I always wanted one father for all my children," she said. "That's why I left Barbados, so that we could be one family, together. This is not the way it was supposed to be.

"My three boys were always to be with me. I wanted the three of you to come over so badly. But there was always something. And then I got sick." She explained what might have accounted for the missed opportunities. Why, for example, we never took the flight on the military plane, which she confirmed was possible at the time as other children had used this privilege, why something had always come up to prevent them from sending for us. For this she apologized. And, of course, there was always a new brother or sister who came along. While pregnant with my second sister, she had been struck with meningitis and had undergone emergency surgery to drain an abscess on the brain and help her in fighting the disease. She was so extremely ill that she had been administered final rites in hospital. The operation left her with one side partially paralysed, an epileptic who needed powerful drugs to control the fits. Before she was even fully on her feet from this ordeal came another sister—the fifth child in England. She said she blamed herself. She should have taken better care of herself because her sickness ruined everything. By then the chances, if not her hopes, of our joining her had disappeared. This was the bleak period when we had heard nothing from them, when nobody wrote. Who likes to send home a stream of bad news and no money? This was when the marriage had finally broken under the stress.

Occasionally, she refilled our coffee cups and checked on my younger sisters. She told me about the painful separation, of how her life began to spin out of control when my father left the British Army and the comfortable life it had given them. She said his ruin was that he found religion, becoming a devout member of the Jehovah's Witnesses, refusing to work and forsaking the only thing he knew—his music.

"Where is he living?" I asked.

"I don't know. I haven't seen him since that day in court when we got our divorce and then he had to come back here to get his clothes. He never once came back to look for the children." As she spoke, it was obviously difficult for her to contain the bitterness.

Rays of sunlight were peeking into the room through breaks in the curtain. My mother got up and went to the window. "It's morning," she announced. Maybe it was the jet lag on my part, or the compelling need for both of us to catch up, but we had talked through the night. The time had just slipped by. We had explained, laughed, confided and blamed. We had gotten angry at fate and circumstances. We had praised those who stepped in to fill the voids in our lives. And my mother showed me a cracked picture that must have been taken a year or two after she left. Stephen, Errol and I were standing in Lodge Road, apparently in front of Grandmother's house. I was seeing it for the first time. A scruffy picture, with me and my big knees, next to me Errol, who was a bit taller, and then Stephen, the tallest of us. Three little boys in white shirts and short black pants. That was how she always remembered us, she confided. I told her of the pictures burnt into my imagination, pictures of a young woman in a nurse's uniform, her arms crossed and smiling, wedding pictures of this woman in white and a man in a military uniform, the picture Grandmother posted on a side of the house, which I looked at every day for the first ten years of life and dreamt. Neither that woman in the picture nor the three boys in her treasured cracked photograph existed.

No amount of talking could adequately recreate them or bring them together again. Too much time had passed. Yet we wanted so desperately for the characters in those pictures to come alive, to again become us and allow us to wipe time away and start out afresh, to pick up from the frozen time in those pictures. Talking would not do it. Nothing would. That amorphous something had long withered and died in the sun at the Bridgetown Wharf two decades earlier. Time and experience had produced two individuals different from those in our minds, different from what we had so dearly hoped. Because of time, there was no going back.

I finally went to bed and my mother set about making breakfast for my brothers and sisters. Just the way it always was: me vanishing, this time into the bedroom, like some dream disappearing with the reality of sunlight; my mother taking care of her real family, the boys and girls to whom she didn't have to explain anything, with whom there was a natural bond. From the bedroom, I heard the family awakening to a new day, heard my sisters asking for me and my mother explaining how we had gone through the night talking and they should let me sleep. I tried to sleep, but I felt hollow. Perhaps Stephen and Errol would have had a different feeling. They would have found a way for us to overcome the effects of time, and wipe them away as if their experiences were just a bad dream. Maybe I was too outspoken and straightforward with my questions. If, after a full and intense night with my mother, I was finally home, then why did I feel even more like an intruder? Why was it so much easier and more intimate talking to my grandmothers and aunts?

*   *   *

My father, when we finally met, was unapologetic when answering any questions.

"The best thing we ever did for you boys," he said, all so matter-of-fact that my blood started to boil. Why was he saying it was a good thing he had left the three of us behind? Didn't he think we suffered from the separation?

"Look at yourself. Look at your brother Errol, travelling the world, living in Toronto. Look at Stephen. And then look at your brothers and sisters here in England."

With this he looked around the small cramped room at the dejected faces of my brothers and sisters. We were all pressed into a very narrow room in this rooming house, with a few chairs, some books and newspapers, and most of us sitting on the bed. It was filthy and small and the looks on the faces of my brothers and sisters might have been quite different from what my father thought; they might have been the hurt and disappointment from finding their father living in such squalor. They must have thought he was living in better conditions, somewhat as the three of us living in Barbados had felt the family in England lived in splendour. The truth can be so harsh.

"You three in Barbados didn't have it as tough as these here," my father continued. "You didn't have to live through the fighting, the court appearances, the breaking up of the marriage and family, the scars. You didn't have to live through that."

I had always heard a good defence was to attack. My father, the soldier, had obviously learned this well. Stephen, Errol and I had nothing to complain about, he argued. Certainly not me, he said. I had received a good education, eventually getting to Harrison College, something he could not even have dreamt about as a young boy. I was a journalist, a profession that even in 1977 was essentially closed to black people in England. On and on, he pointed out how advantaged were we, the left-behinds. Nothing to complain about, or nothing we shouldn't have long outlived and outgrown.

Then he moved on to his crowning argument. We in Barbados had a future, living in a young country. We were justifiably arrogant and believed that we had control over our lives. I could even afford to buy a plane ticket and come to England, so life could not be that bad. "Look at your brothers and sisters. Look at the young black people in this country. Look at all the black people in this country. See how beaten down they are. See how they appear to have no hope for the future, because this will never be their country. See how they appear to have no ambition or self-confidence. You are better off than all of them. It was the best thing we did to leave the three of you behind. Do not fall into the trap of emotional paralysis."

Indeed, emotion was the last thing my father showed. Well, he once let his mask slip, for I guess the tough guy image can last for only so long. "Are you still practising the clarinet?" he asked Julie.

"Sometimes," she answered, in almost a whisper.

"You must keep practising. You were so good. And Tony, how is the job?"

Tony explained he had started working at a multinational company, Gestetner, and was optimistic about his prospects. With time, he might even make it into management, he reported.

My father also tried to get a conversation going with Roger and Sandra. Six of his children sitting around him, all of us acting as if we were seeing him for the first time. In some respects, this was true because the English contingent of the family had not seen their dad for years. They had not known where he lived. And it was killing them to find out the conditions under which he lived. They must have felt better not knowing the truth. This was certainly my case. I knew I lived in better conditions in Barbados, but this wasn't what I had expected.

We had received the address for him when my father wrote me at my mother's flat. It was a very formal letter: before leaving Barbados I had found an old address and had written, giving him the dates for my visit. His letter was to make arrangements for me to see him. His action might have been prompted, too, by the intervention of his brother, Uncle John, who had come around to the house a few days after I arrived, and enlivened things for me by taking me to a pub. John played the saxophone in a band there. And he performed for me the night he brought me to the pub. In truth, he played only the first set. When they called him back for the second, Uncle John announced, "Not me. You can't mean me. Play more? No, man, I have my nephew here from Barbados with me. I only played a little bit to let him see I can blow. And I can't even play half as good as his father, Freddie." The band played the rest of the night without Uncle John. He and I stood at the bar with some very generous friends as the collection of glasses of beer in front of me kept extending. I could not drink as fast as the pints of beer were coming.

"Uncle John," I finally capitulated, "I can't drink any more. This is too much, man."

"Okay," Uncle John said, casting a quick glance at this liquid challenge that had defeated me. "You just leave them to me."

To my amazement, Uncle John drained every last one of the pints in front of me, along with every one of the pints offered him, too. It was truly an amazing feat, even better than his saxophone playing, which I thought was very good, too. Still, Uncle John argued that I had not really heard good music until I heard my father.

My mother suspected that Uncle John knew where his brother lived, but he never gave out the address. Mother said she did not recognize the address I had brought from Barbados for my father, and that she would not rest until she had found out where he really lived, so I could visit him. When my father's invitation arrived, Mother decided to send us all off to see our father, with the others ostensibly showing me the way.

"So would you play something for me?" I asked my father, picking up on Uncle John's advice that I must hear my father's music. This was my last frantic bid to reach across time to him. After all, it had started with music, hadn't it? He had said he left the island as he could only grow as a musician by leaving. Only a few minutes earlier he had confirmed this to me, even though he dismissed with a wave of the hand any notion that he was the best musician on the island during his time.

"No." He dropped his voice, emphatically. "I won't play. I've not touched a musical instrument in years. And I swear never to touch one again." Denied again, I thought. Yet another disappointment.

Nothing more was left to say. We filed out and headed back to my mother's house, taking various buses and trains. None of us said a word.

"Lord, what happened over there?" my mother asked when we came into the flat. "All of you look so downcast. What happened? And nobody talking. What happened? I have never seen you children looking so sad."

She had set the table. Fried chicken and rice cooked with pigeon peas I brought from Barbados was supposed to be our feast that evening. She had worked on it while we were out. We sat at the table and ate robot-like. My mother was almost in tears. It was an awful Sunday.

*   *   *

My father eventually related bits and pieces of his story, but always from behind the facade that the past was the past and we should be mindful that, in our search for the truth, we did not become "paralysed by nostalgia and emotion." We should use the truth only for vindication. According to him, he was always captivated by music and the wish to excel in all areas of this artistry. From early in life, music became his calling and he was so fascinated that he wanted to discover all the intricacies, to understand the language and to conquer the art by understanding all there was to know about it.

His search started when as a youth some older man in Barbados gave him a book on the fundamentals of music, a basic introductory study that, apart from whetting his appetite, caused him to dream of becoming the best musician in his homeland but also of excelling abroad. He felt the limitations of living on a small island like Barbados. Actually, he thought that the island was somewhat politically backward, "still in the darkness," he said, where the colour of skin and the different shades of black accounted for too much and where political leadership was suspect. This might be a reason for his never going back once he left the island; why he professed to having no urge to return.

The opportunity to join the British army gave him the chance to get off the island and to follow his dream of studying music at the highest levels. In the army, he played an array of wind instruments and occasionally even the drums. And he enrolled at Trinity College, taking the correspondence course for which the institution was known internationally. The military offered him and my mother a comfortable life, and the chance to bring Stephen, Errol and me to England once he and my mother were settled. This was his goal, he said. But this opportunity would be at a greater personal cost than my father wanted to pay. He never achieved his goal, and because of this, obviously felt compelled to forever prove himself, forever seek what became his ultimate goal—vindication.

Disillusionment quickly set in for him. The down side of his using the military to further his studies in music was that the army had the right to use him in the way that it deploys all soldiers—as a faceless individual in a force sworn to unquestioningly protect the status quo and the interest of the state paying the soldiers' wages. It also wanted people of the same mindset and commitment. This was the difficult part for him. He was a black man in a colonial army, a black man who from his voracious reading and world travel was aware of, and even identified with, the international quest by black and Third World countries for political and economic independence. So, he had great difficulty when the military sent him to places in Africa to help put down local uprisings or to keep an eye on a population made restive by the dream of independence. He felt the British Army was using black soldiers to do its dirty work, and that, worse, the black soldiers were quite happy to be brainwashed into doing the army's bidding. They forgot who they were or did not realise their roles in a colonial struggle, for these black soldiers talked and behaved as if it were natural for them to identify with the goals of the army.

"One night I was on watch," I remember his telling me. I can't recall where he said he was posted, but it might have been in Addis Ababa or in Kenya during the Mau Mau uprisings that were part of that country's independence struggle. "Some replacements came in one evening and among them were a number of blacks, some from Barbados. Some of them came to ask where they should go out on the town, and they started talking about going nigger hunting tonight and coolie hunting, talking just like the other soldiers. I said to them, 'Why are you talking like this? Why don't you look at the backs of your hands and see the colour of your hands; see that it's the same colour as the very people you want to hunt tonight?'"

Such thoughts, he confessed, did not go down well in a military setting. He was considered to be ill-disciplined and not a member of the team. My father spent many days suffering the army's imposed discipline, performing such meaningless tasks as sweeping up tree leaves with a tooth-brush, standing on the same spot for hours or working long hours in the mess room. Or to really rub it in, his superiors would temporarily reassign him to the lowly posi-tion in the band of walking on parade with the bass drum and not allowing him to play the clarinet, saxophone or any wind instrument that was his specialty.

He was also having problems with the military at another level, and this made him distrustful of many of the African and Third World leaders of the newly independent countries. "We would sit around and smile whenever we saw some soldier or military leader from one of the newly independent African countries visiting our quarters. They were usually young and smartly dressed in their uniforms. They would talk with us. Then true enough, a few weeks on, one of us would be reading the newspaper and we would see this familiar face on the front page. Somebody would say, 'Hey, wasn't that the chap who was here a few weeks back?' The fellow would have gone back home and overthrown the government in some coup. It used to be that when we saw them coming through that we just made a mental note and waited." Britain might have granted political independence, but it still pulled the strings by training their favourite military officers on how to grab—and keep—power. These leaders then continued to do the bidding of the former colonial power, essentially reversing the gains of the struggle against colonialism. This was partly why he did not take seriously the offer to join the Kenyan military when he got out of the British Army.

But the disillusionment was happening for other reasons. My father said that his mind began changing when he stumbled onto the discovery that there is no great mystery to understanding music. "I was out walking in Addis Ababa, in what was one of the poorer areas, when I heard music coming from a hut. I was attracted to it by the bass. When I got there, I discovered this wonderful music was being played by a man who couldn't read or write, playing on a crude instrument that was really a sort of bow and string, with him manipulating the string to get the music scale. I realised music was that simple. That was the basis of all music. You don't need all that formal education to understand it."

I suspected that was only part of the story for why he was turned off music. Other things were happening to him and I suspected this "discovery" might have become the convenient excuse for accepting defeat when he realised that he would never fully achieve his dreams. One of these experiences had to do with an interview with the prestigious orchestra for the British Broadcasting Corporation, the orchestra that he had listened to over the airwaves in Barbados as a young man and around the world on assignment with the British army. My father applied to fill some position that came open with the orchestra and my memory suggests that either he or my mother said he might have even applied to become the orchestra's conductor. He got the interviews and believed that he impressed in the tryouts. But he did not get any of the jobs, didn't follow the tradition of moving from the army's musical unit into the orchestra. Had he succeeded, he would have been the only, and perhaps the first, black musician in the orchestra. My father believed that the colour of his skin prevented him from getting the job.

One other experience seemed to cap it all for him. The pain lingered long, for obviously the cut was deep and was still open many years later when he told me about the incident. While still in the army, my father faithfully corresponded with one of his tutors at Trinity Collge. The teacher was very impressed with my father's musical talents. They would exchange arrangements and play around with concepts. The tutor said he wanted to recommend my father to a full-time scholarship at Durham University, one of the top music schools in the British Commonwealth. As they had never met, primarily because my father was posted out of the country, the professor invited him to visit his home when he was in London.

They agreed the professor would meet my father on the platform of the commuter train station nearest to the professor's home. My father had said he would be arriving on the five o'clock train. When the train pulled into the station, the passengers got off. The commuters went about their business and my father remained standing on the platform. A man in a trench coat was standing on the platform, too. Eventually, the area cleared except for these two men. The man in the trench coat came to my father and sheepishly whispered, "You wouldn't be Mr. Goddard, would you?" My father said he was. And the professor turned around and just walked away. "Imagine insulting and offending your scholarship candidate on first sight!" my dad told me.

Against the wishes of my mother, Dad decided not to extend his stay in the military. And he also gave up on music. Instead, he became religious. "Which was a mistake," he said, eventually claiming that religion was mental slavery. He became a Jehovah's Witness, becoming fanatical in his zeal of witnessing on the streets by giving away magazines and tracts, visiting homes for at-the-door preaching, having long prayer sessions in his house, imposing strict discipline on the children and forcing them into Bible study sessions and eventually sleeping apart from my mother because she refused to be converted and was therefore deemed, by him, to be religiously unclean. My mother could not understand these changes. She pressured him to find a job, but I suspect that once he had given up on music, my father had no real skills to fall back on. And this, my mother said, was a reason she didn't want my father to leave the army too soon.

One memorable event for all parties was when Dad's brother, John, scraped together about two hundred pounds and bought a new saxophone. This was to be a gift to my father, to help his beloved brother make the transition from military to civilian life. It was his attempt to get a brother he dearly loved, and a mentor for him, to shake out of his private funk and to use his talents to earn a living for his family. John arrived at the family home, interrupted my father in his prayers and meditation, and shoved the saxophone in his hands.

"I said, 'Here, man, this is for you, man,'" John recalled. "'Take this and do something with your life. For you is a musician, one of the best, and you should use your music to make a living, to help Doris and these children here,' I said to him. The man, my brother, took the brand new saxophone that I bought for him. He took it and blew a few notes on it. He said it was a good instrument. Then, he gave it back to me, saying he's done with music. I said, 'What you mean, done with music: music is the only thing you know. How you can be just *done* with music?'"

My father bodily threw John and the saxophone out of the house. John kept the instrument, pawning it when short of money, and holding onto the hope, for as long as he could, that his brother would come by for the saxophone. Finally, he gave up hoping and sold the instrument. John eventually moved back to Barbados when he retired from his job with Prudential Insurance.

My mother's illness brought on more stress. My father was caring for a sick woman, who had been near death, a wife with whom he obviously had fundamental differences, and he was essentially the sole parent for three girls and two boys. This meant doing everything—from learning how to wash and comb his daughters' thick hair to helping them with school work and cooking and washing for them. He felt alone and abandoned, removed from his cultural moorings without the extended family of supportive relatives and friends. The savings were being whittled away and my father did not have an income. In these circumstances, it is understandable why it was impossible to even think of bringing Stephen, Errol and me from Barbados, why he rarely wrote home. The situation became worse when my mother tried to force my father to work. On the advice of a social worker, a Mrs. Lane, who became a good friend of my mother's and whom my father accused of destroying his family, my mother, tired of relying on social assistance and handouts from her own church and friends, asked the courts to force my father to financially provide for his family. Apparently, the courts could make this imposition only as part of a divorce settlement. My mother filed for divorce and my father fought back, arguing that he was fundamentally opposed to divorce, and that he wanted a chance to make the relationship work.

To get the marriage set aside, my mother had to prove that the relationship had broken down beyond repair. Acting as his own legal counsel, my father testified before the judge that he wanted another chance to save the family. My mother spoke words to the effect that she could not even think of continuing to live in the same house as *this man*. My father felt this was the ultimate put-down. At the back of his mind must have been how low he had fallen, how he had become simply *this man*, that a woman who spent her life chasing him was now testifying in a court of law that she could not stand him, indeed, hated him. My father refused to accept that my mother was expressing her true feelings. My father believed that the words coming from my mother's mouth were authored by Mrs. Lane, the social worker whom he felt had coached my mother so well.

The worst was that the judge gave custody of the children to the mother, with my father getting supervised visiting rights. The judge ruled that a policeman was to accompany my father back to the house. He was to collect his clothes and personal effects and he was not to return. Dad said this was the biggest indignity: a policeman standing at the door while he packed his clothes; for anyone to even suggest that he had to be supervised when he wanted to see his children, children for whom he was once the sole parent, virtually. He went to the house, packed and left, saying nothing but waving goodbye to the stunned children looking on in bewilderment, never to return again. Never to see his children until I arrived in England several years later, and even then the children had to seek him out, resorting to combing municipal records to find him; perhaps never to see his former wife again. Instead, he devoted all his efforts to studying, spending entire days in the library, writing poetry, studying the extensive works of leading philosophers, coming up with his own philosophy on the meaning of life for black people—all for the purpose of vindicating himself. "I haven't got [a] telephone or any of the modern conveniences, as you saw when you were here," he later wrote me. "I would've gone into a monastery, if I'd known how to go about it. I should've gone to India, when I, unlike you, was spat on and falsely imprisoned and injuncted[sic]."

The next time my brothers and sisters saw my father was when I once again "found" him. He had dropped out of sight once more. I returned to England, made enquiries of friends and located him. He later complimented me in a letter for using my "journalism skills to come all the way from Barbados" to track him down, whereas others living in the country could not locate him. I suspect this was as much a dig at my brothers and sisters for not putting out the effort to keep in touch with him—but then they might not have had the same burning desire to know and understand an intriguing part of a puzzle that would explain to them who they were and why they always felt cheated and denied of a birthright.

In his way, my father never gave up reaching out to Stephen, Errol and me, even if he continued to be aloof, never betraying any emotion, and communicating only with written words and heliographic symbols, drawings and cryptic puzzles that read as if they came out of an emotionless computer, sentiments that must have been his recognition that we could never regain what we lost when he and my mother left us behind in Barbados. To me, this was his way of protecting himself, of hiding behind a shield so he would not expose himself to even the possibility of being hurt, of having his dearest dreams trampled on, of feeling unfulfilled at not attaining his true calling. I asked him subsequently why he persisted in writing to grandchildren whom he has never met, sending letters and postcards few of us could understand. He replied that by using difficult language and symbols, he was simply trying to challenge us to higher levels of critical thinking, to make us put out some effort. I think the answer is more than he wants to admit—that he is still struggling with the old role for Caribbean males of never showing emotion, or leaving home and sending back the anticipated letters, but expecting no personal rewards—of figuratively hugging ever so briefly so that nobody would even entertain the thought that the huggers enjoyed holding each other. My mother becomes genuinely emotional when she talks about missing her role as a nurturer. My father, true to this military training but more so still a victim of the Caribbean male tradition, suggests emotion is a luxury we cannot afford.

I have discussed my thoughts and feelings about my father with Errol and Stephen and with several of my generation who were among the left-behinds. We marvel at how so many people from the Caribbean were afflicted by insanity or appeared borderline sane from the experience of living in England. Indeed, this is a debate that is prevalent in Caribbean literature, about all those ambitious young men and women who sailed away from their homelands for greener pastures, but ended up losing their minds, or having their minds developed to such heights that they were beyond comprehension. In either case, they dropped out of society. And looking at the conditions of older Caribbean people in England, I understood why they might be driven to such distractions. Uncle John took me to visit some of his friends and people who knew my father. Many of them lived as if they were still in Barbados, with very few material possessions or little evidence that they were integrated into the English mainstream. They seemed to have no social interaction with the new society, no real social standing and no real commitment to their new community— and in a perverse way they took great pleasure identifying themselves as West Indians, using this as a badge of honour, something that proudly set them apart from all around them and with which they must contend, even delighting in openly celebrating when the vaunted Caribbean cricketers gave an inferior English team an ignominious "blackwashing." Other than that, with the obvious exception of my father, they all talked incessantly of "going back home" to eventually die in a warmer climate, to rest peacefully among people for whom they felt some warmth and affinity. Except for my father, who said he never desired to return to Barbados.

Even though I rarely respond to his letters and postcards, he always writes, carrying on what is really a very cryptic one-sided conversation. He has made only two formal requests. The first was that I change my last name from Foster to Goddard. I didn't and wouldn't. The second is that I consider myself a god, for all of us are gods, he says, if only in the sense, I gather, that we are all capable of achieving great things and controlling our future. Of vindicating ourselves. Maybe, someday, I'll give the request more serious thought—perhaps if I feel the same compelling reason as his to vindicate myself. Until then, I can't grant him that wish either.

I feel a close bond to this man who so torturously restrained himself from openly showing me any emotion, from actually apologising for the separation that hurt me and my two brothers so much. And yet, borrowing from him, from a distance I identify personally with him, although I would never admit this to him. I understand the desire that must have burnt in his guts when he first discovered the joy of producing something artistic. I understand the feeling of confinement from living in a small society and wanting to break out, of feeling trapped and having to do other things so as to make a living and support a family when I would rather indulge in other pursuits closer to my heart. Like him, I like to debate and ponder philosophical questions and politics. And like him, I am prone to asking questions when, perhaps, it might be wiser to accept the status quo or to stay silent. Years after we met, I would eventually know from my own personal experience what caused my father to spend most of his life feeling compelled to vindicate himself. For him the spark was music; for me it was when I realised I could write. I often think that his greatest gift to me is an artistic mind—even if he never hugged me.

*   *   *

I received one more letter from my father while I was in England, suggesting I write him to make an appointment for my next visit. He remarked that while a little book given to him had started his musical journey, it was the smell of onions that started my own quest. The mention of the smell of onions just seemed to be part of the unexplained, another throwaway line.

My mother read the letter. "Is this the best he can offer, and you came all the way from Barbados? Asking you to write to make an appointment. Is this all he can do? Even your Uncle John did better. At least he came and took you to a pub. And then he has to go and mention about the smell of onions. You don't know what that mean, right?" I didn't and she explained to me that when she was a domestic servant in Barbados, my father would walk her home after work—work that left the smell of fried onions on her clothes, a smell my father claimed to have found special and endearing, a smell that reminded him of when he and my mother were young and unencumbered.

From that point, I began counting the day until my return to the serenity and refuge of Barbados. The pressure was off to find answers as I realized there were none, certainly not what I wanted to hear. The rest of the six-week stay, I spent as a tourist, but not straying too far from my mother's house, and getting to know my brothers and sisters better. I seemed to hit it off best with my eldest sister, Julie. When the time came, I was happy to leave England. I did not see my father again on that trip.

The week I returned to Barbados came unexpected news. I had put any thought of going to university out of my mind, but a cable from Jamaica changed my plans. It came from the Friedrich-Ebert Stiftung, a German foundation assisting with adult education in the Caribbean. The cable said that a full scholarship covering academic and living expenses was available to me if I still wanted to enrol in the mass communication program. A ticket was waiting for me at the local offices of BWIA airline.

The morning I left for Jamaica, Aunty Ann came to say goodbye before leaving for work. "I want to wish you all the best and to tell you that we are proud of you going to university. We made a collection in the family to help you out."

The call for financial help had gone out once again, just as it had when I went to high school—this time without my knowledge. Aunty Ann pressed the money into my hand. In only a short time I was again at the airport, carrying the same suitcase with the same clothes I had brought back from England, but I was leaving with totally different expectations.

12

Soldiers and Sedition

"So you're back from Jamaica," Prime Minister J.M.G.M. "Tom" Adams said in the friendliest of voices. As he spoke, he stretched out on the big desk in front of him, his head resting in the crux of his right arm, a very relaxed man. "And now you are writing some good things in the newspaper."

We were sitting on the second floor of the Barbados House of Assembly, an imposing weather-beaten limestone building, the third oldest legislature in the western hemisphere, pre-dated only by the Bermuda Legislature and the House of Burgesses in Virginia. This was the parliament the original colonists had fought and received a guarantee for in 1652 as a protection of liberties. The house that was the prototype for so many parliaments in the New World. Tom Adams had been three years in office and was still fighting to put his imprint on the island, for the legacy of his father, Sir Grantley Adams, and that of his nemesis, Errol Barrow, were still strong. These men had made their names in this building, in this room. Adams' task was to live up to the high expectations of his father and to match Barrow, who, even though he had been kicked out of office, was still very popular. Partially to undermine Barrow's popularity, Adams had called a commission of inquiry into the "financial mismanagement and infelicities" of the previous government, a report that essentially exonerated Barrow and perhaps even further enhanced his image and popularity.

Mere weeks after my return to Barbados, on the first day of the new sitting of the House of Assembly, with all its pomp and circumstance, I was sitting across the desk from the prime minister, informally talking, as if I were an insider.

It was not by accident I was meeting with him. In the chair next to me was Glyne Murray, my editor at the Barbados *Advocate-News*, the man I had been recruited to replace. Murray was a very political editor. His weekly columns were controversial, setting a new style and standard in partisan politics. Tom Adams and his Barbados Labour Party loved them. Errol Barrow and his Democratic Labour Party hated them, even suggesting that Adams wrote, or at least dictated, the columns. When I returned from Jamaica, Robert Best, managing editor of the *Advocate-News*, one of the oldest newspapers in the region, had outlined his plans.

"We know that Glyne will be going on to bigger things soon," he said to me in the interview. At that time, there were rumours Murray was to be posted as a diplomat to Toronto or New York as reward for his service to the party. "So we are going to need an editor to replace Glyne." I was offered the job, raising the prospects that at twenty-four years old, I was going to be one of the youngest, if not the youngest, editor of a major newspaper in the Caribbean.

The first weeks on the job, I shadowed Murray. One of the big assignments was to report on a significant by-election that was to be the first test for the new BLP government at the polls since general elections in 1976. Although the by-election was in a DLP stronghold, the outcome was significant. The DLP not only retained the seat but now had in the winner a charismatic young doctor, Richie Haynes, a potential rival for Tom Adams. Murray's last job was to take me into the prime minister's chambers and generally make provisions for the passing of the torch to me, even if I was not told this was the specific reason. "Come and meet Tom," Murray had said to me. This accounted for my spending the luncheon break with a very relaxed Tom Adams.

"You have been doing some good writing," Adams said, punctuating his words with his trademark snort and snuffle. "I've been reading your stuff." Then he went on to talk more specifically about what I had written, especially my political columns. According to the plan, I was also to take over Murray's spot as the lead columnist in the Sunday newspaper. Flattering me, Adams asked what I thought about the day's proceedings in parliament. He said the opposition had made a strategic mistake. They had not milked the opening of parliament and the presentation of their victorious candidate for their full public relations impact.

"When Richie came into the courtyard of parliament, he had his supporters there. He should have walked through them. Stop and hugged them. Have one of them, a woman, give him a big bunch of flowers. Instead, he walked from the leader of the opposition's office into parliament, not stopping, only waving his hand as he went in." Tom Adams had worked for the British Broadcasting Corporation when he studied law in England. Obviously, he knew the power of the media, especially in a country like Barbados. A winning strike for him came during a televised debate prior to the last general election, a performance that was to become legendary on the island. Accusing the government of corruption, he dramatically produced a series of cancelled cheques incriminating the government, using the moment and the live political broadcast to the maximum, assured of parliamentary privilege against prosecution, and making a name for himself as a master public relations strategist. The performance set him on the way to winning the government.

"But what do you think about your time in Jamaica?" he asked.

Jamaica, especially the capital, Kingston, had been an eye-opener for me, the equivalent of a country boy going to live in the city. Yes, there were so many things that were the same as in Barbados, but still so many things different, the pace of life so much faster, the gulf between the richest and the poorest so wide. It was in Jamaica that I became a man, living on my own, having to budget and plan my life on a daily basis. But it was also where I quickly became aware of many of the harmful effects of political strife and violence and how political instability can destroy a society.

* * *

I was taking a taxi from the Kingston airport to the Mona Campus of the University of the West Indies when I got my first culture shock. This was mere hours after arriving on the island. The car was passing through what I later knew as a small community called Halfway Tree when it turned onto the main road to the university. I must have nodded off, for suddenly I was looking at a small park, with what looked like a statue of a man looking down on the streets, holding a gun. I looked again. It was not a statue, but a soldier standing in green fatigues, the gun pointed down on the streets and the people below. I was startled. I had never seen anything like this. In Barbados, police didn't even carry guns. There wasn't anything seriously considered an army, although the government was in the process of setting up a defence force. I soon found guns were everywhere, with the police and defence forces always having their weapons on display as a show of force, many of the weapons looking well used with the paint rubbed off the barrels where they were palmed.

Jamaica was very different. This was the late 1970s and the battles between the socialist and capitalist forces were fought with real guns. Violence was a way of life, spilling over even onto the university campus, where the local bank and book store were knocked off from time to time. On weekends, I wrote for the Caribbean News Agency, hanging out in the offices of the *Jamaica Daily News*, catching up on the latest unravelling of law and order and the frantic efforts of the government to cope.

On campus, we were warned not to travel late at night and never alone. I noticed that on nights, drivers did not stop at street lights, not even when they were red. Everyone was talking about *the gunman*, a ubiquitous political animal given to a life of crime and intimidating supporters of rival political parties. And the government of the day was giving increased powers to the security forces and the regular courts, and was setting up a special gun court, to deal with the escalating violence. We talked about these developments in our classes, about how, as journalists, we should cover them—whether we should be bold enough to apportion political blame for what was happening. We feared what we were seeing in Jamaica was soon to arrive in the rest of the Caribbean. After all, this might be part of the maturation process as the region asserts its independence and right to self-determination, a test of our political systems.

One night, I was watching television in the common room of Irvine Hall, where I lived on campus, when I had a frightening experience. On the television was the minister of defence, a very blunt-talking Dudley Thompson. He was wearing his trademark black beret and he was speaking directly to *the gunman.* "We are going to come and get you. And when we get you, we will deal with you." The minister said words to this effect. "We'll deal with you. We'll shoot you in the gutter. We'll shoot you in your home. We'll shoot you on the streets, wherever you are." The minister was declaring war on *the gunman* and gangsters. Either they surrender and put down their guns or risk a violent crackdown by the security forces. This must be how some civil wars begin, I thought, but I was so frightened listening to this minister of the crown that I straightaway left the common room and went to my bed. The threats, however, didn't seem to have much effect on *the gunman,* as the carnage continued.

Life in Jamaica was hard for other reasons. Whenever we got the chance, we left the campus and the city to enjoy the beauty, size and diversity of the country. But we were always looking over our shoulders. This was the era of political destablization, according to then prime minister Michael Manley. For this he pointed a finger at the United States. It had decided to undermine the local economy because the Jamaican government was socialist, because it was non-aligned in international politics, because Jamaica had nationalized the assets of American and foreign companies, because the United States did not like the temerity of Jamaica, Barbados, Guyana and Trinidad and Tobago opening diplomatic relations with Cuba, essentially breaking the American trade embargo against Cuba and asserting their right to choose their friends, because America and its cronies in the World Bank and the International Monetary Fund wanted to punish Jamaicans for voting socialist by undermining and devaluing the local currency, wanted to pave the way for the election of a more amenable government, wanted to prevent the influence of the Cubans from spreading beyond Jamaica and Grenada.

These and many more reasons were given for this destablization, a word I had first heard in Barbados in the dying days of the previous government. Late at night, we used to hear planes flying into Barbados. These were Cubana planes refuelling in Barbados, supposedly transporting farmers to Angola. The passengers that got off the planes in Barbados to stretch their legs looked amazingly fit and young for farmers and they were all dressed the same way, in formal suits that appeared to have been cut by the same tailor. And rarely were there any women. As this was usually the last flight before the airport closed for the night, only a few customs and immigrations officials saw these farmers.

As it turned out, the Americans were onto what was happening. They didn't like the idea of Barbados' being a refuelling station for Cuba's sending soldiers across the Atlantic to Africa. The U.S. State Department would later claim that Cuba's deployed up to 50,000 troops in Angola, much of the early deployment coming through Barbados. These soldiers helped liberate Angola and Mozambique in their wars of independence and were responsible for inflicting the first major defeat on the vaunted South African Army, essentially making one of the earliest strikes militarily against apartheid. Barbados' becoming a refuelling point was one of the results of the decision by these Caribbean nations to open diplomatic relations with Cuba—a decision that had some deadly consequences when Cuban exiles living in Miami, and later identified as operatives for the Central Intelligence Agency, placed explosives on board a Cubana plane that blew up in midair shortly after a refuelling stop in Barbados, killing all on board.

The United States protested and flexed its muscles over Cuba's making the transatlantic stops. The Barbados government, having been caught out, claimed it had a choice: either stop the flights or have Uncle Sam destabilize the local economy, the same way it was hitting Jamaica. For the prime minister of Jamaica, Michael Manley, and the prime minister of Barbados, Errol Barrow, were close friends and had supposedly learned their socialism at the London School of Economics, where they were colleagues of the man who was to become prime minister of Canada, Pierre Elliott Trudeau, who also refused to go along with American policy on Cuba. Tom Adams sided with the

Americans. With the issue too hot for him, the Barbadian prime minister stopped the flights through Barbados. Obviously, this was a lesson for the learning: despite all the talk of independence, some countries simply did not have the free choice, or clout, to follow an individualistic foreign policy. And yes, to answer some of those questions raised during the independence debate, size did matter, as did the presence of a powerful military.

But destablization, or just poor economic management, as claimed the main opposition, was destroying life in Jamaica. The economy was grinding down, with many of the intellectual and moneyed classes fleeing to Miami, New York, Toronto or wherever. Airlines were operating shuttle services to Miami, taking people and large bank accounts. Food was in short supply, so that at university we were constantly complaining of a diet of primarily plain rice; we were subject to several electrical blackouts or brown-outs as the Jamaican refineries ran out of fuel. Even laundry soap was in short supply.

Jamaicans were divided on just about every issue. They were solidly in two camps: the socialists with Michael Manley and his People's National Party and the capitalists rallying behind Edward Seaga and his Jamaica Labour Party. In the classroom or in discussions around the campus, we heard the heated debates, and we listened to the phone-in talk shows on the radio. Political disunity seemed to be the main cause of all problems in Jamaica. One of the high points of my stay was the euphoria over a peace rally at the National Stadium in Kingston. This produced the memorable picture of reggae great, Bob Marley, raising the hands of Prime Minister Manley and his opponent Seaga in a peace symbol. That euphoria quickly gave way to more violence, much of it the result of partisan politics.

Ruthless partisan politics was not unique to Jamaica. In our classroom at university we talked about the situation in Guyana and Trinidad and Tobago. In these countries, partisanship was compounded by race. In Guyana, the party of President Forbes Burnham was essentially black, while the opposition was supported by the majority Indian population. We had discussed how, in a bid to hold onto power, Burnham had resorted to rigging elections, primarily by introducing overseas voting. I knew a lot about the situation in Guyana. Over the years, I had interviewed Guyanese opposition leaders in Barbados, where they always complimented us for having a free press. One of these leaders was Dr. Cheddi Jagan, the Marxist chased from power by Britain and the United States to make way for Burnham, but who would later die as president of the Guyanese republic. Jagan always warned us to fight to ensure press freedom, noting that under Burnham he could not even buy newsprint to publish his party newspaper. And in one of its most dastardly deeds, the Burnham regime was suspected of killing one of its main foes, Dr. Walter Rodney, when a bomb exploded in his car. This was the same Rodney for whom many people across the region had protested a decade earlier when he was deported from Jamaica.

In Trinidad, the ruling party which had been in power for an unbroken twenty-five years was also supported by blacks, while the majority Indians were splintered among smaller parties. In both countries, the party in power made no bones about offering jobs and whatever support was

necessary to its partisans, often deliberately leaving opponents without. A similar situation existed also in Antigua,
where the Bird family had used patronage to ensure a long
rule. The rule was broken for five years when George
Walters became premier. First thing back in power, the
natural governing party in Antigua brought corruption
charges against Walters and sent him to prison, essentially
removing the only real challenge to the family. Just about
everyone in the Caribbean believed Walters' biggest sin was
to oppose the Bird dynasty. Partisan politics was his ruin.
Added to this was the coup in Grenada where an elected
government was overthrown and the ruling cadre appeared
unwilling to call new elections, where for the first time the
Caribbean had political prisoners. It seemed as though
violence in its many disguises would wreck the region
unless the people were to take control.

Prime Minister Adams said he agreed with my analysis
and that Barbados should not fall into such instability. The
Barbadian electorate was too smart and there was the
legacy of respecting political institutions on this island.
And while partisanship was strong in Barbados, its practice
was nothing like what was the norm in Jamaica. Barbadians
might disagree politically but they would not settle their
difference with violence. Barbadians did not use politics as
a weapon to hurt one another. And this, he said, was a
legacy we must be careful to protect.

At this point the bell sounded, recalling parliament into
session. "Well, I have to go now," Prime Minister Adams
said, picking up his navy blue jacket. "I want to wish you all
the best as editor of the newspaper when you take over from
Glyne. We should have these chats from time to time."

I went into the House of Assembly for the first report-ing stint after the luncheon break. Within hours, I had blown any chance of becoming editor of the *Advocate-News*. Events were now set in motion for my eventual departure from Barbados.

13

Starving for the Cause

"Did Lammie Craig really say this?" managing editor Robert Best asked across the newsroom, his natural instincts as a long-time newsman pricked by what could only be the makings of a good controversy.

The question was directed at me. We were racing against deadline for the next day's newspaper. Best and his team of copy editors huddled around a table editing the raw news copy, with Best deciding on the spur of the moment where to place the story in the newspaper. "Did he really say this in the House today?" Best asked, his head down as he scratched his editor's notes on the paper with my story.

"Yes," I said, assured by my notes. "He said it."

"Okay, then," Best said, "if you say he said it, it is on the front page. Let's see what will happen."

We did not have to wait long. The next morning all hell broke loose. The island was in a political controversy and I was at the heart of it.

Minutes after leaving the prime minister's chambers, I was sitting at the reporters' table in the House of Assembly, a privileged position on the floor of parliament and ideal for monitoring the cut and thrust of debate. The session was raucous. The opposition, basking in the glow of its by-election victory, was going after the government. It was accusing the ruling party of trying to punish those who didn't vote for it by replacing hundreds of casual workers at the Parks and Beaches Commission with government lack-eys. These workers kept the beaches spruced up to enhance the tourist industry. It was not exactly back-breaking labour and few of the workers seemed to put in a full day's effort. Undoubtedly, there was a lot of feather bedding, a way for the dominant political party to reward supporters by putting them on the government payroll. Now, it was the turn of ruling Barbados Labour Party to prune opponents from the ranks and replace them with its supporters. For this the opposition was self-righteously crying foul.

Suddenly, the government's chief firebrand was on his feet. Lionel Craig was the minister of housing and labour. In political terms, he was a partisan street brawler, not one of the smoother debaters who had received the finishing touches of university or of an upper-middle-class back-ground. Craig learned his politics on the streets, having to sit out in personal hard times the fifteen years in the wilder-ness as he waited for his party to return to power. In the bad days for his party, often he was one of the few to be elected in opposition to the DLP. He had learned to survive by playing tough partisan politics. His initial instincts were to defend his government's record in the face of this assault and to point out that his party's patronage appointments were simply a continuation of political politics on the island. To the victor goes the spoils was the gist of his speech.

But this soldier of many political battles did more. Egged on by the taunts of the opposition, the minister launched into a partisan rant. His government would not offer assistance in any form to opposition supporters. His government would offer jobs and assistance only to those who supported the ruling party. Supporters of his party were to get preference in every way. As far as he was concerned, people who supported the Democratic Labour Party should starve. Indeed, he was going to be so partisan that if anyone approached him and had the misfortune of being named Douglas Leopold Phillips, DLP for short, then that person should starve, would get no work from him. That's how partisan the government would be.

Eventually, a government backbencher, realizing the minister of housing and labour was straying too far, suggested nobody should be allowed to starve in Barbados because of government policy. But, in the heat of battle, through various asides, Craig disagreed with his colleague and other members of his party too timid to be as plain-spoken as he. Yes, they should starve, he insisted. As the minister responsible, he would deprive them of jobs and housing, just because they were associated with the DLP.

As he spoke, I took notes and followed the debate. My colleague from the competing *Nation* newspaper, Albert Brandford, promptly put down his pen and sat back, watching events unfold. This was theatre of the highest. Several times the House had to be brought to order. I was aghast at this behaviour. After all, this was the venerable parliament, the one that we claimed with such pride as the repository of all our rights and freedoms, a place where government ministers announced and set policy, where ultimately they are held accountable. Craig was one of the most senior parliamentarians. He knew the importance of parliament and the significance of what he was saying. Here were all the elements for a good news story, if not to inform the public of an apparent new government policy but to indicate the level of debate in this august House.

When I returned to the office, I paraphrased in a story what Craig had said. My lead, front-page story the next day emphasized the Let-Them-Starve portion of the speech. I followed up the report with an editorial arguing this display of partisanship was responsible for violence and instability in Jamaica and should not be condoned in Barbados. For, in my mind, wasn't this what Tom Adams and I had discussed only minutes before this disgusting speech? One member of Craig's party had even disagreed with him in the House. My report was going to be a reminder of the need to maintain the integrity of the House and, as the prime minister had said to me earlier, to make sure Barbadians didn't descend into the kind of partisanship a minister of government was now proposing. How naive I was!

As to be expected, the opposition jumped on the story. Former prime minister Errol Barrow, who had been at the centre of the debate, said he was surprised to see a journalist with the temerity to write the truth. Various opposition members embellished the story, suggesting I had left out even more incriminating parts of the speech. With great glee, they pointed out that the *Nation* newspaper had reported nothing. For them, this was not only a sign that my presence was like a breath of fresh air in local journalism, as they put it, but proof that the entire media were partisan and censored themselves. And nobody even questioned why the government-owned radio and television service or the local Rediffusion also did not report the speech, for it was expected that they would act this way.

These were heady times for a young reporter. It seemed just about everyone who mattered on the island knew my name. And I felt I was making for myself a reputation that was going to serve me well in the editor's chair. People had to realize that not only did I spot good stories, I was showing I was non-aligned in local politics, a journalist following the age-old professional credo of unbiased reporting and independence of thought. Or so I thought.

It was a different story from the government. When parliament resumed, Craig walked through the courtyard of the building, hand-in-hand with his wife, Maria. Scores of partisans were on hand. He slowly walked through his throng of supporters, stopping to hug some of them, finally receiving a big bunch of flowers, all of this happening as the news photographers snapped away. Who would have been the mastermind choreographer? Inside the House, the opposition demanded a suspension of the day's regular business. They wanted a discussion of urgent importance because of a newly announced government policy on job patronage that would lead to people starving.

Craig said he had been badly misquoted and that his privilege in parliament had been violated. Various government members rose on points of privilege demanding that I be punished for an erroneous report, also for breaching their privilege as Members of Parliament, for to breach the privilege of one was to do it to all. This precedent had been set so many hundreds of years ago, they claimed, citing the various parliamentary traditions going back to the Magna Carta in England and possibly beyond. The solution, they suggested, was to call me before the bar of the house, when the entire parliament became a court, to deal with my transgression. There I was to be charged with contempt of parliament, the government members argued, with the possible punishment that I be held in prison indefinitely until I was purged of my contempt. I sat at the reporters' table, writing down all that was being said about this article, which was according to parliamentary parlance a published report purporting to be a true report of what had happened in the House and supposedly written by one Cecil Foster, or someone claiming to be a Cecil Foster, or some stranger to the House named Cecil Foster. I was uncertain of what was to happen next, but I knew that matters could not get too far out of hand, as the prime minister had not spoken on the issue and had not even turned up in parliament. After all, in light of what we had discussed, how could he not understand why I wrote the story or even defend me behind closed doors, if not publicly?

Prime Minister Adams soon let me know how he felt about the story. The following evening I was reporting on a speech he gave at a local hotel. When I arrived, I ran into Lady Grace Adams, mother of the prime minister and my former teacher. She was cool and distant, but at least we talked, never mentioning the controversy of the day. When the prime minister finished speaking, a group of reporters approached him and I asked for a copy of his notes. "I don't think you'd be interested in anything I had to say. In it nobody didn't say anything about letting anybody starve." He fixed me with a deep gaze, the light dancing off his wire-rimmed glasses, the lenses of which were always well polished. It was a wilting look.

With the pressure building on me, fate intervened to give me a temporary respite. The opposition barbs that the *Nation* newspaper was in the government's pocket, and that this accounted for his ignoring Craig's statement, stung Albert Brandford. He decided to strike back by proving that he had not really missed a major story but that I might have been deluded or simply made too much of a non-issue. His solution was to publish a copy of Hansard, the official verbatim record of the day's sitting. The *Nation* carried the official report, and there was no mention of the controversial words *let them starve.* This might have been a result of some timely editing. In accordance with parliamentary tradition, MPs are given a draft of their speeches, called the blues (originally, from the colour of one of the layers of the paper on which the speech had been typed in triplicate). They can edit or add to the speeches. The approved and possibly sanitized version of the speech is entered as the record and later issued as a document of the House. Only then is it the record official.

By publishing the speech, Brandford ran afoul of the speaker of the House for not getting permission to publish the early versions of Hansard. In a fit of rage, the speaker imposed a ban for life on Brandford. By now the controversy had truly deepened. It was now not only a question of partisan politics but of press freedom. Could a speaker

unilaterally ban anyone for life, possibly flouting parliamentary tradition by binding future speakers with his decision: and whose life was he talking about, the life of the
reporter, the life of the speaker or the life of the current
parliament? As the focus shifted to discussing the niceties
of parliamentary tradition, giving credence to those who
argued that political independence showed we were simply
mimic men and women, some of the heat was taken off me,
if only temporarily. More importantly, it was because of the
heavy-handedness of the speaker and the resulting public
outcry that I was spared the threat of being officially hauled
before the bar of the House of Assembly.

Instead, I felt the suffocating pressure of government in
other ways. Everything I wrote was scrutinized by the
government and the opposition. Every morning the prime
minister's office called to complain to the publisher about
my stories. Monday morning complaints were less subtle.
The prime minister's press secretary, Denzil Agard, often
turned up in person to meet with the publisher to
complain. People in the business were asking me to "cool
it" for my own good. I should take the sting out of my writing until the situation settled. They reminded me of two
important things. First, there were limited job opportunities on the island for anyone on the wrong side of the
government. The government owned outright the sole television station and one of the two radio stations. It had the
other radio station on a short leash, awarding it one-year
licence renewal. The *Advocate-News* was under pressure to
fire me and it was unlikely I would be employed by the
Nation because its ownership was supposedly government
supporters.

Second, they reminded me of what had happened to two other journalists on the wrong side of the government. A brilliant young journalist and friend, Yussuff Haniff, had to seek refuge at CANA when his job prospects dried up after he criticized the government. So, too, did Trevor Simpson, fired by the government from his news anchoring job at the local television, and also seeking refuge at CANA. It was unlikely CANA could take a third refugee. Just as important, some nasty rumours were sweeping the island of what could happen to opponents of the government. The police were dealing with two high-profile murders and had failed to make an arrest in either case. Rumours suggested that the victims had paid the ultimate price for tangling with the government. Supposedly, this was not a government to mess with.

It was not easy reporting from parliament. While I sat in the House of Assembly, government members often made snide remarks, as if inviting me to respond and run afoul of the rules of the parliament. With this pressure, I was very conscious of what I wrote, for I was often reminded by them that many on the government benches were lawyers and that they were willing to sue me if I ever misquoted them. Obviously, I was not bearing up well under this relentless pressure.

One night parliament met late, and I suffered through many of the taunts and asides. On my way out, Henry Forde, the back-bench lawyer who had tried to steer Craig back to safety in the initial debate, offered me a ride home. We talked candidly. He told me to be careful and to take the advice of "cooling things" and said that I should try not to get hit by the cross-fire between the two parties.

And he seemed to be saying that he liked the integrity I was bringing to the job, but that sometimes it was better to retreat to fight again. So I should let things cool down, he suggested. Over the years, I wondered whether Forde, who later become one of the finest attorneys general on the island, a leader of the party and was finally made Sir Henry, was acting on his own or whether my family had spoken to him. An aunt was one of his strongest supporters and canvassers in his constituency. I figured my name and her connection to me must have come up when they spoke.

But the issue of my reporting and Craig's statement had taken on a life of its own. One night I was walking towards a public meeting by the opposition DLP when I heard in the distance the former prime minister talking disparagingly about journalists on the island. "Cecil Foster is the only journalist among them with any sense." I stopped in my tracks. The statement reverberated for miles around, possibly picked up by government. This was like pouring gasoline on fire. Now I was likely to be even more marked by the government, I thought. Worse, the DLP had taken to publishing columns in the local newspapers and to claiming they were written by someone named Douglas Leopold Phillips. Almost twenty years later, the party was still using this pen name. Douglas Leopold Phillips had entered into the local folklore. Then, two things happened in quick succession to make me realize I was really in big trouble with the government.

Robert Best strolled into the newsroom talking at the top of his voice. We heard him before he physically entered the room.

"Okay, Cecil. I know what I am going to do," he announced to one and all. "'Cause this is *bere* foolishness. They have to realize there is a difference between them as a government hitting out at you and your criticizing them. So from next week, I'm going to take you out of the line of fire. You ain't going into the House any more."

The next week, I was transferred to the courts. I also gave up my political column. It was some time before I found out what had caused this sudden change, before some media officials attending let me in on a secret.

Prime Minister Adams had gone on national television to warn of an attempt to overthrow his government. A gunrunner, Barbadian Sydney Burnett-Alleyne, who supposedly had never forgiven Adams for creating a public scandal by dramatically revealing on television, from parliament, cancelled cheques from Burnett-Alleyne to former government members, had been arrested in Martinique with a shipload of weapons. Apparently, he claimed he was planning to overthrow the Adams government. In light of what had happened in Grenada and in Dominica, where a group of white power racist mercenaries from North America was intercepted on route to attacking the government, the threat announced by Adams was taken seriously.

Before going on television, Adams called the top media officials on the island for a meeting. Those attending were sworn in under the Official Secrets Act, which prohibited them from divulging what was said behind closed doors. Adams took them into his confidence over the threat against his government and suggested that they temper their reports so as not to spook the general population. Finally, he suggested that the meeting might be a good opportunity for the government and media to mend fences and to enter a period of co-operation. These had been testy times for all, with the banning of reporters and discussions about the erosion of press freedom, he said.

"Well, it's not only the banning of one reporter," one of the journalists said. "What about the treatment of Foster?"

"Foster is a different story," Adams said. "We will get even with him."

Although he never explained it, Best was responding to this statement when he came into the newsroom and assigned me to the courts, hoping the fury would blow over with me no longer a political reporter. Switching me to the court beat didn't change much, although it got me out of the line of political fire. For the change was too sudden and it became as much political fodder as what I used to write about. The issue of press freedom was raised among politicians and other government critics. The government didn't like getting blamed for forcing this change and I became even more of an albatross for them.

In the courts, some of the leading legal minds in the country befriended me and we would discuss my situation in the corridors. Of course, most of these lawyers were themselves politicians. One of them was Bobby Clarke, a friend of Maurice Bishop, then prime minister of Grenada. Another was the garrulous and plain-speaking lawyer and one-time luminary in the former government, Frederick (Sleepy) Smith. His advice to me the first day I showed up to report from the courts was always to make sure I reported both sides of a case and not to fall into the trap of presenting the Crown's case only. The case of the Crown should always be suspect until proven and I should remember the defence also had its own story. Failure to present both sides—something many reporters often did, according to him—could leave me open to a charge of contempt of court. Having narrowly missed a charge of contempt of parliament, I took to heart his advice. Sir Frederick, later knighted for his outstanding legal work, went on to become the chief justice of the Eastern Caribbean, but I will always remember him for that morning he purposely came over to me sitting in the press section, perhaps looking bewildered at all that had suddenly enveloped me, and offered his support and a figurative pat on the back.

Eventually, Glyne Murray decided to leave the newspaper and to accept the government's patronage appointment. Everyone was invited to a farewell party at a house about five minutes' walk from an apartment I was renting. I turned up at the party.

About midnight, with the music wailing, people dancing and the food and drinks flowing, Prime Minister Adams showed up. Like me, he was not much of a dancer and eventually the two of us were standing side by side across from the dance floor.

"You are not a bad reporter," Adams said. "But I do think you are easier on the opposition than you are on the government." He proceeded to tell me of all the stories I had written, recalling from memory minute details, slights of his government and praise for his opponents, suggesting that like most reporters on the island I had missed the salient points of the commission of enquiry that essentially exonerated members of the previous government of corruption. We chatted for a long time, with Adams suggesting it was time for us to forget our differences. Ever conscious of the pressure on me, this was music to my ears. I wanted to be free of this war of attrition.

"With the estimates coming up we have some initiatives you might find interesting to write about," he said. "You might want to report on them." Once again he tried flattery, suggesting I was a natural political reporter and better understood what was happening on the island than many of the reporters. For this reason, he wanted to see me return to what I did best.

As we talked, we watched Lionel Craig, minister of labour and housing, waltzing *pretty, pretty* across the floor, the perspiration flowing down his face and soaking his multi-coloured shirt. Craig had steered his partner in front of us and was within listening distance over the blaring music.

"Lionel," Adams called to him. "Lionel, I was telling Mr. Foster here about some of our plans. You might want to explain to Mr. Foster some of the finer points of the initiatives for your ministry that we are planning."

"Mister P.M.," Craig shouted, ending his dance and stylishly taking a handkerchief to wipe the sweat from his face. "I ain't having nothing to do with that man. 'Cause I'm going to get even with him. He writing that I say let people starve. Well, I am going to get even with him." Still wiping his face, he started talking directly to me. "If you ever cross my path, it's good night nurse. I'll feed you with a long spoon. It's going to be *bere* pressure in yuh chest from me. 'Cause you hurt me and I'm going to hurt you back and I'm going to hurt you worse than you hurt me. If I ever catch you on the wrong side, it's all over, lights out for you. If you or any member of your family get into my way, it's all over for them, too."

It must have been the alcohol in my head, but I was not backing down from Craig. We were standing toe-to-toe shouting at each other and ready to come to blows. The party was now stopped. Everyone was looking on. We were standing, waiting for one of us to throw the first blow. Suddenly, I was saved. I felt several strong slaps on my shoulder. Someone was saying: "Cut this out. Cut this out. Cut this out. This is not the place for this kind of behaviour. This is not the place for this kind of discussion. Cut this out." The strong hand steered me away. It was Robert Best. I looked for Prime Minister Adams. He had gone, slipping away and disappearing into the night. I could never decide whether he had deliberately set me up for the confrontation with Craig.

Robert Best took me away to a corner, while talking loudly to defuse the situation. It must have worked and sobered me up. For standing in the corner, I realized I was never much of a fighter and the thought of fighting with a cabinet minister was indicative of what the daily pressures were doing to me. It was at that point that I realized I was in really big trouble.

When nobody was looking, I slipped into the darkness and walked home, looking over my shoulder frequently to make sure nobody was following me. Errol must have been sleeping when he answered the telephone in Toronto.

"You *gotta* help me get off this island," I said as soon as he answered. With that, I explained what had happened. I needed him to sponsor me to Canada and could he possibly make some enquiries soon with Canadian Immigration, perhaps as soon as the sun came up in a few hours.

Errol promised to act right away and asked me to take care of myself. But before hanging up, he asked questions that of late I had been asking myself. "Why didn't you keep your mouth shut like everybody else? Why did you have to write that story, let them starve? Why couldn't you be like that reporter who wrote nothing?"

I had no answers. Must have been something I had learned in school, something about being a maverick, the lone wolf, and feeling compelled to speak truthfully. Perhaps something ingrained in me that we, the young people of a young nation, had been entrusted with the fragile future of a country others didn't believe, I had taken perhaps too seriously the admonition that we had to consciously fight and sacrifice to build a better society. Within the people and their institutions had to be the checks and balances. In the schools, they had told us these things. I was a product of the new and supposedly post-colonial education system. I would not have become a reporter and columnist, someone talking and arguing about matters of state with prime ministers and men and women on the streets, someone considered by the leaders of my nation and some of the best minds among us as having some potential, if I had not been rescued by education. But in my frightened state, even that wasn't an adequate answer. For once again, I was back to yearning deeply for the opportunity to flee my island and to have a new start in somebody else's country.

14

Flying Alone

Within days Errol got back to me by phone and said he and his wife had visited Canadian Immigration in Toronto, filled out some forms and were told there shouldn't be much problem sponsoring me to come to Canada.

And sure enough, a few weeks later I received a letter from the Canadian High Commission in Bridgetown, setting a date for an interview with the Canadian officials. I felt the pressure easing off me. Still, there was no guarantee of a visa to Canada, so I told only my immediate family about my plans. I went to the headquarters of the Royal Barbados Police Force and had the mandatory fingerprints taken and an affidavit saying I had no criminal record. For the interview I took along my bank statement book showing I had the equivalent of $750 U.S. dollars.

The interview was with a bearded Canadian who nonchalantly smoked his pipe. It did not last long. Working from a long form, he ticked off some questions and filled in some spaces, then consulted a manual that told him how many points to award me for job prospects and work experience, for my education, my ability to speak English and to understand a few words and phrases in French, and for having a brother willing to assist me.

"Well, you qualify for a visa as an independent immigrant," he said. "Now, you can take your medicals and when everything is complete we'll send you your visa. I hope you like it in Toronto, Mr. Foster."

I walked out of the interview with a load lifted off my shoulders. The medical examination should be no problem and wasn't. Still, I decided not to tell anyone of my plans to immigrate to Canada. However, to save money, I moved back home. Although they never told me this, I got the feeling that members of my family were glad to have me back under their roof, perhaps so they could keep an eye on me until I was out of the country.

In an unexplained move, Robert Best sent me back to report from parliament. I was extremely cautious in my reports and when I saw colleagues put down their pens, I did likewise. Often, I put down my pen before they did. Still, there was controversy, even if I had nothing to do with it. One day I was sitting at home when a vendor came around selling a sensational newspaper from Trinidad called the *Bomb*. Everyone in Barbados was talking about what the *Bomb* was reporting. The newspaper claimed it had uncovered evidence of a political scandal in Barbados, information that it claimed the local journalists were afraid to touch. As I sat reading, obviously engrossed and even intrigued by the report, I heard the stern voice.

"You are not going to touch that one, you hear me? You will not write about that." It was Mervin. "Let somebody else write about them things. You've done your bit." Mervin had never spoken to me like that before even though he was essentially the only man in any of the houses I grew up in. It was the voice of someone who genuinely cared, who didn't want me to feel some misplaced obligation to get involved and bring further grief on myself. At that moment he sounded just like what in my mind I figured a father would, the right mixture of concern and firm authoritative reproach.

"No, I won't," I mumbled. "I'm just reading."

We said nothing more about the subject. I was not going to create waves. Unfortunately, everybody did not trust me not to make trouble, which meant my trials weren't over just yet.

* * *

The House of Assembly was to resume sitting after the luncheon break. We were walking to our positions at the reporters' desk, a route that took us directly behind the government benches. The voice was loud and clear and what it said was so unexpected it startled us and froze me with fear.

"Mr. Foster," it thundered. "So you planning to go up to Canada. I hear that before you leave you plan to write some bad things about me and my government. Well, let me tell you, if you think you can write anything bad about my government and run away to Toronto, Canada, I want you to know we can reach you up there. We can get you up there. All I can say is good riddance to you and the sooner you get out the better, but don't think you can say anything bad about me or my ministers and run. We'll get to you." It was Prime Minister Adams, standing in the place reserved for holders of his office in parliament.

"Wow," said Trevor Simpson, a reporter with the Caribbean News Agency and a news anchor with the government-owned Caribbean Broadcasting Corporation television station until he was fired at the bidding of this prime minister. "I wish I had what he just said to you on tape. That would be such a story. A prime minister saying that to a member of the press. But you know how these people are. If you don't have them on tape, they'll deny it and say they never said it."

To be threatened so openly was not the only reason I was scared. My mind kept wondering how the prime minister of Barbados knew I was planning to immigrate to Canada. I had told nobody but family members, had not even informed Robert Best that I was quitting the job, and I believed the Canadian High Commission handled all applications in confidence. Why would a prime minister be so interested in my plans and what else did he know? At that moment, all the warnings from people telling me to be careful and to cool things overwhelmed me. I decided to take everybody's advice, especially the prime minister's.

For that afternoon, I simply listened to the debates. My pen spent most of the time resting on my notebook. The next day, I called the Canadian High Commission to ask if there was any word on my visa.

The officer handling the case wasn't in a great mood when the receptionist put through the call to him. He didn't like having to field these calls, he said, and apparently there were many. When everything was ready, he said, the visa will be sent to me from Trinidad. "In any case, it's winter in Toronto," he offered. "You wouldn't want to be walking the streets of Toronto looking for a job in winter. Spring would be a good time to be in Toronto. So relax and wait." If only he knew the reason for my urgency.

* * *

Returning from lunch, I found a note waiting for me with the receptionist at the *Advocate-News*. I had received my visa and was marking time until I left for Toronto. Errol had told me to telephone him when I got my visa. He had sent me the dates he was planning to vacation at home. We could fly to Toronto together. But I couldn't wait to double-check anything with him when my landed immigrant papers arrived. I straightaway booked a flight on Air Canada—one way—to leave on the day Errol planned his return from Barbados to Toronto. I assumed that naturally Errol was going to travel on Air Canada. Wrong, he was travelling on the charter airline Wardair and it was too late to change tickets. Now, everything was in place for me to leave.

The message left with the receptionist was scribbled in pencil. "Mama real bad in hospital. Help us how you can." It was signed Jasmine, Aunt Princess' real name. Later, David confirmed the bad news. Grandmother was terminally ill in hospital with cancer. He was visiting her every day, but the doctors had given up hope. David also told me of plans well underway for him to immigrate to New York and join his mother. Both of us were looking forward to new beginnings in North America. We said our goodbyes, realizing we might not see each other before I left and promising to keep in touch when we both were up north. I also promised to visit Grandmother before leaving.

I walked into the public ward at the Queen Elizabeth Hospital, having put off visiting until the very last moment. I never liked hospitals or their strange disinfectant smells. Something about them always reminded me of my friend Ian Nurse. The nurse on duty pointed out the cot to me. I approached gingerly. Stretched out on the cot was a figure I didn't recognize. It was in a white gown, the face turned away from the direction in which I was approaching. The person looked emaciated, not the strong Grandmother I knew. She had a scarf tied loosely around her head, but I could tell she had no hair, possibly from the radiation treatment. The woman on the cot must have been in a light sleep, for she was groaning and rhythmically raising one foot and letting it drop.

I stood next to her cot for a while. I had no voice. I stood and watched her, her foot rising and falling; groaning. Then I turned away.

"What happened? Didn't you say you came here to visit Mrs. Goddard?" the nurse asked.

"Yes. But I can't wake her."

"Why not? She might only be sleeping."

"I don't have the heart to wake her," I explained in an uncertain voice, hoping the conversation would not wake the woman on the cot. "Could you give her a message for me? Tell her for me that her grandson, Cecil, was here to see her."

"You sure you don't want to tell her yourself? Go ahead, man, wake her," she said.

"No, no, no. I can't. Tell her for me that on Sunday I am going to Toronto, Canada, to live and that I came by to say goodbye but that she was sleeping."

"I am sure she would be glad to hear you tell her that yourself. Especially since you're going away for good." The nurse was speaking gently. "But if you can't . . ."

I shook my head, wrote my name on the piece of paper the nurse handed me, wiped from my eyes whatever was causing them to mist up and walked away, unable to look back. I knew I was never going to see Grandmother again. David would write me in Toronto and tell me she had died. I didn't want to see Grandmother so frail. That was not the memory of her I wanted to take away with me, not when I was so unsure of my future.

I wanted to remember Grandmother as the strong woman of my early years in Lodge Road, of the endless times I fell asleep on her lap, making her a surrogate mother; when she joked and often stole from her pot the wet rice that she mixed with salted butter and gave me to eat when I was too hungry to wait for the full meal; when she always promised me with such surety that I would grow up to be a strong young gentleman who would go overseas and make her proud, as long as I kept asking God to grant me wisdom and understanding. I wanted to remember the Grandmother before the pressures of trying to survive in this society changed her, some of the same pressures I had handled just as badly and which were forcing me instinctually to return to those early dreams she instilled in me. I wanted to remember those dreams of succeeding overseas, of how moving to a foreign country would ease my pains and stop me from crying. I needed to adopt her strategy of appearing brave and strong on the outside when bullies threatened and frightened us, when the powerful made us cower at night, but in the morning we had to awake with a smile on our face and try to get through another day. I wanted the strength of this woman when she was really strong, and I hope she forgave me for not waking her and saying goodbye.

*   *   *

Easter Sunday 1979, we are assembled for the family lunch. Aunty Ann was putting on a spread. Easter is a day of celebration in Barbados, part of the Christian tradition of celebrating rebirth, resurrection and new life. A day of hope. This lunch was traditional, but also different. It was to be the final time for only God knew how long that all of us who had shared this small house in Kendal Hill over the past fourteen years were going to be sharing a meal. Errol and I were leaving for Toronto in hours. The atmosphere was tinged with sadness. Grand-Grand was invoking God's blessing on me and suggesting that in all things I put God first. She, too, was happy to have me leaving the island. It was for the better, she promised.

After the meal, with the planes already waiting at the airport about half an hour's drive away, our luggage packed, it was time to bid farewell to those members of the family and close friends not going to the airport.

"Don't worry about Cecil," Errol said, speaking directly to Aunty Ann. "I will take care of him in Toronto. He will do well in Toronto once this is behind him. He will enjoy Toronto."

"I hope so," Aunty Ann said, trying to force a laugh. "I know you'll take care of him."

"But I know you'll worry," he said.

We hugged all around and headed with our luggage for the cars taking us to the airport.

Errol's flight on Wardair left first. Minutes before boarding, he came over to me. "Don't worry. I'll see you in Toronto. If for some reason your flight arrives before mine, wait for me. Otherwise, I'll come over from my terminal to yours and get you." Then, he reminded me to buy from the duty free shop the maximum amount of rum I was allowed into Canada. Friends in Toronto will be expecting that much, he said.

Finally, it was time for me to leave. Stephen hugged me. "Do you realize this is the first time the three of us who were left behind are really going to be separated, and this time I'll be the one still left behind." He was trying to joke and lighten my spirits. "You will do well in Canada," he said. "Remember when that headmaster at Harrison College said you weren't good enough for his school? You will do well. All I ask of you is that you always remain humble and have humility, let us always remember where the three o' we came from." Then, he tried for another joke. "Now you are going to be living in Canada, you can go and try out for the Canadian cricket team. You know, you weren't all that bad as a batsman and it looks like just about anybody can make the Canadian cricket team."

We hugged again. I smiled and waved at my family. Then, I turned and walked through security and onto the tarmac, but not before stopping by the duty free shop.

At the top of the stairs to the aircraft, I stopped for a moment to take one last look at the island and to wave to my family. As a little boy, I had always wondered what would be my thoughts as I entered an aircraft knowing I was leaving the island permanently. I didn't expect to have so many mixed feelings. I was looking forward to living in a new country, but I knew it was not going to be easy. I was not a Canadian. I was a very nationalistic Barbadian and Caribbean person. I knew few people in Toronto. The most I could hope for was that I would land quickly on my feet, maybe, if I were lucky, getting a job as journalist. In my luggage was a folder with clippings of various reports.

But I also knew this was not the way I had hoped to leave Barbados. I never believed I would be on the run. Even as I was boarding the plane, I was hoping that I would soon return to Barbados, even if friends had told me to rest a while in Toronto until the political situation blew over. (Meeting months later with Grenada's prime minister, Maurice Bishop, in Toronto, he said, "Fost, man, Bobby Clarke tells me Tom Adams ran you out of the country. Do you know you are probably the only Bajan in political exile?" Bishop was joking, or that was what I wanted to believe, for he and Tom Adams had become enemies, publicly denouncing each another. Adams had taken to accusing Bishop of having political prisoners in Grenada. Still, his statement hurt, for I could not make up my mind if I had been in physical danger. Perhaps I was still too naive. There was a lot of truth in the joke and it hurt.)

But I also realized that in my lifetime something profound had happened on this island. While life looked casual in Barbados and the Caribbean, big and possibly lasting changes were at work. The people of the region and my island were adjusting to the harsh realities of living independently on their own, like the children who had left home with so many ideas and dreams swimming in their heads, but who had to face up to the stark reality of their times, of trying to remain committed to their dreams while trying to earn a living. Yes, they were standing on their own, but life was tough, even if there had been improvements in our lifestyle and the style and numbers of our creature comforts.

I could think of my own case, how for me education had offered so much. There was a time when for most the dream was to pass the Common Entrance Examination and get to a grammar school, then to get a few passes at the General Certificate of Education examination to get a civil service job or to work in a bank.

But in only a decade since independence, life had changed remarkably. The dreams were bigger, and more people were jumping over the bars that previously looked so high and insurmountable, but which now looked so narrow and unchallenging. A short while earlier, a young woman and I were the first to pass five GCE subjects at Christ Church High School and that was considered historic in terms of the school. Since then, many more students from the same school had surpassed us. The same had happened at the various schools across the country. Education and the ability to see dreams within reach were now available to just about everyone.

But while an independent Barbados was producing a better educated and qualified population, it still was not generating the number of jobs to satisfy the demand; the jobs still weren't challenging enough. Many of us still had to consider immigrating. For some, even a university degree was no longer a guarantee of a good job and income. Many with well-trained minds were left with the luxury of time to question the society and what it offered, to analyse the lots of certain groups and to more aggressively agitate in institutions they better understood for improvements. The calibre of politicians, if not always the level of discussion, had risen.

The push out of the island for ambitious young men and women was still just as strong as when my mother and father looked to England for their self-fulfilment. And there were the political tensions. It appeared to me that the political leaders of the day were lacking vision, unable or unwilling to galvanize and unite the people behind a single idea or concept, such as how independence was more than just an idea, but also a reason for enduring tough times because independence promised a better day. It raised expectations, even if the expectations were different from person to person, from class to class. At least everybody seemed to be talking about and even working for the same purpose.

There wasn't the excitement of reaching for a goal, no flamboyant display of pride like what had first roared through the island and region when new flags first flapped in the air, seemingly daring the world to accept us, to notice our arrival. Ten tough years of adjusting and living on our own had wrung dry some of that enthusiasm. Politics seemed to be concerned with the mundane, as politicians readjusted their philosophies and looked for solutions to seemingly intractable problems such as solving high unemployment and diversifying the economy from its dependence on one crop or industry.

And there was a sense of anger in the region. A blood-less coup had overthrown a government in Grenada, there was talk of attempted or planned coups against govern-ments in Barbados, Dominica and Trinidad and Tobago. Jamaica was battling with all sorts of domestic and imported problems. In Guyana, human rights and the stan-dard of living were in sharp decline. Even one island, Anguilla, had voted to go against the trend of political inde-pendence by choosing to remain a British colony.

The region appeared headed for an explosion, perhaps as momentous as the eruption of Mount Soufriere in St. Vincent that dumped tons of ash on us in Barbados and neighbouring islands days before I left, the same kind of anger that erupted into a bottle throwing incident in Barbados when spectators abruptly ended a cricket test match between the West Indies and Pakistan. They had disagreed with an umpire's decision. And this was in Barbados, an island where the people were supposedly so placid, tolerant and law abiding.

The Caribbean and my island appeared to be at a junc-ture: they could slide into what might be considered to be typical Third World disease of lawlessness, as some had predicted before independence, or they could adjust and realign expectations with reality. Whatever the choice, I realized I was going to view it through the filter of distance. I was not going to be one of the young reporters chroni-cling the first draft of history. I was not going to be one of the voters making these decisions.

Still, it was Easter, a time of new beginnings, at least for me. I took one last look at the island, took a deep breath and entered the aircraft. As we travelled across the Atlantic, the captain drew to our attention the ash from Mount Soufriere that providentially seemed to be travelling out of the region, going with us to North America.

Over the decades, thousands of us escaped this way. We always took something with us—a defiance and a strong belief in ourselves, something that appeared peculiar to Caribbean people who tended to arrive in their adopted country with the strong belief that they belonged, that they can contribute, make changes to benefit everyone and then, if all went well, go back home in retirement. A belief that brought self-assuredness, no different from the visionaries, who from international capitals dreamt about a postcolonial nirvana in the Caribbean and returned to instill the dream in the young.

It was no different from those who from foreign lands looked back and felt a strengthening of the bond with those back home, who felt that to claim sovereignty and political independence was the culmination of one long struggle, perhaps going back as far as in 1651 in Barbados in Oistins, a small town on whose beach I used to walk. A struggle that took the peoples of this region through emancipation from slavery and indenture service, through riots for the right for poor people to vote, to the day when they not only voted but could be elected to parliament, when they could aspire to be their own rulers, prime ministers, presidents and governors-general.

This was why other blacks living in North America for several generations considered those of us from the Caribbean as uppity, as the King George Negroes, as Coconut Heads, as we were called by African Americans in the United States and by blacks in Canada. This early social and political training was partly why Caribbean blacks were considered so assertive.

Six hours later I was in Toronto. It was just over two decades since my father and then my mother had left Barbados, and now I was finally leaving, too, carrying on my search for some ties that could bind me to anyone, or anything. Perhaps I had finally taken my island wings. At various times, I had dreamt that my future rested with a new country, *new* not only in terms of remaking or modernizing the old, but as in different. *New* as in the type and choices of opportunities available to me. This was still the case. Except that the country in which I hoped to spread my wings and soar was now Canada.